# ERIC NEWBY

Eric Newby was born in London in 1919 and was educated at St Paul's School. In 1938 he joined the four-masted Finnish barque *Moshulu* as an apprentice and sailed in the last Grain Race from Australia to Europe by way of Cape Horn. During the Second World War he served in the Black Watch and Special Boat Section, and was prisoner-of-war from 1942 to 1945. After the war his world expanded still further – into the fashion business and book publishing. Whatever else he was doing, he always travelled on a grand scale, either under his own steam or as Travel Editor of the *Observer*. He was made CBE in 1994.

# A MERRY DANCE
# AROUND THE WORLD

*The Best of*

# ERIC NEWBY

PICADOR

First published in Great Britain 1995 by HarperCollins Publishers

This edition published 1996 by Picador
an imprint of Macmillan Publishers Ltd
25 Eccleston Place, London SW1W 9NF
and Basingstoke

Associated companies throughout the world

ISBN 0 330 34903 1

1 3 5 7 9 8 6 4 2

A CIP catalogue record for this book is available from
the British Library.

Printed and bound in Great Britain by
Mackays of Chatham plc, Chatham, Kent

# Contents

# First Steps

## BIRTH OF A TRAVELLER

*Births, Marriages, Deaths*
NEWBY. – On the 6th December at 3 Castelnau
Mansions, Barnes, SW13, to Hilda Newby, wife
of Geo. A. Newby – a son.

IN THIS EXTRAVAGANT fashion – altogether it cost 50p ($1.95)*, at
a time when Lady Secretaries with shorthand and typing were earning
around £3.50 ($13.65) a week – my arrival was announced on the
following Tuesday, 9 December, in *The Times* and the *Daily Telegraph*,
two of the daily newspapers my father 'took in' at that period. The
other was the *Daily Mirror*, then a rather genteel paper, which he
ordered for my mother, but never looked at himself, and which she
passed on to the cook/housekeeper when she had finished with it. From
then on it was also passed on to a nurse.

At 3.45 a.m., the ghastly hour I chose, or rather the doctor chose,
for my arrival – I had to be hauled out by the head – conditions must
have been pretty beastly in Barnes. It was a dark and stormy night,
with a fresh wind from the west whose gusts would have been strong
enough to blow clouds of spray from the big reservoir (which was
opposite our flat by the bridge and which has now been filled in to
make playing fields for St Paul's School) over the pavement and right
across the main road (which was called Castelnau but which all the
inhabitants knew and know to this day as Castlenore) as it always did

* All sums of sterling have been converted from pounds, shillings and pence to
their decimal equivalents and to American currency of the time.

'when the wind was strong from that particular quarter, sometimes, but rarely at 3.45 a.m. wetting unwary pedestrians and people travelling in open motor cars.

And it was certainly dark, although the moon had been up for more than thirteen hours and was only a day off full. It would be nice, more romantic, altogether more appropriate for a potential traveller, to think of myself arriving astride the Centaur, and, Sagittarius being in the ascendant, perhaps carrying the latter's arrows for him, as we moved across a firmament in which ragged clouds were racing across the path of a huge and brilliant moon; but it was not to be. It was ordained that I should be a child not only of darkness but of utter darkness, of ten-tenths cloud.

When it dawned, the day was even more rumbustious than the night. And when the sun rose, just before eight o'clock, like the moon, it remained invisible. Thunderstorms visited many parts of the country, accompanied by hail, sleet or snow and west or north-westerly winds which reached gale force in high places. In Lincolnshire, the Belvoir Hunt, having 'chopped a fox' in Foston Spinney (seized it before it fairly got away from cover), 'were hunting another from Allington when scent was totally swept away by a tremendous rainstorm'.

'Flying Prospects' on my birthday were not good, according to *The Times*. It is now difficult to imagine that a pilot, or even a passenger, might actually buy a newspaper in order to find out whether it was safe to 'go up', but it must have been so, otherwise there would have been no point in publishing the information at all. 'Unsuitable for aviation or fit only for short distance flying by the heaviest sort of machine' was what the communiqué said. 'Sea Passages' were equally disagreeable. The English Channel was rough, with winds reaching forty miles an hour, and there was extensive flooding in France.

But if the weather was disturbed that Saturday, it was as nothing compared with the state of great chunks of Europe and northern Asia. In spite of the fact that the advertising department of *The Times* had chosen this particular Saturday to announce 'PRESENTS SUGGESTIONS FOR THE GREAT PEACE CHRISTMAS', on it Latvians were fighting Germans, on whom they had declared war a week previously on 28 November, and so were the Lithuanians. In Russia, on the Don and between Voronezh and Kirsk and in Asia, beyond the Urals, along the line of the Trans-Siberian Railway, where typhus was raging, Bolsheviks and White Russians were engaged in a civil war of the utmost ferocity. Meanwhile, that same Saturday, while their fellow countrymen were destroying one another, with their country in ruins and becoming every day more ruinous, Lenin and Trotsky and the 1109 delegates of the Seventh All-Russian Congress of Soviets passed a resolution to the effect that 'The Soviet Union Desires to Live in Peace with All Peoples'. On that day, too, Lenin told the Congress that 'Communistic Principles were being utterly disregarded by the Russian peasantry.'

That day, too, much nearer home, while I was taking my first nourishment, as it were, in the open air, French Army units with heavy guns were rumbling across the Rhine bridges in order to force the Germans to ratify the peace treaty which they had signed at Versailles in June; and in the same issue of *The Times* which carried the headline about 'THE GREAT PEACE CHRISTMAS', there were other headlines such as 'GUNS ACROSS THE RHINE' and 'WAR IMMINENT', although who was to fight another war with millions killed and wounded, armies in a state of semi-demobilization, and millions more dying or soon to die from sickness and starvation was not clear. Nevertheless, that weekend, the only thing, theoretically, that stood between the protagonists and another outbreak of war, was the Armistice, signed in a French railway carriage parked in a wood, thirteen months previously, so that, equally theoretically, it would simply have meant carrying on with the old one. That weekend, too, the Americans quitted the peace conference.

There was, altogether, a lot about death in the papers that Saturday. It was as if Death the Reaper, an entity embodied by cartoonists in their drawings as a hideous, skeletal figure, and it would have been difficult to have lived through the last five years without thinking of death as such, had become dissatisfied with his efforts, had once again sharpened his scythe and was already cutting fresh, preliminary swathes through the debilitated populations of the vanquished powers, as if the great influenza epidemic, which reached its peak in Britain in March 1919, and which altogether killed more people in Europe than all the shot and shell of four and a half years of war, had not been enough.

In Britain, that Saturday, things were rather different. Bank rate was six per cent, exports were booming. On Friday, the US dollar closed at $3.90 to the pound. The only disquieting news that morning, and that was more or less a rumour, was that there was a possibility of a number of pits being forced to close in the South Wales anthracite fields.

Altogether, for many people that Saturday, life seems to have gone on much as it had done before the Deluge. Giddy and Giddy, House Agents, offered a luxuriously furnished town house, facing Hyde Park, with thirteen bed and dressing-rooms for £26.25 ($102.40) a week. Harrods announced Laroche champagne, 1911, the last vintage generally available (shipped) since the war, at £6.50 ($25.35) a dozen. Very old vintage port (Tuke Holdsworth) was £4.50 ($17.55) a dozen. Not advertised in *The Times* or the *Daily Telegraph*, but still listed in Harrods' enormous current catalogue, (and for some years to come) under 'Livery', were red plush breeches for footmen.

Domestic servants were still comparatively inexpensive, although more difficult to find, than they had been before the war. That Saturday Lady Baldwin, of 37 Cavendish Square, advertised for a housemaid, 'five maids and a boy kept, wages £28-£30 ($109-$117) a year'. And there were vacancies for live-in under nurses, at £25 ($97.50) a year, the price of a high-class baby carriage of the sort that my mother had acquired for me.

That Saturday, too, wholesale garment manufacturers, at what was, and still is, known as 'the better end of the trade', the sort of firm my father was a partner in, were advertising jobs in their workrooms for bodice and skirt makers at around £2.50 ($9.75) for a five and a half day, forty-nine hour week (8.30 a.m. to 5.30 p.m. week-days, 8.30 a.m to 12.30 p.m. Saturdays), £130 ($507) a year, which made the 50p spent on announcing my birthday seem hideously extravagant.

That Saturday some London fashion houses, including the then ultra-fashionable Lucile, in Hanover Square, were advertising for 'Model Girls', in emulation of Paul Poiret, the Parisian designer, who had just returned from the army and for the first time showed clothes on living models.

A sketch in *The Times* that Saturday shows that clothes were good-looking, if not positively saucy. Dresses, according to their fashion correspondent, were '*décolleté*, sometimes dangerously low', in brilliant colours, with tight, mid-calf-length skirts. Jet was high fashion for the evening: embroidered on coloured velvet, used for making girdles and shoulder straps. Feathers, which had been used for years for making headdresses for evening, were being replaced by flowers, 'as little like nature as possible?', although another couple of years were to pass before the Importation of Plumage (Prohibition) Act became law. The ultra-fashionable were already wearing the long, skimpy jerseys which were to become a sort of hallmark of the 1920s; but there was nothing about them in the papers the day I was born.

Yet in spite of all this display of what an American politician described as 'normalcy', 'The Great War', as it would still be referred to by the British far into the next one, although over, must have seemed terribly close to most people, as it still must do today to anyone reading some of the classified advertisements which appeared in the quality papers that Saturday. The request for a lady or gentleman to play once a week at a *thé dansant* in a hospital for shell-shocked officers. The offers to keep soldiers' graves trimmed and lay headstones in the neighbourhood of Albert, Bapaume and Péronne – the dead had not yet been gathered together in communal cemeteries. The endless columns of advertisements inserted by ex-servicemen, under 'Situations Wanted' (there were 350,000 of them unemployed), part of the huge citizen army of the still living that was being demobilized into a world in which, in spite of there being whole generations of dead, there was not enough work for all. Such advertisements, inserted by ex-officers, warrant officers, petty officers, NCOs and men of superior education (the labouring classes did not advertise their services in this way), were some of them despairing, some of them pathetic, some of them hopeless:

EX-SERVICE MAN. Loss of right arm, seeks situation as Window Dresser or Shopwalker.

DEMOBILIZED OFFICER. Aged 21, *4½ years' service* [my italics]. Good education. Left school to join up, therefore no experience. Accept small salary until proficient.

Will anyone lend DEMOBILIZED OFFICER, DSO, just starting work again, £5000 ($19,500) for one year? Highest

references. Applicant desperately pressed by money-lenders.
No Agents. Write Box J.28.

Money-lenders were so numerous that they had whole classified sections to themselves. Most of them offered 'immediate advances on
note of hand alone'. Their advertisements make repulsive reading, even
across such a gulf of years.

A far more prominent advertisement than any of these announced
the setting up of what was called the Bemersyde Fund, opened by the
Lord Mayor of London and the Right Honourable Lord Glenconner,
'to acquire the estates of Bemersyde from its owner and have the same
conveyed to Field-Marshal Earl Haig, a member of the well-known
whisky distilling family, as a personal gift from the people of the British
Empire – the consideration for the purchase being £53,700 ($209,430)'.

Altogether – leaving present for the headmaster (the Estates of
Bemersyde), although he had not been a very good headmaster, the
boys (or what was left of them, for it had been rather a rough school
with a lot of mud in the playing fields) now going out into the world
to seek their fortunes – there was a distinctly end-of-term feeling in
the air. But in spite of this there was no singing of 'Lord Dismiss Us
With Thy Blessing' as one would perhaps expect on such occasions
and as there was at the schools I later attended. Possibly because the
only songs the boys knew were not hymns but songs that had become
dirges: 'Pack Up Your Troubles', 'Tipperary', 'It's a Long Long Trail
A'Winding' and 'I Don't Want To Join The Army'.

Even the Ministry of Munitions and the Admiralty were selling up.
That day and every day there were offers for sale by auction of aero-
dromes, enormous munition factories, equally enormous hutted camps,
and of minesweepers, motor charabancs, fleets of ambulances, ships'
boilers, railway engines, enough barbed wire to encircle the earth,
millions of cigarettes in lots, miles and miles of ships' hawser,
inexhaustible supplies of bell tents, cereal ovens, lower fruit standard
jam, wicker-covered stoneware jars, torpedo boats, with and without
engines and part-worn and unworn issue clothing, etc., etc., etc., so
inexhaustible that many items were still being sold off twenty years
later on the eve of the next world war, when the whole stocking up
process began all over again. Everything, except projectiles and the

means of discharging them, was open to offer and even these would eventually come on the market, but for export only.

In fact the world was changing with a rapidity that would have been unbelievable in 1914, even though it was still possible to buy red plush breeches for footmen and under nurses could still be acquired with comparative ease. Yet it was, one sees in retrospect, only a temporary acceleration. If it had continued at the rate envisaged in 1919 man would probably have stood on the moon by 1939.

That afternoon the muffin man ringing his bell went down Riverview Gardens, the side road outside 'Ther Mansions' as the local tradesmen who dealt with my mother called them, in which there were other blocks of flats, carrying his muffins in a wooden tray covered with a green baize cloth, which he balanced on his head; and the lamplighter came and went on his bicycle (lighting-up time that evening was 4.21 p.m.), lancing the gas lamps in the street into flame with a long bamboo pole.

And so ended my birthday. For all concerned it had been a jolly long one.

\*     \*     \*

The truth is that babies do not like travel, and I was no exception. Babies are unadventurous. Babies act as grapnels to prevent 'the family' dragging its ground. That is why they were invented. Perversely, their desire for fresh horizons comes much later when they have already begun to 'attract' fares, and can no longer travel free; by which time they are no longer babies at all.

I remember the Isle of Wight as the place where I first sat in the side-car of a motor cycle, at Easter 1923, but much more I remember it as being the Place Where God Lived, although this was later, some time in the summer or autumn of 1925. It must have been during one of those interpolated holidays my mother was so adept at arranging at an instant's notice if my father had to go abroad without her, on the grounds that a change of air would do me good. He often used to go to Holland to sell enormous coats and costumes to the Dutch. With her she took her sister, my Auntie May, who loved travel, however banal.

On one occasion we made an excursion to a place near the middle of the island and some time in the afternoon of what I remember as a very hot day we arrived at our destination, a village of thatched houses that were clustered about the foot of a green hill, on the summit of which stood what seemed a very small church.* From where we stood it was silhouetted against the now declining sun, the rays of which shone through its windows, producing an unearthly effect.

There was no time to climb the hill to the church and have tea as well. If there had been, I am sure that my mother and my aunt, both of whom were interested in 'old things', would have done so. Instead, we had the tea, in the garden of one of the cottages, and while we were having it I heard my mother and my aunt talking about the place and how nice it was, which they called Godshill.

I was very excited. Godshill. If this was Godshill then God must live on it. God to me at this time and for long years to come was a very old, but very fit, version of Jesus and much less meek-looking. He had a long white beard, was dressed in a white sheet and was all shiny, as if he was on fire. He also had a seat in the front row of the dress circle, as it were, so that he could see immediately if one was doing wrong. This was the God to whom I prayed each night, either with my mother's help or with whoever was looking after me.

'Does he live on it?' I asked my mother.

'Yes,' said my mother, 'that's where he lives, darling, on top of the hill.'

I was filled with an immense feeling of happiness that this radiant

---

* It was originally intended that the church should be built at the foot of the hill near the site of the present village. However, when work was begun on it, the plan was vetoed by a band of local fairies. As a practical expression of their objection whenever the walls reached a particular height they proceeded to knock them down and carry the stones up to the top of the hill where they rebuilt the walls, after which they danced round them in a ring. After this had happened three times, the workmen who had on each occasion been forced to demolish the walls, carry the stones back down the hill and then build them up again in the low ground, lost heart and decided to build the church where the fairies wanted it to be built. As a result of this wise decision there was much jubilation among the fairies and when the church was finally completed they held a great *fête* on top of the hill to celebrate their victory, the sounds of their revelry being audible at a considerable distance.

being, whom I had never actually seen but who was always either just around the corner or else hovering directly overhead but always invisible, should live in such a shining, beautiful place; and I asked if we could climb the hill and see him. Unfortunately, the train was due and we had to hurry to the station. I cried all the way to it and most of the way back to Bembridge. I never went back to Godshill and I never will.

I can remember, in July 1923, being carried high on my father's head through the bracken in the combes that led down to the beaches on Sark, and once having reached them I can remember falling down constantly on the rocks and hurting myself, I considered, badly. And it was on Sark that I had my first remembered nightmare, in the annexe to Stock's Hotel, a charming, ivy-clad, farmlike building. I awoke screaming in what was still broad daylight with the sun shining outside my first-floor room in which the blinds were drawn, to think myself abandoned to a dreadful fate by my parents who were dining only a few feet away in the hotel, certain that I had 'gone off' to sleep. It was a nightmare of peculiar horror, because it was founded on fact; so horrible and at the same time so difficult to explain to anyone that for years I dared not confide the details to anyone, and to my parents I never did, although it recurred throughout my childhood, together with an almost equally awful one about falling down an endless shaft.

## WESTWARD HO!

In 1925, when I was five and a half, we embarked on what, so far as I was concerned, was the most ambitious holiday I had ever had. In summer my father took a cottage at Branscombe, at that time a very rural and comparatively unvisited village in South Devon, between Seaton and Sidmouth. It promised to be a particularly exciting time as my father had decided that we should travel there from Barnes by motor. This meant that most of our luggage had to be sent in advance by train from Waterloo to Honiton, a market town on the main line to Exeter; at Honiton it was picked up by a carrier and transported the ten miles or so to Branscombe by horse and cart. Others taking part in this holiday, although they did not travel with us, being already foregathered there, were my Auntie May (the aunt who had accompanied my mother and me on the memorable visit to Godshill) and her husband, Uncle Reg. Before the war Uncle Reg had worked as a journalist in Dover on the local paper and in this capacity had been present in 1909 when Blériot landed on the cliffs, having flown the Channel. During the war he had been in the navy in some department connected with propaganda. Later he became editor of the *Gaumont British Film News*. He was very urbane and elegant. He was later on good terms with the Prince of Wales for whom he used to arrange film shows at Fort Belvedere, and for the Royal Family at Balmoral. For these services he was presented with cufflinks and cigarette cases from Plantin, the court jeweller, as well as other mementoes. He preferred to be called Reginald rather than Reg, but no one ever did so. They put up in the village pub where we, too, were to take our meals.

The third party was made up of three fashion buyers for London stores, Beryl, Mercia and Mimi Bamford, all of whom were friends of my mother, particularly Mimi, and their mother. All three were unimaginably elegant, often almost identically dressed in long, clinging jerseys and strings of amber beads, and they were surrounded by what seemed to be hordes of extremely grumpy Pekingese who did not take kindly to the country. Their mother, who did not take kindly to the country either, was even more formidable. She owned a Boston Bulldog called Bogey, which had had its ears clipped, a practice by then declared illegal. Like her daughters she was immensely tall, and must at one time have been as personable as her daughters, but even I could recognize that she was incredibly tough, if not common.

'She didn't ought to 'ave 'ad 'im,' was the comment she made about me, by now a boisterous, active little boy, to my Auntie May while we were at Branscombe, 'she' being my mother; an anecdote that my aunt eventually told me, which she did with an excellent imitation of the old lady's gravelly voice, having put off doing so until only a few years before her own death in 1974 in order, as she put it, to spare my feelings.

Neither Beryl nor Mercia nor their mother ever went to the beach, or even set eyes on the sea, the whole time they were at Branscombe.

For Beryl and Mercia the seaside was Deauville. What Branscombe
was to them is difficult to imagine, or they to the inhabitants. Only
Mimi relished the simple life. The journey to Branscombe, a stately
progression in an open motor, took two days.

At Branscombe, behind the Mason's Arms, the pub which stood next
door to the cottage my father had taken for the summer and of which
it formed a part, there was a yard surrounded by various dilapidated
outbuildings and a piece of ground overgrown with grass and nettles
which concealed various interesting pieces of rusted, outmoded
machinery, the most important of which was an old motor car smelling
of decaying rubber and dirty engine oil. The stuffing of what was left
of its buttoned leather upholstery was a home for a large family of
mice. This yard was to be the scene of some of the more memorable
games I played with my best friend in the village, Peter Hutchings,
whose mother kept a grocery, confectionery and hardware shop on the
corner opposite Mr Hayman, the butcher's. It was from Peter Hutchings, who was killed while serving as a soldier in the Second World
War, and whose name is inscribed with the names of fourteen other
village boys who died in the two great wars on the war memorial at
the entrance to Branscombe churchyard, that I learned the broad local
dialect which was so broad that by the end of that first summer at
Branscombe no one except a local inhabitant could understand what I
was saying. 'Sweatin' like a bull 'er be,' was how Peter Hutchings
described to me one day the state of his sister, Betty, confined to
bed with a temperature, and it was in this form that I passed on this
important piece of news to my parents.

There in the inn yard, in the long summer evenings, we used to sit
in the old motor car, either myself or Peter at the wheel, taking it in
turn, the driver making BRRR-ing noises, the one sitting next to him
in the front making honking noises – the horn had long since ceased
to be – as we roared round imaginary corners, narrowly missing
imaginary vehicles coming in the opposite direction, driving through
an imaginary world to an imaginary destination on an imaginary road,
a pair of armchair travellers. In the back we used to put Betty Hutchings, if she was available, who wore a white beret, was placid, said
nothing, apart from an occasional BRR, and was in fact an ideal

back-seat passenger. Sometimes, if we felt like doing something 'rude', we used to stop the car and pee on the seats in the back, and Betty would pee too. This gave us a sense of power, at least I know it did to me, as I would not have dared to pee on the upholstery of a real motor car belonging to real people. Less courageous than my wife, who confessed to having peed on the back seat of a 'real' very expensive motor car stopped outside her parents' house at her birthplace in the Carso, *and* smeared it with cow dung.

When we got tired of driving our car we ourselves used to become motor cars, tearing up and down the street outside making BRRR-ing noises of varying intensity as we changed gear, disturbing the elderly ladies who used to sit at their cottage doors making Honiton lace, pillow lace, appliqué and guipure, the principal manufacture of the village. Close by, over the hill at Beer where there were stone quarries, the quarry men's wives had made the lace for Queen Victoria's wedding dress in 1839, something that was still talked about in the neighbour-hood more or less as if it had happened yesterday. It was these hideous BRRR-ing noises that no doubt prompted old Mrs Bamford, whose cottage also faced the main street, to utter the words, 'She didn't ought to 'ave 'ad 'im.'

But all this was in the future, that first day of our holiday.

The next morning I woke at what must have been an early hour and, obeying some mysterious summons, dressed myself in the clothes that I had worn the previous afternoon – white shirt, shorts, socks and white sun hat (I couldn't manage the tie unaided), brown lace-up shoes from Daniel Neal's in Kensington High Street (soon to be replaced by hobnail boots, bought for me at my earnest request so that I could be a real country boy, which took me ages to tie) and my pride and joy, a hideous red and green striped blazer with brass buttons that I had persuaded my mother to buy for me, much against her will, from Messrs Charles Baker, Outfitters, of King Street, Hammersmith, so that I should look more like what I described as 'a real schoolboy' rather than an infant member of the kindergarten at the Froebel School in Barons Court. As school blazers were not made to fit persons as small as I was, when I was wearing it my short trousers were scarcely visible at all. Not even Messrs Baker appeared to know which school it was, if any, that had red and virulent green stripes as its colours.

Then, having picked up a stout stick that I had acquired the previous day, I stole downstairs and let myself out into the village street which was deserted as it was Sunday morning.

At the side of the road, opposite what I was soon to know as Mrs Hutchings's shop, a little stream purled down from one of the side valleys, one of several such streams that, united, reach the sea at Branscombe Mouth; and there, under a brick arch, it issued from a pipe which supplied this lower end of the village with water, before burrowing under the road to reappear once more outside the shop. From here it ran away downhill over stones along the edge of a little lane with an old, ivy-clad wall on one side of it, chattering merrily to itself as it ran over the stones in a way that seemed almost human.

Here, in this narrow lane, the water had what looked to me like watercress growing in it, and it was so clear and delicious-looking that I got down and had a drink of it, only to find that it was not delicious at all and that it had a nasty smell. Later I discovered that Betty Hutchings used to drink from this crystal stream if she was not watched which was probably the reason why she sweated like a bull.

I continued to follow the stream, racing twigs down it, until it vanished into a sort of tunnel from which proceeded a delightful roaring sound. At the other end it emerged beyond a wicket gate to flow more placidly under a little bridge and in these calmer waters I spent some time stirring up the bottom with my stick and frightening some water beetles, the air about me filled with the droning of innumerable insects.

From this point it ran to join the main stream in the middle of the valley and here the path turned away from it to the left beyond a five-barred gate which, because I could not open it unaided, I squeezed underneath, to find myself in a beautiful and what seemed to me immense green meadow, hemmed in by hedgerows and huge trees and filled with buttercups, while high above it to the right were the hanging woods we had seen the previous morning from the car, the open down above them alive with gorse.

At the far end of this field the now augmented stream was spanned by a small wooden footbridge with a white painted handrail. When I eventually reached the stream, in spite of all these distractions and making a number of more or less unsuccessful attempts to spear on the end of my stick some of the older, harder sorts of cow flop in

which the field abounded, and launch them into the air, the water tasted
even funnier than it had done in the village outside Mrs Hutchings's
shop and I stung myself on the nettles getting down to it.

Beyond the bridge the path continued uphill, dappled with sunlight
under the trees, and here the air struck chill after the heat of the
meadow. Then it dipped and suddenly I found myself out in the sun
on the edge of an immense shingle beach which had some boats hauled
out on it, and in my ears there was the roar of the sea as with every
wave it displaced and replaced millions upon millions of pebbles. To
the left it stretched to where a cluster of ivy-covered white pinnacles
rising above a landslip marked the last chalk cliffs in southern England;
to the right to the brilliant red cliffs around Sidmouth; and beyond it,
out to sea, on what was a near horizon, for there was already a haze
of heat out in Lyme Bay, I could see the slightly blurred outlines
of what Harry Hansford, the local fisherman who lived opposite the
blacksmith's shop, would soon teach me to identify as a Brixham
trawler, ghosting along under full sail.

> 'Then felt I like some watcher of the skies
> When a new planet swims into his ken;
> Or like stout Cortez when with eagle eyes
> He star'd at the Pacific – and all his men
> Look'd at each other with a wild surmise –
> Silent, upon a peak in Darien.'

Many years were to pass before I read these words of Keats, but when
I did the memory of that morning came flooding back.

There was a sound of feet slithering on the pebbles behind me. It was
Kathy, my mother's help, panting slightly, as she had been running.
'Whatever did you do that for, Eric, you naughty little boy, without
telling me?' she said. 'Your mum's ever so worried, and your dad, too.
He'll be ever so cross if he finds out where you've been. You'd better
keep quiet when you get back. I'll say I found you in the field.'

Together, hand in hand, we went back up the hill towards the village
where the church bells were now beginning to announce the early
service.

## LANDS AND PEOPLES

By the time I was eight years old, apart from a visit to the Channel
Islands in 1923, I had never been out of England, not even to visit
Scotland, Ireland or Wales. Yet, in spite of this, I already knew a good
deal about these places and their inhabitants, as well as the wider world
beyond the British Isles.

This was because, some time in the 1920s, my parents took out on
my behalf a subscription to *The Children's Colour Book of Lands and
Peoples*, a glossy magazine edited by Arthur Mee, at that time a well-
known writer who was also responsible for the to me rather boring
*Children's Newspaper*, which I had given up buying in favour of more
trashy, exciting comics. *Lands and Peoples*, according to the advertisements which heralded its publication, was to come out at regular intervals and when complete the publishers would bind it up for you to
form six massive volumes.

What excitement I felt when *Lands and Peoples* came thudding
through the letter-box, in its pristine magazine form. To me, turning
its pages in SW13 was rather like being taken to the top of a mountain
from which the world could be seen spread out below, a much more
interesting world than the one my father read bits out about from
his *Morning Post* to my mother while she was still in bed, a captive
audience, sipping her early morning tea.

*Lands and Peoples* was addressed to 'The Generation whose business
it is to save Mankind' – mine presumably, although I had no suggestions to make about how it should be done. 'We are marching,' Mee
wrote, an incurable optimist, apparently envisaging a pacific version
of the Children's Crusade, with the children waving white flags instead
of brandishing crucifixes, 'towards a friendlier and better world, a
world of love in place of hate, of peace instead of war, and one thing
is needful – an understanding of each other . . . it is the purpose of this
book so to familiarize us with the lands and peoples of the world that
we can cherish no ill-will for them. We are one great human family,
and this is the book of our brothers and sisters.'

I never read the text. All the efforts of what was presumably an
army of experts in their various fields, painfully adapting their ways
of writing to render them intelligible to infant minds, were totally

wasted on me. All I did, and still do, for I still have the six volumes,
was to look at the photographs, of which there were thousands in black
and white besides the seven hundred or so in colour, and read the
captions and the short descriptions below them of a world which, if it
ever existed in the form in which it was here portrayed, is now no
more. What I saw was a world at peace, one from which violence,
even well-intentioned sorts, such as ritual murder and cannibalism, had
been banished, or at least as long as the parts kept coming.

In Merrie England, donkeys carried the Royal Mail through the
cobbled streets of Clovelly, milkmaids in floppy hats churned butter
by hand in the Isle of Wight, swan uppers upped swans on the River
Thames, genial bearded fishermen in sou'westers mended nets on the
Suffolk coast, town criers rang their bells, and choirboys wearing
mortarboards, using long switches, beat the bounds of St Clement
Danes.

In the Land of the Cymry, which is how *Lands and Peoples* described
Wales, ancient dames wearing chimney-pot hats stopped outside their
whitewashed cottages to pass the time of day with more modern,
marcel-waved neighbours, and cloth-capped salmon fishers paddled
their coracles on the River Dee.

In Bonnie Scotland, brawny, kilted athletes tossed the caber, border
shepherds carried weakling lambs to shelter from the winter snows,
women ground corn with stone hand-mills in the Inner Hebrides and,
far out in the Atlantic, on St Kilda, the loneliest of the inhabited British
Isles, men wearing tam-o'shanters and bushy beards were photographed returning homewards with seabirds taken on its fearsome
cliffs.

In the Emerald Isle, bare-footed, flannel-petticoated colleens drew
water from brawling streams, or knitted socks in cabins in Connemara,
while little boys in the Aran Islands wore skirts to protect them from
being kidnapped by the fairies.

Further afield, as I turned the pages, covering them with Bovril (for
one of my greatest pleasures was to go to bed early with *Lands and
Peoples* and at the same time eat Bovril sandwiches), I came upon
Czechs and Slovaks and Hungarians wearing embroidered petticoats
irrespective of sex, and incredible hats – in Rumania there were men
who wore garters with little bells on them, who looked like sissies to

me. I also saw fellers of proud giants in the Canadian forest; savages
of New Guinea – their hair plastered with grease and mud; Jews in
Poland – a new state with a glorious past; sun-loving Negroes in South
Africa; happy Negro children romping in the 'Coloured Section' of
New York; Kirghiz tribesmen on the 'Roof of the World'; Orthodox
scholars wearing arm thongs and phylacteries studying the ancient laws
of their people; penguin rookeries in the Great White South; geishas
negotiating stepping stones in Cherry Blossom Land; hardy Indian
women on beds of nails at Benares; laughter-loving girls of the Abruzzi;
Flemings and Walloons – little Belgium's two sturdy races; Macedonian
women weaving fine cloth with deft fingers; haughty-looking redskins
decked in eagle's feathers and wampum; Germany – rich country of
an industrious nation; and so on, and so on.

Everywhere in *Lands and Peoples* there were photographs of schools
and schoolchildren; ruinous-looking schools in which little Negroes
were learning to add up, schools in Japan with the pupils marching
round in circles dressed in military-looking uniforms, clinical-looking
schools in the United States in which the children were being inspected
for dental decay, children brandishing enormously long slates in
Burma, memorizing the Koran in oases, going to school in wheelbarrows in China, learning to read in lonely Labrador and being basti-
nadoed in Persia, one of the only examples of violence in the entire
work. That children had to put up with going to school in other countries besides my own I found encouraging. And here at home they
didn't have the bastinado, even at Colet Court.

Each time I got through all six volumes of the *Children's Colour Book
of Lands and Peoples* I began again, in much the same way as the Scots-
men of Bonnie Scotland, sturdy independent folk, who painted the
Forth Bridge, would start all over again as soon as they had applied
the final brush strokes to that miracle of Scottish engineering.

At St Paul's I became a Scout in order to avoid being drafted into the
Officers' Training Corps, the OTC, which would have meant wearing
an insufferably itchy uniform that was blanket thick. As a Scout I
learned to light a fire with one match and to use a felling axe without
dismembering myself. On Saturdays we engaged in bloody night
battles with other troops of Scouts in the swamps of Wimbledon

Common. In the holidays we went camping in the beautiful parks of
gentlemen's country seats. Because I got on with Jews – I still do, I
think they find my lack of subtlety restful – I was given command of
a Jewish patrol. One of them, who was as prickly as a present-day
Israeli, refused to wear Scout uniform and appeared at our open-air
meetings wearing a double-breasted overcoat, a bowler hat and carrying a rolled umbrella. Another, who used to charge his mother half a
crown to kiss him good night, was always loaded down with silver.
On one occasion, when there was a danger of our losing one of the
outdoor games known as 'wide games' (which necessitated covering
large tracts of ground on foot) another member of my patrol whose
family owned a huge limousine in which he used to arrive at wherever
was the meeting place, summoned the chauffeur who was parked round
the corner, and six scouts whirred away in it to certain victory.

In the spring of 1936, when I was sixteen years old, my father
announced that, as it appeared unlikely I would pass the School Certifi-
cate Examination (the then equivalent of O-levels), in mathematics, a
subject in which it was obligatory to pass, he had decided to take me
away from St Paul's at the end of the summer term and 'put me into
business'. I did fail. I was sorry about this decision. I was good at
English, History, even Divinity, and I had dreamed of reading History
at Oxford.

Apart from an innate inability to cope with mathematics the only
disadvantage I laboured under at St Paul's, and being a Scout made not
the slightest difference, was that I had a curious sense of humour which
meant that if anything came up in class with a suggestion of *double
entendre* it caused me to dissolve into hysterics, for which I was
punished, sometimes quite severely. In other words I had a dirty
mind.

For instance, on one occasion, when we were reading Scott's *Marmion*
aloud, it became obvious to myself and everyone else in the classroom
that by the working of some hideously unfair natural process of selection it would fall to me to read a completely unreadable part of the
romance in Canto Two, entitled 'The Convent', which concerned the
blind Bishop of Lindisfarne. And you could have heard a pin drop
when I got to my feet.

'No hand was moved, no word was said
Till thus the Abbot's doom was given.
Raising his sightless balls to heaven . . .'

was all I could manage before going off into peals of mad laughter and
to be beaten by John Bell, the High Master, a hedonist who showed
in as marked a way as possible in the circumstances where his sympa-
thies lay by beating me as hard as anyone else sent to him for punishment, and then giving me a shilling. I have never forgiven Scott.

# In and Out of Advertising

IN THE SUMMER OF 1936, my father took me away from school and put me into a large, West End advertising agency.

Two years later, on the day we lost the Cereal Account, I finally decided to go to sea.

'You've 'ad it,' said the Porter with gloomy relish as I clocked in a little after the appointed hour. I was not surprised. My father had known the Chairman, George Wurzel, in his earlier, more uncomplicated days and had placed me with him in the fond belief that the sooner I got down to learning business methods the better. By now they were beginning to feel that they might have been wrong. Wurzel's had long held a similar opinion. Since I had ridden a bicycle into the office of Miss Phrygian, the secretary of the managing director, they had been more than cool. Julian Pringle, the most rebellious copywriter Wurzel's ever had, bet me that I could not ride it round the entire building without dismounting. The coast had been clear, the numerous swing doors held open, and the bicycle, which was being sketched for the front page of the *Daily Mail*, borrowed from the Art Department.

I had started my uneasy career in the Checking Department at the age of sixteen. Miss Phrygian had escorted me there. On the way we passed the Porter's cubby hole; inside, half a dozen evil-looking messenger boys were waiting to take blocks to Fleet Street. There were more seats than messenger boys and I found Miss Phrygian casting a speculative look at the empty places. For a moment I thought she was going to enlist me in their ranks, but she must have remembered my father's insistence on the value of the business methods I was going to learn, and we passed on.

In the narrow, airless transepts of the Checking Department, where the electric lights burned permanently, I thumbed my way through the newspapers and periodicals of the world to make sure that our advertisements were appearing on schedule and the right way up, which they failed to do quite frequently in some of the more unsophisticated newspapers from rugged and distant parts of the globe. Some of the advertisements had to be cut out and pasted in a book. We always cut out Carter's Little Liver Pills, but I never discovered the reason. Turning the pages of thousands of newspapers day after day, I accumulated knowledge of the most recondite subjects – croquet matches between missionaries in Basutoland, reports of conventions of undertakers at South Bend, Indiana, great exhibitions for tram ticket collectors in the Midlands – the world spread out before me.

When I was not speculating about what I read, I would fight with Stan, a great dark brute of a boy, one of the two assistants in the Department, to whom I had become quite attached. Both Stan and Les, the second assistant, called me 'Noob'.

''Ere, Noob, what abaht a pummel?' Stan would croak invitingly, and we would pummel one another until Miss Phrygian banged furiously on the frosted glass of her office door to stop the din.

From time to time we would be visited by the Contact Men who dealt personally with Wurzel's clients and handled the advertising accounts. They would stand gingerly in our den and turn the pages of the glossy magazines with beautifully manicured fingers. They were all youngish, perfectly dressed in Hawes and Curtis suits, and they smelled of bay rum. The amorous complications of their private lives were hair-raising. One of them owned a Bentley. They all wore clove carnations every day except Saturdays when they were in tweeds and went to the 'country' around Sunningdale. I always felt a clod in their presence and for some time after their visits disinclined to pummel. More popular were the visits of the typists. Wurzel's was run on pseudo-American lines and had a splendid collection. Two of the most popular were Lettice Rundle and Lilly Reidenfelt. Lilly was the more provocative of the two. It was generally conceded that Lettice was the sort of girl you married and had children by after trying Miss Reidenfelt, who was expected to run to fat.

When Miss Reidenfelt entered the Checking Department, Stan, the Man of Action, would be stricken dumb and with eyes cast down would trace bashful circles amongst the waste paper with his toe. Les,

Socialite and Dreamer, knew better how to please, and, more forth-
coming, usually succeeded in pinching her. At such times what little
air there was would be so heavy with lust that I would develop an
enormous headache of the kind usually brought on by thundery
weather. When Miss Reidenfelt had finally minced away inviolate, Stan
would fling himself at the piles of newspaper in the steel fixtures and
punch them in torment, crying: 'Oh, you lovely bit of gravy.'

With such experiences behind me it was easy to believe the Porter when
he said I was going to be sacked, and when I went into the main office
through the swing doors in the reception counter I was filled with
strangely pleasant forebodings. By this time the place would normally
have been a Babel, but this morning the atmosphere was chilly, tragic,
and unnaturally quiet. Lettice Rundle was having a good cry over her
Remington and the group of young men who handled the Cereal
Account were shovelling piles of proofs and stereos into a dustbin and
removing their personal belongings from drawers. Years later I was to
witness similar scenes in Cairo when Middle East headquarters became
a great funeral pyre of burning documents as the Germans moved
towards the Delta. But this was my first experience of an evacuation.
    It was easy to see that besides myself quite a number of people were
about to leave. Those remaining pored over their tasks with unnatural
solicitude and averted their eyes from their unfortunate fellows. I had
no personal possessions to put together. My hat was in the cloakroom
where it had remained for two years. I had never taken it out but
sometimes I dusted it, as Mr McBean from time to time checked up
on the whereabouts of the more junior and unstable members of the
staff by identifying the hats in the cloakroom. This was my alibi; with
my hat in its place I was permanently somewhere in the building.
    Before they left I asked them why I had not been sacked with the
rest of them. Robbie only called you 'old boy' in moments of stress.
He was reluctant to answer my question. He called me 'old boy' now.
    'Well, old boy, they did think about it but they decided that it cost
them so little that it didn't make any difference whether you stayed
or not.'
    I was furious. The Porter had been wrong and I hadn't ''ad it'. I
was perhaps the only member of the staff who would have actively

welcomed the sack. Wurzel's was a prison to me. All the way home in the Underground I seethed . . . too unimportant to be sacked . . . At Piccadilly the train was full but the guards packed in more and more people. At Knightsbridge two of them tried to force an inoffensive little man into the train by putting their shoulders to the back of his head and shoving. Someone began to Baa loudly and hysterically. There was an embarrassed silence and nobody laughed. We were all too much like real sheep to find it funny.

At Hammersmith where I emerged sticky and wretched from the train, I found that we had been so closely packed that somebody had taken my handkerchief out of my pocket, used it, and put it back under the impression that it was his own.

I bought an evening paper. It had some very depressing headlines about the breakdown of Runciman's negotiations at Prague.

The next day I went to Salcombe for my holiday. During that fortnight while swimming in Starehole Bay I dived down and saw beneath me the remains of the four-masted barque *Herzogin Cecilie* lying broken-backed, half buried in the sand.

On my way back to London there was an hour to wait for the connection at Newton Abbot, and wandering up the hot and empty street in the afternoon sunshine I went into a café and wrote to Gustav Erikson of Mariehamn for a place on one of his grain ships.

I never went back to Wurzel's.

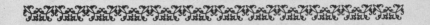

# Around the World in a
# Four-masted Barque

WHEN I RETURNED from my holiday, events started to happen with
increasing momentum so that I began to feel like the central figure in
one of those films of the twenties, in which the actors flash in and out
of buildings in the twinkling of an eye. With suspicious promptness a
letter arrived from Gustav Erikson in Mariehamn, in which that man
of iron told me to get in touch with his London Agents, Messrs H.
Clarkson of Bishopsgate.

Captain Gustav Erikson of Mariehamn, 'Ploddy Gustav' as he was
known more or less affectionately by the men and boys who sailed
his ships, was in 1938 the owner of the largest fleet of square-rigged
deep-water sailing vessels in the world. The great French sailing fleet
of Dom Borde Fils of Bordeaux had melted away upon the withdrawal
of government subsidies in the twenties; only two barques, *Padua* and
*Priwall*, still belonged to the once great house of Laeisz of Hamburg;
Erikson remained. He was not only the proprietor of twelve four- and
three-masted barques, he also owned a number of wooden barquentines
and schooners, the majority of which were engaged in the 'onker'
(timber) trade in the Baltic and across the North Sea.

There were still in 1938 thirteen vessels entirely propelled by sail,
engaged in carrying grain from South Australia to Europe by way of
Cape Horn. There were other cargoes for these ships: timber from
Finland to East Africa, guano (a sinister kind of bird dung) from Maur-
itius and the Seychelles to New Zealand, and very rarely, for the two
remaining German barques, cargoes of nitrate from Tocopilla, Mejil-
lones, and other ports on the Chilean Coast to be carried round the
Horn to Hamburg. But for the most part the outward voyages from
Europe to South Australia round the Cape of Good Hope and across
the Southern Indian Ocean were ballast passages. Grain was the staple

cargo. If that failed most of these thirteen ships would soon be rusting at forgotten anchorages.

The survival of the big sailing ships in this trade was due to several favourable circumstances. Grain was not dependent on season, neither was it perishable. In the primitive ports of the Spencer Gulf, where the grain was brought down from the back blocks in sacks, steamers found it difficult to load a cargo in an economical time. Although at some ports there were mile-long jetties, in most places the grain had to be brought alongside the ships in lightering ketches and slung into the hold with the vessel's own gear, which might, and frequently did, take weeks. But a sailing ship run with utmost economy and a low-paid crew could still in 1938 take six weeks to load her cargo of grain, reach Falmouth or Queenstown for orders after 120 days on passage and still make a profit on a round voyage of about 30,000 miles, the outward 15,000 having been made in ballast.

At the time I went to sea Erikson was sixty-five years old. Unlike most twentieth-century shipowners he had been a sailor with wide practical experience before he had become a shipowner. At the age of nine he had shipped as a boy aboard a vessel engaged in the North Sea trade. Ten years later he had his first command in the same traffic and then, for six years, he had shipped as mate in ocean-going ships. Between 1902 and 1913, when he finally left the sea to concentrate on being an owner, he was master of a number of square-rigged vessels.

If I had imagined that Clarkson would be impressed when I approached them, I should have been disappointed. I was one of a number of Englishmen who applied to join the Grain Fleet every year, and Clarkson could not know that I was to be one of the last. From this small mahogany-bound office, saved from being prosaic by the numerous pictures of sailing ships on the walls, they looked after the destinies of practically every grain sailer in the world. Even the Germans came to Clarkson. In 1937 they fixed the high freight of 42s 6d a ton for the *Kommodore Johnsen*. Most cargoes were for British ports and Clarkson fixed the freights. Erikson was well served by them.

I learned some of these things from a little white-haired man, who said that to make the voyage at all I must be bound apprentice and pay a premium of fifty pounds. He made no suggestions except that I would probably be better advised not to go at all. I left Bishopsgate with a

form of indenture which among other provisions stipulated that my
parents were to bind me to the owner for eighteen months or a round
voyage; that if I deserted the ship in any foreign port my premium
would be forfeited; that if I died or became incapacitated, a pro-rata
repayment of premium could be claimed; that I should receive 120
Fin-marks (10s) a month, and that I should be subject to Finnish law
and custom.

This document my father reluctantly signed after hopelessly trying
to discover something about Finnish law and custom. I remember that
he was particularly concerned to find out whether the death penalty
was still enforced and in what manner it was carried out. Even more
reluctantly he paid out £50 and sent off the Indentures with two doctors'
certificates attesting that I was robust enough for the voyage, and one
from a clergyman which stated that I was of good moral character. By
this time I began to feel that I was destined for Roedean rather than
the fo'c'sle of a barque.

Then, towards the end of September, I received a letter from the
owner's agents telling me to join the four-masted barque *Moshulu* which
was discharging its cargo of grain in Belfast.

S/V *Moshulu*, East Side,

York Dock,

Belfast

26 September 1938

Dear Mummy and Daddy,
. . . I was up on deck on the steamer from Heysham about
6.30 just in time to see the terrifically high masts of the
*Moshulu* rising high above the dock sheds and looking very
cold and remote in the early morning. After breakfast in the
steamer I took a very ancient taxi that was practically falling
to pieces to the ship and when it arrived alongside it was so
big that I felt like a midget. It is more than three thousand
tons and is the biggest sailing ship in commission in the
world.

I went up a gang plank and spoke to a very tough-looking
boy with slant eyes like a Mongolian who was oiling a don-

key engine, and asked him if he would help me with my enormous trunk. He picked it up, having made threatening gestures at the taxi man who was trying to overcharge me, and carried it up the plank on his back all by himself!

Meanwhile, sacks of grain were being hoisted out of the hold and weighed before being taken ashore and into the sheds – altogether the ship brought back more than sixty-two thousand sacks from South Australia on this last voyage and was a hundred and twenty days at sea, which is rather slow. A hundred days from Australia to Britain is good, anything under a hundred, very good.

Then my new friend, Jansson, who comes from the Åland Islands, took me into the starboard fo'c'sle where I am to live until the watches are appointed, which will be on the day we go to sea. It is about thirty feet long and about thirteen feet wide, with wooden bunks from floor to ceiling, one above the other, like coffins with open sides. I am not sure how many but will tell you later. The boys seem pleasant enough, but not exactly gushing. About three-quarters of them speak only about a dozen words of English and some of those are swear words, which is twelve words more than I speak of Swedish which is the language in which all orders are given, rather than Finnish, which would be too difficult for non-Finns, I suppose. Swedish/Finns from the Åland Islands and Finns make up the majority of the crew.

They gave me some coffee and then I was told the second mate wanted to see me on the bridge deck, which is amidships above the fo'c'sles, where the ship is steered from, not from the poop. He was a pale, thin fellow and after asking me my name suddenly said, 'Op the rigging!'

I simply couldn't believe this. I thought they would give one a bit of time to get used to being in a ship. I was wearing my Harris tweed jacket, grey flannel trousers and those leather shoes with slippery soles which I took the nails out of because I thought they might damage the decks! He wouldn't allow me to change, not even my shoes, just take off my jacket and shirt. I was in a sort of daze. I swung out over

the ship's side and started to climb the ratlines, wooden rungs
lashed to the shrouds which hold the mast up, quite wide at
the bottom but only a few inches wide when you get under
what is known as the 'top', where it was difficult to get feet
as large as mine on to them. The top is a platform and to
get on to it I had to climb outwards on rope ratlines, like a
fly on a ceiling, and when I got on to it, looking down I
almost fainted.

I thought this was enough, but 'Go on op,' he shouted,
and so I went on 'op' by rope ratlines, some of them very
rotten after the long voyage – you have to hold on to the
shrouds, not the ratlines, in case they break. These ratlines
ended at the cross trees, which are made of steel and form
a sort of open platform, like glass with my slippery shoes
on, a hundred and thirty feet up with Belfast spread out
below.

'Op to the Royal Yard,' was the next command. This was
forty feet or so of nearly vertical and very trembly ratlines
to just below the Royal Yard, the topmost one, on which
the Royal Sail is bent at sea. Here, there were no more ratlines, and I had to haul myself up on to it, all covered with
grease from something like a vertical railway line [a mast
track on which the yard is raised and lowered by a halliard]
on the face of the mast.

This yard was about fifty feet long, and made of steel, like
all the other yards and masts. It had an iron rail along the
top [a jackstay] to which the sail is bent and underneath it is
a steel footrope [the 'horse'] on which my shoes skidded in
opposite directions, so that I looked like a ballet dancer doing
the splits. At the yardarm I was – I learned the heights when
I got down – about a hundred and sixty feet over the dock
sheds, which had glass roofs – what a crash, I thought, if
I fell off! It was better looking further afield. There were
marvellous views of the Antrim Hills and down Belfast
Lough towards the Irish Sea.

Back at the mast, thinking thank goodness that's over, I
heard the mate's voice telling me to climb to the very top of

the main mast [the main truck]; but I couldn't do this with
such slippery shoes on, as there were only two or three very
rotten-looking ratlines on the stays [seized across the royal
backstays], and then nothing but about six feet of absolutely
bare pole to the cap. So I took off my shoes and socks, which
were even more slippery than the shoes, left them on the
yard and then shinned up, past caring what happened, more
frightened of the mate than anything else, until I could touch
the cap which was like a round, wooden bun. This cap I
have discovered is nearly two hundred feet above the keel,
much higher than Nelson's column [which is only a hundred
and forty-five feet high].

Now he was shouting to me to sit on the top; but I would
have rather died than do that and so I pretended not to hear
him. When I got down he was angry because he said it was
unseamanlike to take off my shoes and socks, and also that
the shoes might have fallen and injured somebody. I think
the part about sitting on the cap must have been a joke,
because he never mentioned it and none of the others have
done it. Then he sent me to clean the lavatories; but I was
allowed to change first. My trousers got awfully dirty with
Belfast soot up in the rigging and will have to be cleaned.

I am not writing this to worry you but only because I feel
that I will be alright in the rigging from now on. It was
probably a good idea to get it over. Anyway, it is much
better than cleaning the lavatories.

Please do not send anything but letters and money as I
have no room for anything in my bunk except myself.

This evening we are going ashore for what the boys call
a 'liddle trink' at a pub called the Rotterdam Bar, a farewell
party for the boys who are leaving the ship and going home.
I never imagined that one day I would go to a pub called the
Rotterdam Bar and be a sailor.

All my love,
Eric

S/V *Moshulu*,
Belfast

11 October 1938

Dear Mummy and Daddy,

We are now loading ballast, mostly rock and sand used in blast foundries, and paving stones and the best part of an old house. Altogether about fifteen hundred tons. There is bad news about George White, the nice American boy. He fell into the hold through the tonnage opening in the between-decks below Number Three Hatch when there was no ballast in it and broke one of his legs and various other things, so he won't be able to sail with us. I've just spent a wonderful time with Ivy [a friend of my parents] and her husband at their house. The butler, called Taggart, brought me an enormous breakfast in bed and all my clothes were laundered for me, goodness knows how in the time.

My other friends are Jansson, the boy who put my trunk on board, a Dutch boy, called Kroner, and a Lithuanian named Vytautas Bagdanavicius, who sailed on the previous voyage. We go to gruesome pubs and drink porter, a weak version of Guinness and we eat fish and chips and go to the Salvation Army Hostel for wonderful hot baths. Don't worry about mean night adventures in the streets. They are much too wet, and we haven't got any money. The only one who tried a Matros, an AB [able-bodied seaman] got a nasty disease which he is treating himself, with a syringe. I wish he was elsewhere . . .

All my love,
Eric

This letter is from my father and is dated 16 October 1938. It was sent to Belfast but, having arrived too late, was forwarded to Australia.

My dear Eric,

I feel that you are on the eve of your departure for the open sea, and so I take leave to bid you a fond farewell. You have chosen a difficult job and are beginning life again on the bottom rung.

I enclose a German Text Book for Travellers which may help you with some words you have forgotten. I could not get one in Swedish or Finnish and I did not think Norwegian would be much good.

That fellow with the venereal disease sounds a rotten blighter. I should complain to the captain about him . . .

Good luck to you, my dear boy, and a safe journey.

Your loving father.

PS. Your mother is writing separately.

We sailed for Australia on 18 October 1938 with a crew of twenty-eight.

At two in the morning on 11 December, fifty-four days out from Belfast when we were in Latitude 39° South, Longitude 9° East in the South Atlantic, our watch was called on deck to square up the yards and sheet home the fore-and-aft sail on the port side. There was a new movement in the ship now: she was rocking slightly from stem to stern.

'Kom die Väst Vind,' said Tria as we ground away at the Jarvis brace winches. By noon that day the westerlies were blowing strongly, lumping the rollers up behind. This was a memorable day because we ran 293 miles, and Alvar dropped our dinner on the way from the galley.

On the 13th we crossed the longitude of the Cape of Good Hope and entered the Southern Indian Ocean in 40° 33' South Latitude. Whilst running eastward we edged south to 42° and finally to 43° 47'. Sometimes the West Wind blew strongly, sometimes we were nearly becalmed. Always the drift was carrying us eastwards, thirty to forty miles a day. In the course of this outward voyage we only made one landfall, Inaccessible Island, one of the Tristran da Cunha group.

By five o'clock that evening *Moshulu* was sailing fifteen knots. The wind was on the quarter and there was a big sea running. When Sedelquist and I took over there were already two men at the wheel. (Sedelquist was helmsman and I was help wheel.)

'Going to be deefecult,' he said in an unusual access of friendliness, as we stumbled out on deck, immense in our thick pilot coats, 'going to be von bastard.'

We took over from Hilbert and Hörglund, a wild-looking but capable team. Although it was quite cold with occasional squalls of hail, I noticed that their faces were glistening with perspiration in the light of the binnacle.

'Törn om,' said Sedelquist, as he stepped up beside Hilbert on the weather side.

'Törn om,' I echoed as I mounted the platform to leeward.

'Ostsydost,' said Hilbert and then more quietly as the Captain was close by, 'proper strongbody for vind, Kapten.'

The ship was a strongbody too, she was a fury, and as soon as we took over we both knew that it was going to be a fight to hold her.

Sedelquist was a first-class helmsman – very cool and calm and sure of himself. I too was on my mettle to give him all the help I could, not for reasons of prestige but because a mistake on a night like this might finish us all.

Being at the wheel was a remarkable sensation. It was as if the ship had wings. The seas were big, but they never caught up with her to drag at her and slow her down. Instead they bore her up and flung her forward.

Steering was very hard work; heaving on the spokes, at Sedelquist's direction, I was soon sweating. There was no time to speak, nor was it permitted. Only when I made 7 bells at half-past seven did Sedelquist shout out of the corner of his mouth:

'Oh you noh, Kryss Royal going in a meenit.'

The Captain, the First Mate, and Tria were all on deck, the Captain constantly gazing aloft at the upper sails. At a quarter to eight with our trick nearly over, when I was congratulating myself that we had come through, we suddenly lost control of her and she began to run up into the wind.

'Kom on, kom on,' Sedelquist roared, but it was too late. Our combined strength was not enough to move the wheel.

*Moshulu* continued to shoot up, the yards began to swing, a big sea came over the waist, then another bigger still. There was a shout of 'Look out, man!' Then there was a great smashing sound as the Captain jumped at the after wheel and brought his whole weight upon it. Tria and the First Mate were on the other side. Spoke by spoke we fought the wheel while from above came an awful rumbling sound as the yards chafed and reared in their slings, until the ship's head began to point her course again.

The danger was past, but as the Captain turned away, pale and trembling, I heard him sob: 'O Christ.'

Suddenly I felt sick at the thought of what might have happened if she had broached-to.

'O Yesus,' muttered Sedelquist, his assurance gone, 'I tought the masts were coming down out of heem.'

The clock in the charthouse began to strike. Before it had finished, more than anxious to be gone, I had made eight bells, but the Mate was already blowing his whistle for all hands. The Captain had had enough, and before Sedelquist and I were relieved at the wheel the royals came in, all the higher fore-and-aft sails, and the mizzen course. It was now 8.30 p.m. Between 4 and 8 *Moshulu* logged 63 miles, and the same distance again between eight and midnight.

### 'GOD JUL'

For many days we had been thinking of Christmas, which this year fell on a Sunday. There had been a good deal of grumbling about this in the fo'c'sle, but even Sedelquist, who knew his rights, and was always threatening to complain to the Finnish Consul over imaginary infringements, wasn't able to suggest any satisfactory plan for moving Christmas Day to the following Monday in order to get an extra day's holiday.

In the week before Christmas I was 'Backstern'* for the second time on the voyage. My job was to wash up for the twenty occupants of the three fo'c'sles whenever mine was a working watch. Kroner performed the same service when I was free. Besides being a romantic, Kroner was a great grumbler and every day he told me I had forgotten

* 'Backlagsman' – Mess man.

to dry the dishcloths in the galley. Every day I told him the same thing. Very often, on the occasions when we did remember to hang them over the range, they were knocked down by the coal-carrying party and trampled in the coal-dust. Kroner drew my washing-up water; I drew his.

To get sea-water for washing-up I tied a rope to a bucket, stood in the lee rigging of the foremast, and dropped it into the sea. Bäckmann had been the first person to do 'Backstern' in our watch and he had cast a new teak bucket into the sea on the evening of our spectacular dash into the Atlantic. With *Moshulu* running thirteen to fourteen knots it was lucky that he had not known how to attach the rope to the bucket in a seamanlike manner; if he had, the tremendous jerk when it fetched up at the end of a lot of slack would probably have pulled him over the side. As it was, the knot came undone and the bucket sank before the eyes of the First Mate and the Captain, who were interested spectators. I had been charged for a hammer. Bäckman was put down for a teak bucket.

With the water safely on deck my troubles were not over, for it still had to be heated over the galley fire, and if the 'Kock' didn't like you he would move it as far as possible from the hot part of the stove. Like all cooks he was subject to sudden glooms and rages. It was unfortunate that he had taken a dislike to Kroner, who had been rude to him about some bacon instead of keeping his mouth shut and throwing it over the side, but he had nothing against me. Thanks to the 'Kock's' misplaced malevolence, Kroner enjoyed a week of scalding and abundant water whilst I suffered lukewarm water one day, total loss on another, and on a third found a long sea-boot stocking stewing merrily away in a bucket topped with a yeasty-looking froth.

The washing-up basin was a kerosene can sawn in half, the sharp edges beaten down so that it looked like some revolting curio from an oriental bazaar. These were the days before detergents, and their place was taken by sand, with some ropeyarn as a scourer. The everyday work on the ship had already battered my hands beyond recognition so that they resembled bloodstained hooks; and now the salt water penetrated cuts and scratches, making them swell and split. There was a vivid and appropriate name for these sores which never seemed to heal.

It was an unspoken rule that the 'Backstern' washed up first in his own fo'c'sle in case he was called on deck by 'två vissel' – two whistles. After the port side was finished, he washed up for the starboard watch. Then for the daymen amidships. Theirs was a gloomy hole, without ports and filled with stale cigarette smoke, its only natural illumination a skylight, rarely opened, shedding a permanent dusk into it. To one side was a tiny rectangular table piled high with the most ghastly debris of *après déjeuner*: islands of porridge; lakes of coffee in which cigarette ends were slowly sinking; great mounds of uneaten salt bacon; squashed putty-coloured fish-balls, and, in the tropics, almost phosphorescent herring. At other meals mountains of bones and a warm feral smell made the fo'c'sle more like a lair of wild beasts than a human habitation.

On the Monday of Christmas week washing-up had been terrible. There was heavy rain and it had come on to blow hard. 'Like sonofa-beetch, like *helvete*,' said Sandell as he came from the wheel. I was pressed for time as I had second look-out, which meant washing up three fo'c'sles in less than an hour. Kroner, the damn fool, had forgotten to put the drying-up cloths in the galley and there was only one tin of hot water instead of three. To make things worse the ship was heeling at such an angle that it was impossible to stand upright.

I tore the tail off a good shirt, wedged the kerosene can against the rim of the table, and put each wet irreplaceable piece of crockery in the locker as I washed it. When I finished I took them all out, dried them, and put them back piece by piece. Around me the bunks were full of men trying to sleep, but the ship was a pandemonium of noise, the wind roaring in the rigging, the footsteps of the Officer of the Watch thumping overhead, the wheel thudding and juddering, and the fo'c'sle itself filled with the squeaks and groans of stressed rivets. From the hold came a deep rumbling sound as though the ballast was shifting. I dropped a spoon and five angry heads appeared from behind little curtains and told me to 'Shot op.' Eight bells sounded and it was my 'utkik', the hour of lookout on the fo'c'sle head.

There was a fearful sunset. The ship was driving towards a wall of black storm cloud tinged with bright ochre where the sun touched it. About us was a wild, tumbling yellow sea. South of us two great concentric rainbows spanned the sky and dropped unbroken into the sea. At intervals everything was blotted out by squalls of rain and hailstones as big and hard as dried peas. It only needed a waterspout to complete the scene.

Soon I became clammy and forlorn, gazing into the murk. It was dark now and the rain was freezing in the squalls. Above the curve of the foresail everything was black, and from the rigging, right up the heights of the masts came the endless rushing of the wind. To warm my hands I pushed them into the pockets of my oilskin coat and found two deep cold puddles. In one of them was my last handkerchief.

After an hour of 'utkik' I in my turn became 'påpass', the man who called the watch on deck if it was necessary and woke the next man relieving the helmsman. During my spell on the foredeck there were 'två vissel'. Welcoming the opportunity to exercise my frozen limbs I flung open the fo'c'sle door and screamed, 'Two vistle, ut på däck' in the most hair-raising voice I could manage.

Inside, water was swirling pieces of newspaper and bread about the floor. It broke over Yonny Valker and Alvar, those primitive men sleeping down there, awash and shining like whales. The other five members of our watch were dozing perilously on the benches. Everyone was fully dressed in oilskins, too wet to get into their bunks. The oil-lamp was canting at an alarming angle and Bäckmann hit his head on it as he started up from the table. He didn't feel anything because he was still asleep. One by one the others lurched out of the fo'c'sle, and as they encountered the blast on deck they cursed the owner for owning *Moshulu*, the Captain for bringing us here, the Mate for blowing his 'vissel', and me for being 'påpass' and hearing it.

Little Taanila was at the wheel, clinging to it like a flea, while the Mate tried to prevent it spinning and hurling him over the top on to the deck.

'Två män till rors,' shouted the Mate, and Bäckmann went as help wheel to Taanila.

'Mesan,' said the Mate and we tailed on to the downhaul of the largest of the three fore-and-aft sails on the jigger mast. It jammed, but we continued to take the strain. Suddenly it broke and we rolled in a wet heap in the scuppers.

'That ploddy Gustav,' said Sedelquist, speaking unlovingly of the owner who was reputed to be very close with ropes. 'He vonts—'

By Friday the rain was wearing us all down. Breakfast was terrible.

Black beans and fried salt bacon from the pickle cask. The margarine and sugar had both given out on Wednesday. We were ravenous and talked of nothing but food. But at noon Sandell reported that the hens had disappeared from the henhouse and that the Cook was making huge puddings. I saw them myself when I was fetching the washing-up water. They looked like sand castles. We were agog.

At last it was Saturday, 24th December, Christmas Eve. Christmas Eve was the principal Finnish celebration. It was our free watch in the morning, and now came the opportunity for the great 'Vask' in the slimy little 'Vaskrum'; but the joy of putting on clean clothes was worth the discomfort. Even Yonny and Alvar had a 'Vask', and some of us whose beards had not been a success shaved. Then we put on our best clothes: clean dungarees, home-knitted jerseys, and new woollen caps. Bäckmann even put on a collar and tie. This was too much for the more rugged members of the watch, and a committee was formed to discuss the question. They were very serious about it and decided he was improperly dressed for the time and place. Nevertheless he continued to wear a tie, and presently I put one on myself, with a tennis shirt and flannel trousers with the mud of Devon lanes still on the turn-ups. It was wonderful to wear clothes that followed the contours of the body after so many weeks of damp, ill-fitting garments. In the splendour of our new robes we slept till noon. Then, except for wheel and look-out, work ceased for everyone.

Like the apprentices in *A Christmas Carol* preparing the warehouse for the party, we put the finishing touches to the fo'c'sle. Bäckmann washed the paint with hot water and green soap. I removed a large number of bugs from the bunkboards and drowned the eggs. Taanila scrubbed the floor; Hermansonn polished our door-knob, while the others removed horrid debris from the unoccupied bunks and shook all the blankets on deck. The floor and tables were washed with hot soda and burnished white with sand. Then we sat down and looked around at what we had done. It did seem more like home. It would need to for tonight to be a success. 'Like home,' said Sedelquist. 'Like hell.'

At half past one I threw the last lot of washing-up water over the side. My week of 'Backstern' was over for a whole month, and I was heartily sick of it. Cleaning the 'skit hus' was preferable. From three

until four I was at the wheel. The wind was ENE and the ship steered
herself except for a slight touch from time to time. The afternoon was
cold, the decks were deserted. Everyone was below having haircuts,
shaving, trimming beards, or squeezing pimples. Just before I was
relieved the First Mate came on deck. A startling transformation had
been effected in him. He was no longer grimy-looking; the ginger
beard and moustaches that had given him so much the appearance of
a Cheshire Cat had disappeared. Instead he was very stiff and self-
conscious in a gold-braided reefer suit, his head bowed beneath an
enormous peaked cap, also gold-braided, on which was pinned the
white house badge, a white flag with G.E. in black letters on it. With
dismay I realized that without the beard his was not the sort of face I
cared for at all. Indecently bare, it was shorn of its strength. I think he
realized this, for he giggled, almost apologetically. This moment
marked the beginning of a certain coolness in our relationship.

'Coffee-time' brought the first fragments of a great avalanche of
food. On Saturdays the bread was always different; today it arrived in
the shape of scones. There were a great number, they were very good,
and we ate the lot in seven minutes.

As the dinner hour approached the agony of waiting became almost
unbearable. We roamed about the fo'c'sles like hungry lions. Outside,
the rain beat down on the deck. The weather had broken up soon after
five, but the wind blew steadily and we were all confident that there
would be no work on deck unless it shifted. Otherwise the ship would
carry topgallants and topmast staysails throughout the night. When it
grew dark, at seven o'clock, 'tre vissel' summoned all hands. We
crowded the well-deck. Looking down on us was the Captain, all braid
and smiles; the First and Second Mates, less braid and fewer smiles;
and Tria, no braid but more smiles than all of them put together. I had
never seen such splendid uniforms.

The Captain made a little speech. Addressing us as 'Pojkar' (Boys),
he wished us 'God Jul' and told us to come aft to his saloon after
dinner. When he had finished we tipped our caps to him, mumbled
our thanks, and made a rush below. Two sheets were produced and
spread on the table. We gathered all our lamps and lanterns and hung
them round the bulkheads.

The food was brought in from the galley. Great steaming bowls of rice and meat; pastry, sardines, salmon, corned beef, apricots, things we had forgotten. A bottle of Akvavit and the set piece, a huge ginger pudding, its summit wreathed in steam.

There were maddening moments of delay while I took what proved to be a series of unsuccessful photographs. Then we made a dash for the table. From then on there were few sounds other than the smacking of eight pairs of lips and an occasional grunted request to pass a dish. We had been hungry for weeks and now our chance had come. After the traditional Finnish rice-porridge I worked through potato pastry, chopped fish, and methodically round the table to the ginger pudding, which was sublime, the zenith of the evening. Alvar, appointed wine steward, circled the table allowing us half a mug of Akvavit each, and the starboard watch, who had already eaten, came in in bunches to cry 'God Jul, Pojkar!'

When the others had given up, Sandell and I were still plugging on steadily. He turned to me, his face distorted by a great piece of pudding, a little rice gleaming in his black beard. 'To spik notting and eat, is bettair,' he said and carved himself a slice of Dutch cheese. We all loved one another now. Even Sedelquist offered me an old *Tatler* containing a photograph of the Duchess in Newmarket boots and raincoat at a very wet point-to-point.

'Oh, say you. I think he is fon in bed, yes?'

'No.'

I took a good look at the Duke gazing myopically over her shoulder before I remembered that Sedelquist always got his genders mixed.

Each of us had been given a green tin of Abdullah cigarettes. Shaped to fit the pocket, they held fifty; on the lid, in large letters, was inscribed 'Imperial Preference'. There were additional charms: each one contained a coloured picture of a girl in an inviting posture, more accessible than the Duchess. After dinner brisk business was done in exchanging one for another, and Sedelquist emerged with the best collection. Although I didn't really like cigarettes I smoked half-a-dozen in rapid succession in order not to miss anything.

From the midships fo'c'sle came the sound of a Christmas hymn being sung rather well in Swedish and we all went to listen. The singers were seated with their backs to the bulkhead near the Christmas tree which 'Doonkey' had made from teased-out rope yarns. There were five of them sharing three hymn books and they all sang with great earnestness. Among them were Kisstar the Carpenter, the light of the oil-lamp softening the deep lines on his face; Reino Hörglund with his great black beard; and Jansson, thick-lipped and tousled. Half of the fo'c'sle was in shadow and I stood in darkness by the huge trunk of the mainmast; next to me stood Yonny Valker, hands clasped before him like a peasant before a roadside altar. We were all very homesick.

At nine o'clock we queued up outside the Captain's stateroom to receive our Christmas presents from the Missions to Seamen. This was the first time I had seen the Officers' quarters, which seemed very warm and substantial compared with our own. From somewhere the almost legendary wireless was emitting dance music with the background of peculiar rushing and whining sounds that accompany music across great expanses of ocean. Whilst we waited in this unaccustomed place I noticed with envy the magnificence of the washing-up arrangements, the scullery with an elaborate draining-board, and the abundance of dry dish-cloths. I thought then how easy it would be to provide something similar for the fo'c'sles, how much saving of time.

When it was my turn to enter the 'Great Hall' I felt very serf-like and nervous, but my premonitions were soon dispersed. Inside it was all red plush, banquettes, and brass rails, very like the old Café Royal. I almost expected to see Epstein instead of the smiling and very youthful-looking Captain seated at the mahogany table, his officers around him. He held out a hat to me, full of pieces of paper. The one I took was Number 7. 'Number 7 for England's Hope,' said the Captain, and the Steward who was kneeling on the floor surrounded by parcels handed me the one with 7 on it. I wished everybody 'God Jul' and backed out of the stateroom in fine feudal fashion, stepping heavily on the toes of the man behind me, and dashed eagerly back to the fo'c'sle to open it.

Inside the paper wrappings was a fine blue knitted scarf, a pair of grey mittens, and a pair of stout brown socks. When I picked up the scarf three bits of paper fell out. One of these was a Christmas card with 'Jultiden' in prominent red lettering on one side and on the other, in ink, 'och Gott Nytt År, onskar Aina Karlsson, Esplanadgarten 8, Mariehamn.' On the other two pieces was the text of St John, Chapter 20, in Finnish, and the good wishes of the Missions to Seamen who had sent the parcel. Right at the bottom was a hand mirror and comb.

I thought of Åina Karlsson knitting woollies with loving care for unknown sailors in sailing ships. We all eagerly compared our presents. Some had thicker garments, some larger. Sedelquist said that the Mates had already appropriated the best, but no one paid any attention to this. Among us Taanila had the finest haul – a woollen helmet that pulled over head and ears with a long scarf attached. It made him look like a fiendish Finnish gnome.

In the midships fo'c'sle there were two miserable people, Essin and Pipinen. Essin, the Sailmaker's assistant, had broken one of his molars in the general struggle to eat everything within reach. He now lay groaning in his bunk, his face swathed in mufflers. I tried to plug the cavity with gutta-percha, which on the advice of my dentist I had brought with me in anticipation of such an emergency. It had looked easy in Wimpole Street when he demonstrated how to do it: he put a little vaseline on a plugger, heated the gutta-percha and popped it in the hole. Now, overcome with wine and food, in a swaying ship, by the murky light of a hurricane lamp I felt like a tipsy surgeon about to perform a major operation. Worse still, the patient kept flinching and I dropped a blob of bubbling hot gutta-percha on his tongue. He leapt into the air screaming and three boys had to hold him down while I tried to push a cooler piece into the hole. But it would not stay in, and I gave him an overdose of aspirin and hoped for the best. The operation had not been successful.

Pipinen, the other casualty, had cut his hand badly while opening a tin of apricots and Karma, the unpredictable Finn, was fixing it with fathoms of bandage. Hilbert told me that Karma would not cut the bandage because he had bought it for himself. When I left, Pipinen's hand was as big as a football and Karma still had yards left.

I went in search of my bunk. It was 9.45. By some miracle I was neither 'rorsman' (helmsman), 'utkik', nor 'påpass'. I crawled into my bag and slept dreamlessly until four in the morning, when a voice cried 'resa upp'; but Sandell closed the curtains and I slept on until half past seven. There were loud cheers when I woke. I had slept 'like sonofabeetch, like peeg in straw'. Ten hours – the longest sleep I ever had in *Moshulu*, or anywhere else. I was quite thrilled.

On Christmas morning the weather was cold and brilliant. Big following seas were charging up astern in endless succession. They surged beneath the ship, bearing her up, filling the air with whistling spray as their great heads tore out from under and ahead to leave her in a trough as black and polished as basalt except where, under the stern post, the angle of the rudder made the water bubble jade-green, as if from a spring. From the mizzen yardarm, where I hung festooned with photographic apparatus, I could see the whole midships of *Moshulu*. On the flying bridge above the main deck the Captain and the three Mates were being photographed by the Steward, solemn and black as crows in their best uniforms.

Rigid with cold I descended to eat Christmas dinner, for which the 'Kock' had made an extra sustaining fruit soup. For breakfast we had had Palethorpe's tinned sausages which were very well received; at 'Coffee-time' apple tarts and buns but not enough of either; and for supper, rice, pastry, and jam. At four a.m. on what would have been Boxing Day in England we were setting royals once more. The party was over.

Eighty-two days out from Belfast we anchored in Spencer Gulf in south Australia, having sailed 15,000 sea miles. We were three months in Australia. At first sweltering at anchorage waiting for a freight to be fixed, so that we could load a cargo of grain somewhere in Spencer Gulf, which runs up into the heart of the wheat belt, then, when hope had almost been given up of fixing a freight for any of the ships, and we had visions of sailing home in ballast or being sold with the ships like a lot of slaves, all the ships got freights and *Moshulu* was ordered to load a cargo at Port Victoria on the other side of the gulf at £1.37½ ($6.34) a ton – in 1938 she had loaded nearly five thousand tons at £2.06 ($10.30) a ton. The Spencer Gulf was a hell of a place, wherever you were in it in summer, plagued by flies and an appalling wind as hot as a blast furnace which poured down through it from the deserts of the interior, causing *Moshulu* and other ships to drag their anchors. To go ashore, we rowed and sailed eight miles to Port Lincoln and eight miles back. I found a lot of letters waiting for me and I sent my parents a telegram which read 'Muscular, happy, penniless' and got some money by return.

We sailed from Port Victoria at 6.30 a.m. on 11 March 1939, our destination Queenstown in southern Ireland (now Cobh), for orders,

*Above:* My father and mother at Henley before the first war.

*Right:* Picnic with my mother in Surrey, aged two.

*Left:* At the helm of *Moshulu*, in 1938. There were twin wheels which could be manned by four men in an emergency. Two men at the wheel was a normal occurrence in rough weather.

*Below:* Painting the hull in Belfast before sailing for Australia, October 1938. Every morning while we were in port we went over the side to chip rust and to red-lead the shell plating before painting it.

*Above:* Unloading ballast – which contained two dead dogs – off Port Victoria, Spencer's Gulf, with the temperature in the hold up to 120°F. The ballast, 1500 tons of it, consisted of coarse dark sand used in the manufacture of pig-iron, huge lumps of paving stone, granite blocks, the best part of a small house, and the two dead dogs, added by the Belfast stevedores, which we eventually located and spooned up with our shovels.

*Right:* Starboard watch knocked out after shifting ballast.

Starboard watch hauling on the mizzen royal halliard to raise the yard.

*Opposite top:* Dartmoor in August 1939, the summer before the war.

*Opposite bottom:* Wedding day in Florence in the spring of 1946.

*Opposite:* Village in the Apennines.

*Right and below:* Shepherdess in the Apennines near the village of Pracchiola.

Wanda's mother with friends in Slovenia.

by way of Cape Horn. We were, in fact, taking part in the 1939 sailings of what was known as the Grain Race. This year turned out to be the Last Grain Race.

On the second Friday (having crossed the 180th meridian – the international dateline – there were two Fridays), running the easting down, *Moshulu*'s noon position was 51°S, 176°W, 13 days and 2440 nautical miles out from Port Victoria. In 23½ hours she had sailed 296 miles, the best day's sailing with cargo she ever had with Erikson.* At 5.30 in the morning, *Moshulu*, still carrying her upper topgallants, began to labour under the onslaught of the heavy seas which were flooding on to the deck like a mill race. It was quite dark as six of us clewed-up the mizzen lower topgallant, and although from where I was at the tail of the rope I could see nothing at all except the hunched shoulders of Jansson ahead of me, I could hear Tria at the head of the line exhorting us. The sail was almost up when the wind fell quite suddenly and we all knew that we were in the trough of a wave far bigger than anything we had yet experienced. It was far too dark to see it at a distance, we could only sense its coming as the ship rolled slightly to port to meet it.

'Hoold . . .' someone began to shout as the darkness became darker still and the sea came looming over the rail. I was end man. There was just time to take a turn with the clewline round my middle and a good hold, the next moment it was on top of us. The rope was not torn from me; instead it was as though a gentle giant had smoothed his hands over my knuckles. They simply opened of their own accord and I unravelled from it like a cotton reel from the end of a thread and was swept away. As I went another body bumped me, and I received a blow in the eye from a seaboot. Then I was alone, rushing onwards and turning over and over. My head was filled with bright lights like a by-pass at night, and the air was full of the sounds of a large orchestra playing out of tune. In spite of this there was time to think and I thought: 'I'm done for.' At the same time the words of a sea poem, 'ten men hauling the lee fore brace . . . seven when she rose at last',

---

* When running to the east in southerly latitudes a day, noon to noon, is about 23½ hours.

came back to me with peculiar aptness. But only for an instant because now I was turning full somersaults, hitting myself violently again and again as I met something flat which might have been the coaming of No. 4 hatch, or the top of the charthouse, for all I knew. Then I was over it, full of water and very frightened, thinking 'Is this what it's like to drown?' No more obstructions now but still going very fast and still under water, perhaps no longer in the ship, washed overboard, alone in the Southern Ocean. Quite suddenly there was a parting of water, a terrific crash as my head hit something solid, and I felt myself aground.

Finding myself in the lee scuppers with my head forced right through a freeing port so that the last of the great sea behind me spurted about my ears, I was in a panic that a second wave might come aboard and squeeze me through it like a sausage, to finish me off.

Staggering to my feet, my oilskins ballooning with water, too stupid from the blow on my head to be frightened, I had just enough sense to jump for the starboard lifeline when the next wave came boiling over the port quarter and obliterated everything from view.

Swinging above the deck on the lifeline with the sea sucking greedily at my seaboots, I began to realize what a fortunate escape I had had from serious injury, for the alacrity with which I had leapt for the lifeline in spite of the great weight of sea-water inside my oilskins had convinced me that I had suffered no damage except the bang on the head.

The sea had taken me and swept me from the pin rail of the mizzen rigging, where I had been working, diagonally across the deck for fifty feet past the Jarvis brace winches, on the long handles of which I could so easily have been speared, over the fife rails of the mizzen mast, right over the top of No. 3 hatch and into the scuppers by the main braces outside the Captain's quarters.

'Where you bin?' demanded Tria accusingly, when I managed to join the little knot of survivors who were forcing their way waist deep across the deck, spluttering, cursing, and spitting sea-water as they came.

'Paddling,' I said, relieved to find that there were still six of us.

'Orlright, don' be all bloody day,' he added unsympathetically.

'Tag i gigtåget. One more now. Ooh – ah, oh, bräck dem.'

'What happened?' I asked Jansson.

'That goddam Valker let her come up too mooch,' said Jansson. 'I bin all over the bloddy deck in that sea.'

The fore upper topsail was the most difficult. All the buntlines jammed and more than half the robands securing the topsail to the jackstay had gone. The outer buntline block had broken loose and was flailing in the air, so that when we reached the lowered yard eighty feet above the sea, we hesitated a moment before the 'Horry ops' of the Mates behind us drove us out on to the footropes, hesitated because the bunt of the sail was beating back over the yard. The wind was immense. It no longer blew in the accepted sense of the word at all; instead it seemed to be tearing apart the very substance of the atmosphere. Nor was the sound of it any longer definable in ordinary terms. It no longer roared, screamed, sobbed, or sang according to the various levels on which it was encountered. The power and noise of this wind was now more vast and all-comprehending, in its way as big as the sky, bigger than the sea itself, making something that the mind balked at, so that it took refuge in blankness.

It was in this negative state of mind that could accept anything without qualm, even the possibility of death, that I fell off the yard backwards. I was the last man out on the weather side and was engaged in casting loose a gasket before we started to work on the sail, when without warning it flicked up, half the foot of a topsail, 40 feet of canvas as hard as corrugated iron, and knocked me clean off the footrope.

There was no interval for reflection, no sudden upsurge of remorse for past sins, nor did my life pass in rapid review before my eyes. Instead there was a delightful jerk and I found myself entangled in the weather rigging some five feet below the yard, and as soon as I could I climbed back to the yard and carried on with my job. I felt no fear at all until much later on.

It needed three-quarters of an hour to make fast the weather side. Time and time again we nearly had the sail to the yard when the wind tore it from our fingers.

My companion aloft was Alvar.

'What happened?' he said when we reached the deck.

'I fell.'

'I din' see,' he said in a disappointed way. 'I don' believe.'

'I'm damned if I'm going to do it again just because you didn't
see it.'

'I don' believe.'

'Orlright,' I said. 'The next time I'll tell you when I'm going to fall
off.'

'Dot's bettair,' said Alvar.

\*               \*               \*

At noon on Saturday, the 25th, our position was 50° 7' S, 164° 21' W.
In the 23½ hours from noon on the 24th *Moshulu* had sailed 241 miles
and made 228 between observed positions. Her previous day's runs
were 296 and 282, but the violence of the sea and the necessary
reduction in canvas were slowing her increasingly.

The barometer fell and fell, 746, 742, 737 millimetres. The sun went
down astern, shedding a pale watery yellow light on the undersides of
the deep black clouds hurrying above the ship. It was extremely cold,
colder than it had ever been, blowing a strong gale, force 9. Big seas
were coming aboard. I felt very lonely. The ship that had seemed huge
and powerful was nothing now, a speck in the Great Southern Ocean,
two thousand miles eastwards of New Zealand, three thousand from
the coast of South America, separated to the North from the nearest
inhabited land, the Cook Islands and Tahiti, by two thousand miles of
open sea; to the South there was nothing but the Antarctic ice and
darkness. She was running before seas that were being generated in the
greatest expanse of open ocean, of a power and size unparalleled because
there was no impediment to them as they drove eastwards round the
world. She was made pygmy too by the wind, the wind that was
already indescribable, that Tria said had only now begun to blow.

We rounded Cape Horn on 10 April, Easter Monday, having sailed
more than six thousand miles, and were fifty-five days to the Line. We
were one day ahead of *Parma*'s record-breaking passage of eighty-three
days from Port Victoria to Falmouth in 1933. That year she had been
thirty days to the Horn, twenty-five to the Line, but in 31°N 47°W
our luck deserted us and we failed to pick up the strong westerlies we
needed to beat her.

On 9 June at 8 p.m., ninety days out from Port Victoria, we raised the Fastnet Rock, fifteen miles to the north-east. We had smelt the land for days. The following morning and until evening we were becalmed near the Rock. Five men rowed out to us from Crookhaven, near Mizen Head, nine miles. The Captain made them drunk on rum and we left them drifting into the sunset in the direction of the New World. (More than twenty-five years later I got drunk in Crookhaven with the survivors of this long row.) Then a breeze came up and took us ghosting along the coast of Southern Ireland, past Cape Clear. Nothing could have been more beautiful to us than this country at this moment.

The following day at 5 a.m., the wind shifted from NW through W to WSW, the best sort of wind and we squared away for Queenstown. At about eleven o'clock we took a pilot from a black and white cutter, heaving-to for him to come across to us in a rowing-boat. Then both watches went to the fore braces, boarded the fore tack and began to clew up the remaining course sails, before racing aloft to see which watch could be the first to furl the Main and Mizzen. We won, in the port watch.

We came to anchorage off the narrow entrance to Queenstown under a couple of topsails and staysails. It was twelve o'clock ship's time on Saturday, 10 June 1939, and we were ninety-one days out from Port Victoria, having sailed a round voyage of more than thirty thousand miles.

The Pilot told us that we were first home, and although we did not know it at the time, we had won the Last Grain Race.

On the 19th June *Moshulu* was ordered to Glasgow and a tug was sent to tow us. It seemed an ignoble end to such a venture. On the 21st the tug appeared. 'Kommer bogserbåten,' everyone said. The 'bogserbåt' took us out into a nasty sea with a head wind in which we only made 5 miles in an hour. Steering behind the tug on a dark night in the Irish Sea was as bad as anything in the West Wind and much more dangerous.

At last on the 27th June we were warped with infinite difficulty into Queen's Dock, in Glasgow.

'Coming again?' asked the Captain some days later, after some good parties, as he inked in my discharge as Ordinary Seaman and handed over some fragments of pay. 'Make a man of you next time.'

'I'll think it over,' I answered.

My trunk was loaded on to a taxi. Suddenly those of the crew still on board seemed remote and once more strangers.

Now we were turning through the dock gates into the main road where the trams rattled and swayed. I looked back at *Moshulu* whose masts and yards towered above the sheds in the June sunshine.

I never saw her again.

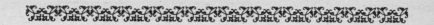

# A Short History of the
# Second World War

ONE MORNING IN August 1940 'A' Company, Infantry Wing, was
on parade outside the Old Buildings at the Royal Military College,
Camberley. Company Sergeant-Major Clegg, a foxy looking Grenadier, was addressing us '. . . THERE WILL BE NO WEEK-END LEAF,'
he screamed with satisfaction. (There never had been.) 'That means no
women for Mr Pont, Mr Pont (there were two Mr Ponts – cousins).
Take that smile off your face Mr Newby or you'll be inside. Wiring
and Demolition Practice at 1100 hours is cancelled for Number One
Platoon. Instead there will be Bridging Practice. Bridging Equipment
will be drawn at 1030 hours. CUMPNEE . . . CUMPNEEEE . . .
SHAAH!'

'Heaven,' said the Ponts as we doubled smartly to our rooms to
change for P.T. 'There's nothing more ghastly than all that wire.'

I, too, was glad that there was to be no Wiring and Demolition.
Both took place in a damp, dark wood. Wiring was hell at any rate and
Demolition for some mysterious reason was conducted by a civilian. It
always seemed to me the last thing a civilian should have a hand in
and I was not surprised when, later in the war, he disappeared in a
puff of smoke, hoist by one of his own petards.

In June 1940, after six months of happy oblivion as a private soldier,
I had been sent to Sandhurst to be converted into an officer.

Pressure of events had forced the Royal Military College to convert
itself into an OCTU, an Officer Cadet Training Unit, and the permanent staff still referred meaningfully in the presence of the new intakes
to a golden age 'when the gennulmen cadets were 'ere'.

'Ere' we learned to drill in an impressive fashion and our ability to
command was strengthened by the Adjutant, magnificent in breeches
and riding boots from Maxwell, who had us stationed in pairs on the

closely mown lawns that sloped gently to the lake. A quarter of a mile apart, he made us screech at one another, marching and counter-marching imaginary battalions by the left, by the right and by the centre until our voices broke under the strain and whirred away into nothingness.

Less well we carried out a drill with enormous military bicycles as complex as the evolutions performed by Lippizanas at the Spanish Riding School. On these treadmills which each weighed between sixty and seventy pounds, we used to wobble off into the surrounding pine plantations, which we shared uneasily with working parties of lunatics from the asylum at Broadmoor, for TEWTs – Tactical Exercises Without Troops.

Whether moving backwards or forwards the TEWT world was a strange, isolated one in which the lunatics who used to wave to us as we laid down imaginary fields of fire against an imaginary enemy might have been equally at home. In it aircraft were rarely mentioned, tanks never. We were members of the Infantry Wing. There was an Armoured Wing for those who were interested in such things as tanks and armoured cars and the authorities had no intention of allowing the two departments to mingle. Gradually we succumbed to the pervasive unreality.

'I want to bring home to you the meaning of this war,' said a visiting General. 'In four months those of you who are not RTU'd – Returned to your Units – will be platoon commanders. In six months' time most of you will be dead.'

And we believed him. Our numbers were already depleted by a mysterious outbreak of bed-wetting – an RTU-able offence. In a military trance we imagined ourselves waving ashplants, charging machine-gun nests at the head of our men. The Carrara marble pillars, which supported the roof of the chapel in which we carried out our militant devotions, were scarcely sufficient to contain the names of all those other 'gennulmen' who, in the earlier war, had died in the mud at Passchendaele and among the wire on the forward slopes of the Hohen-zollern Redoubt. They had sat where we were sitting and their names were set out in neat columns on the pillars like debit entries in some terrible ledger.

This dream of Death or Glory affected our leisure. Most of us had

passed our formative years in the outer suburbs. Now, to make ourselves more acceptable to our employers we took up beagling (the
College had the Eton Beagles for the duration); ordered shirts we
couldn't afford from expensive shirtmakers in Jermyn Street and drank
Black Velvet in the Hotel. The snugger pubs were out of bounds for
fear we might meet a barmaid who 'did it'. No one but a maniac would
have wanted to do it with the one at the Hotel.

The bridging equipment was housed in a low, sinister-looking shed
near the lake on which we were to practise. This was not the ornamental
lake in front of the Old Buildings on which, in peace time, playful
cadets used to float chamber pots containing lighted candles – a practice
now forbidden by the blackout regulations. It was an inferior lake,
little more than a pond; from it rose a dank smell of rotting vegetation.

Inside the shed there were a number of small decked-in pontoons
and strips of heavy teak grating which were intended to form the
footway. Blocks and tackle hung in great swathes from the roof; presumably they were to hold the bridge steady in a swiftly flowing
stream. Everything seemed unnecessarily heavy, as though it was part
of the gear of a wooden ship-of-the-line.

There was every sign that the bridge had not been used for years –
if at all. The custodian, a grumpy old pensioner rooted out of his
cottage to open the door, confirmed this.

'What yer think yer going to do with it, cross the Channel?' he
croaked.

The Staff Sergeant detailed to instruct us in the use of the bridge was
uneasy. He had never seen anything like it before. It bore no resemblance to any kind of bridge that he had encountered.

'It's not an ISSUE BRIDGE,' he kept repeating, plaintively. 'Gennulmen, you *must* help me.' We were deaf to him. The Army had seldom
been kind to us; it was too late to call us gentlemen.

Finally, after rooting in the darkness he discovered a battered manual
hanging on a nail behind the door. It confirmed our suspicions that
the bridge had been constructed at the time of the Boer War. No surprise at the Royal Military College where a whole literature of the
same period – text books filled with drawings of blockhouses with
corrugated-iron roofs; men with droopy moustaches peering through

loopholes; and armoured trains that I associated with the early life of Mr Winston Churchill – were piled high on the tops of cupboards in the lecture rooms and had obviously only recently fallen into disuse.

With the manual in his hand the Sergeant was once more on familiar ground – if one can use such an expression in connection with a bridge. His spirits rose still further when he discovered that there was a drill laid down for assembling the monstrous thing.

'On the command "One" the even numbers of the front ranks will about turn, grasp the Caissons with both hands and advance into the water. On the command "Two" the odd numbers of the front rank will peg out the Guys, Retaining Caisson. On the command "Three" the even numbers of the rear rank will pick up the Sections, Decking' . . . and so on.

On the command 'One' the Caisson Party, of which I was one, moved gingerly into the water, which was surprisingly warm. Some of the more frivolous cadets began to splash one another, but were rebuked by the Sergeant. After some twenty minutes all the Caissons were in position, secured by block and tackle.

'Caisson Party, about turn, quick march!' To the accompaniment of weird sucking noises we squelched ashore.

'Decking Party, advance!' The Decking Party staggered forward under its appalling load. Standing on the bank, with the water streaming from the bottoms of our trousers, we watched them go.

'It all seems rather pointless when we've already walked across,' someone said.

'Quiet!' said the Sergeant. 'The next cadet who speaks goes on a charge.' He was looking at his watch, apprehensively.

'Decking Party and Caisson Party will retire and unpile arms,' he went on. We had already performed the complicated operation of piling arms. It was one of the things we really knew how to do. 'Now then, get a move on.'

We had just completed the unpiling when Sergeant-Major Clegg appeared on the far side of the lake, stiff as a ramrod, jerkily propelling one of our gigantic bicycles. Dismounted, standing half-hidden in the undergrowth, he looked more foxy than ever.

He addressed us and the world in that high-pitched sustained scream

that even now, when I recall it at dead of night years later, makes me
come to attention even when lying in my bed.

'SAAAAN ALUN!'

'SAAAAH!'

'DOZEEEE . . . DOZEEEE . . . GET THOSE DOZY, IDUL GEN-
NULMEN OVER THE BRIDGE . . . AT . . . THER . . . DUB-
BOOOOL!'

'SAAAAH!' shrieked Sergeant Allen and wheeled upon us with a face
bereft of all humanity. 'PLATOOOON, PLATOOOON WILL CROSS
THE BRIDGE AT THER DUBOOL – DUBOOOOL!'

Armed to the teeth, bowed down by gas masks, capes anti-gas, token
anti-tank rifles and 2″ mortars made of wood (all the real ones had been
taken away from us after Dunkirk), we thundered down the bank and
on to the bridge.

The weight of thirty men was too much for it; there was a noise like
a succession of pistol shots as the Guys, Retaining Caisson parted, the
central span of the bridge surged away and the whole body of us crashed
into the water. It was like the end of the Gadarene Swine, the Tay
Bridge Disaster and the Crossing of the Beresina reproduced in
miniature.

As we came to the surface, ornamented with weed and surrounded
by the token wooden weapons which, surprisingly, in spite of their
weight, floated, we began to laugh hysterically and what had begun as
a military operation ended as a water frolic. The caissons became rafts
on which were spread-eagled the waterlogged figures of what had until
recently been officer cadets, who now resembled nothing more than a
band of lascivious Tritons. People were ducking one another; the Ponts
were floating calmly, contemplating the sky as if offshore at noon at
Eden Roc . . .

Gradually the laughter ceased and a terrible silence descended on us.
A tall ascetic figure was looking down on us with a mixture of incred-
ulity and disgust from an ornamental bridge in the rustic taste. The
Sergeant was saluting furiously; Sergeant-Major Clegg, foxy to the
last, had slipped away into the undergrowth – only his bicycle, propped
against a tree, showed that he had ever been there. The face on the
bridge was a very well-known face.

Without a word General de Gaulle turned on his heel and went off, followed by a train of officers of high rank. His visit had been unannounced at his special request so that he could see us working under natural conditions. What he must have thought is unimaginable. France had just fallen. It must have confirmed his worst suspicions of the British Army. Perhaps the intransigence that was later to become a characteristic was born there on that bright morning beside a steamy little lake in Surrey.

For Sergeant Allen the morning's work had a more immediate significance. His career seemed blasted.

'You've gone and done me in,' he said sadly, as we fell in to squelch back to the Old Buildings.

\*　　　　　\*　　　　　\*

In the autumn of 1941 I arrived in the Middle East from India. There I joined the Special Boat Section, whose job it was to land from submarines on hostile coasts in order to carry out acts of sabotage against railway systems, attack enemy airfields, and put ashore and take off secret agents. Members of the SBS had also made sorties into enemy harbours with the intention of sticking limpets (magnetic mines) on ships at anchor and blowing them up.

My interview for this job took place on board HMS *Medway* in the harbour at Alexandria, the depot ship of the First Submarine Flotilla which provided the SBS with transportation to its target areas. The interviewer was Roger Courtney, the founder of the Special Boat Section, an astonishing officer who had been a white hunter in East Africa and had canoed down the Nile. Over his desk was displayed a notice which read ARE YOU TOUGH? IF SO GET OUT. I NEED BUGGERS WITH INTELLIGENCE. This notice made me fear that I would not be accepted, but I was.

I spent the next few weeks at the Combined Operations Centre at Kabrit on the Suez Canal, learning to handle folboats and explosives, how to sink shipping, and how to blow up aircraft and trains or otherwise render them inoperative. Learning to sink ships involved swimming at night in the Bitter Lakes – which lived up to their name in the depths of winter – covered with grease and wearing long woollen naval issue underwear, and pushing a limpet towards whichever merchant ship lying at anchor had been chosen as the target, the limpet being supported by an inflated car inner tube with a net inside it. This was Britain's primitive equivalent to the highly sophisticated two-man submarines of the Italian Tenth Light Flotilla, which in December that year succeeded in entering the harbour at Alexandria and exploding charges under the battleships *Queen Elizabeth* and *Valiant*. Both ships were disabled and put out of action for months, seriously affecting the balance of sea power in the Mediterranean.

On my first practice attempt I was sent to attack a Dutch merchant ship at anchor in one of the Bitter Lakes. I reached it, thinking myself undetected in brilliant moonlight but wondering how anyone on board could possibly fail to hear the noise made by my chattering teeth. To set the limpet in its correct position on the ship's side it was necessary to dive deeply and as I did so I found myself enveloped in the contents of an entire Dutch lavatory pan which someone with a grotesque sense of fun and a remarkable sense of timing had released by pulling the chain.

'Better luck next time, *mynheer*,' a voice from the deck said as I came up spluttering. 'I should joose a dark night, if I was you, and dry not to make so much noise, even if it is so cold.'

Next door to our camp at Kabrit was David Stirling with his SAS, Special Air Service. As his success and power increased, David sometimes gave the impression that he was contemplating a takeover bid for SBS. We used to make use of some of his training facilities – he had a testy genius in charge of his explosives department, a Royal Engineer called Bill Cumper. He also had a lofty tower from which embryonic parachutists were expected to launch themselves parachuteless, and they also had to jump off the back of trucks going at about thirty miles an hour. His camp was definitely no place for the chicken-hearted. There was also a band of anarchists from Barcelona whom no one knew what to do with. They had murdered so many Egyptian taximen and buried them in the sand, instead of paying their fares like any normal persons, that it was now almost impossible to get a taxi from Kabrit to Ismailia and back during the hours of darkness, which was a bore.

One day, having climbed this tower to admire the extensive view and counting myself lucky that I was not called upon to jump from it,

I was about to descend by the way I had come when I heard the voice of one of David's sergeants from far below say in Caterham* accents, 'No officer or man, sir, who has ever climbed that tower, has ever walked down the stairs! Once up there you have to jump, sir!'

So I jumped. I had no choice, and because I had not learned the basic facts about parachuting (which was not a condition of membership of the SBS), I hurt myself.

That winter, as part of a detachment of SBS, I was sent to Tobruk to operate with a flotilla of motor-torpedo-boats. While we were there four of us received orders to report without delay to the Directorate of Combined Operations at GHQ in Cairo; its Director was an excellent sailor, popular with the SBS, named Admiral Maund. We reached it late in the afternoon of the day we set off from Tobruk, after a hair-raising drive of more than four hundred miles down the desert road, or what was left of it, in a thirty hundredweight Bedford truck.

At the DCO we were only asked if we possessed prismatic compasses, and told to report to the Naval Officer in Charge, NOIC, at Beirut without delay. Before the shops shut in Cairo that evening I bought two guide books, one to Palestine, the other to Syria and the Lebanon, and *The Quest for Corvo*, by A. J. A. Symonds.

Early on the morning of the second day out from Tobruk, we arrived at Gaza: we had covered about eight hundred miles since setting out from Tobruk, which was not bad, considering the terrible state of the desert road.

Then we were in Palestine and suddenly it was spring: the country-side in the coastal plain was a green paradise with burgeoning fields of wheat and barley; meadows and gentle hillsides were scattered with wild flowers; and everywhere there were groves of lemons and oranges, of which we bought whole box-loads, afraid that this other Eden might be only a temporary phenomenon and might be succeeded by yet another dusty wilderness as we drove northwards. After the Western Desert, where it was still winter, after Sinai, where we had lain

---

* Caterham in Surrey was a training depot of the Foot Guards, where the characteristic high-pitched word of command peculiar to these regiments was taught, practised and perfected.

shivering in the cold grey hours before the dawn in the duffel coats
we had wangled from the navy, to be in Palestine was to be born again.
Armed with the guide book to Palestine, I was able to persuade my
companions to make a number of short detours from the main road in
order to visit places, some of which I had learned about in Divinity at
school, none of which I had ever expected to set eyes on.

By this time, as a result of haggling for boxes of oranges, shopping
in Tel Aviv, which I thought had a distinctly Eastern European air
about it (although I had never been to Eastern Europe), visiting ruins,
in fact generally behaving in a thoroughly unmilitary way, some of
the impetus had gone out of our expedition.

When we reached Caesarea the sun was setting, drenching everything, including the remains of a Roman aqueduct which stood among
the dunes that had engulfed what remained of the ancient city, in a
brilliant ochrous yellow light. Waves were breaking over the remnants
of the ancient harbour works, and down on the foreshore where the
air was full of flying spume, a man on a camel, dressed in rags which
were streaming in the wind, was the only other human being in sight.
It was here that I began rooting about underfoot with a stick, turning
up potsherds and iridescent fragments of what may have been Roman
or Byzantine glass. In the meantime, whoever was driving kept the
motor running and a brother officer shouted as he had done all day
whenever I had found a ruin to my taste, 'For Christ's sake get a move
on, Eric, we can't stay here all bloody night!' while the sergeant cried
rather more plaintively, 'Oh, do come on, sir!'

The next day, the third since leaving Tobruk, we drove on northwards. At Acre we looked down into a dungeon in which the despot
Jezzar Pasha, who had successfully defended the place against Napoleon, used to pelt his prisoners with cannon balls through a hole in the
ceiling. It was a tough campaign. In the course of it Napoleon ordered
the mass executions of prisoners by firing squads. As we flashed by on
what had been the Roman road to Syria we saw milestones, inscriptions
recording innumerable wars and conquests, fragments of altars, gaping
catacombs, plundered sarcophagi and other ruins of the past.

At Beirut we received from the NOIC the details of *Operation
Aluite*. To us *Operation Aluite* seemed pretty defeatist. It implied
that a German advance into Syria through Turkey, a recurrent British

nightmare, one brought on by the continued presence of von Papen as German ambassador at Ankara, would be followed inevitably by the Allied evacuation of Syria and the Lebanon, probably that of Palestine, and eventually, by implication, that of Egypt.

In an endeavour to stem such an invasion a great fortress was being built near the port of Tripoli, north of Beirut, where the northern arm of the Iraqi pipeline came in. In the event of such an invasion being successful, it would be the task of the SBS, working from Cyprus, if Cyprus had not itself fallen, to act as guerrillas and sabotage the German lines of communication. In anticipation of such a disaster, we were to sound every inlet in which a clandestine landing could be made, to map the hinterland leading up to the main road and the railway, and to make an assessment of every bridge and other important installations with a view to blowing them up, on the two hundred and fifty miles of coast between the Turkish-Syrian frontier and the Lebanese-Palestinian frontier, north of Haifa. We were also to seek out suitable hiding places for caches of explosive and ammunition. All this had to be done without the knowledge of our French allies in these parts, which seemed impossible.

In order to assist in the concealment of such dumps, an enormous quantity of artificial, lightweight rock of the same colour and texture as that found on the coasts of Syria and the Lebanon had been manufactured from papier-mâché. What conclusion a wandering goatherd or even a German *feldwebel* would come to when he found himself walking on artificial rocks made from papier-mâché will never be known as they were never put to the test.

'Personally, I think the whole thing's rather a waste of time,' the NOIC said, 'although you should have fun. Nevertheless I don't envy you. As you know, the Free French have only recently taken over the country from Vichy and some of the permanent members of the administration are thoroughly untrustworthy and hostile and loyal to what they call "La France de la Metropole". The coastguards are said to be particularly trigger happy. If they shoot at you I should shoot back and ask questions afterwards. Oh, and take plenty of rubbers and pencils.'

The following morning the four of us, including the sergeant who had said 'Oh, do come on, sir!' in such a pained voice, now himself transformed into an enthusiastic ruin-fancier, left Beirut in the thirty hundredweight truck to start work on mapping the section of coast south of the Turkish frontier, while others began on the coast south of Beirut. We had been given enough money to enable us to live off the country without having recourse to other military organizations, so much in fact that we decided to take with us a Sten gun as well as pistols, just in case there were robbers about.

All that day we drove north, crossing the Nahr el Kelb, the Dog River, guarded in ancient times by a savage dog with a bark so loud that it could be heard six miles off. In its gorge, where it entered the sea, we saw inscribed slabs recording the passage of Egyptian Pharaohs, Assyrians, Babylonians, Greeks and Romans, the Emperor Caracalla and the Third Gallic Legion, British and French troops in July 1918, and a triumphant one recording the entry of the French into Damascus in July 1920 when they expelled King Feisal and the Arabs. Seeing these great *steles* I realized that we were just another band of marauding soldiers. We saw the ruins of ancient Byblos, the principal city of the Giblites, claimed by an ancient Greek, Philo, to be the oldest town in the world, with a square Crusader castle above it on a hill, ruins among which we later lived for some days while making our survey.

On the outskirts of Tripoli work was proceeding on the construction of the fortress, which looked pretty feeble to us, and all along the coast hordes of men were working away on the Naquara-Beirut-Tripoli railway which we were already making plans to destroy.

The next weeks were the best that any of us had so far experienced in the course of the war, and the best that many of us were ever likely to experience: swimming about in lonely coves, taking soundings with long canes cut in some convenient plantation; pacing out base lines and using our compasses to make triangulations across the fields of wheat and barley; searching out caves and rock tombs, in which the coast abounded, that might serve as caches for explosives; swinging about like apes among the girders of railway bridges; meeting primitive-looking goatherds, one of whom, a rather elderly Sunnite Muslim I found sitting on a rock, had been an itinerant pedlar in the United States before returning home to marry a Syrian girl, a marriage which he said he had arranged by post.

In the course of our travels we encountered a remarkable diversity of religions and nationalities. There were Alawites, Druzes and Ismailites, whose religions contained elements of Muslim, Christian, Indian and Persian beliefs. There were Armenians who had either been deported from Turkey during the First World War by the Turks or who had left it of their own volition to avoid being slaughtered – it was some Armenian Orthodox Gregorians who invited us to a village near the Turkish frontier for a play in Armenian lasting eight hours, which was a kind thought but a great trial to all of us. There were Armenian Catholics and Maronites and Greek-Catholic Melkites and Syrian-Catholic Syriacs and Chaldean Catholics and Roman Catholics and Greek Orthodox and Syrian Orthodox, which included Jacobites and Nestorians, and there were even some Protestants. There were Sephardic Jews and there were Sunni and Shiah Muslims, the latter so fanatical that if they were forced to feed an infidel they destroyed the crockery as soon as the visitor had departed. And in Syria there were some very odd people indeed, whom we never saw, called Yezidis, who believed that God had passed the administration of the world over to the Devil, which on second thoughts did not seem odd at all. None of these conflicting sects seemed particularly fond of one another.

One night we slept among the ruins of Marqab, one of the castles of the Knights Hospitallers. Built of black basalt and reached by a spiral track nearly four miles long, it occupied a fantastic situation, high on a spur of an extinct volcano. It looked impregnable but it had finally been captured by Qalaun in 1285 after a forty-day siege, although it had food supplies for five years; but even so it was a much better site for a fortress than the one that was being built down the hill in Tripoli, as good as Monte Cassino, and as difficult to take.

In its chapels, halls and passages and on its circuit walks, sheep and goats wandered. It was cool up there and we built a great fire in one of the rather smelly halls. We thought the flickering of the light on the walls and the giant shadows highly romantic until we were infested by bats, attracted by the flames, which were so numerous that they eventually forced us to retreat to one of the roofless towers. There we passed the rest of the night free of them and the rotten-chocolate smell of their excrement.

We used to start work as soon as it was light, then rest in the heat

of the day. We had soon lost most of our external military character-
istics. Down on the shore, under the mountains, it was much too hot
to wear anything but shorts and sandals and straw hats, and the sergeant
acquired a long, lean hunting dog. We were dressed like this, the sergeant with his dog on a rope leash and carrying the Sten gun, the others
armed with pistols and the long canes we used for taking soundings,
when one morning the Duke of Gloucester, on a tour of inspection
with a convoy of military big-wigs, looked down incredulously on us
from his motor car as he whizzed past, covering us with dust.

During the hot, midday hours we used to sprawl in the shelter of
an ilex or an over-size boxwood tree in which the coast abounded,
more often than not surrounded by ruins – we soon learned that the
ancients had already identified for us all the best landing places, however insignificant. There we reclined drinking wine, eating chickens
we had bought from some cook shop, carving up big loaves of bread
that looked as if they might have been baked by Phoenicians, dreamily
listening to the droning of unidentifiable insects, the shrill screaming
of the cicadas or the endless din set up by the frogs in some nearby
marsh, and sniffing the pungent smelly *maquis*.

We worked at Ibn Hani, a place lost among olive groves, where
there were the remains of a temple and an amphitheatre, and at Ras
Shamrah, the site of Ugarit, a famous city of the Phoenicians but with
origins far older, going back to 5000 BC, perhaps further. Much of
Ugarit was buried under Ras Shamrah, but a French expedition had
continued to excavate it until the war put an end to their labours. Now
it was completely unprotected – there were no custodians to harass us
– and unvisited. In places one could look down, strata on strata, fifty
feet or so, through different levels of civilization to where people had
lived who had worshipped Baal, the God of Rain, and Dagon, to levels
at which the inhabitants had had relations with Egypt and Crete in the
seventeenth and eighteenth centuries before Christ; to where later, in
the fifteenth and fourteenth centuries, they had installed sanitation and
constructed burial vaults; and to the level where, in the thirteenth century, the Mycenaeans had lived in it until its final extinction by some
peoples of the sea in the twelfth century. It was here at Ras Shamrah
that, scrabbling among the rubble in the fearful afternoon heat with my
stick, keeping watch while the others slept, I discovered two exquisite

miniature bronze bulls which subsequently reached England, only to
be stolen from over a fireplace in a drawing-room while we were
having a Christmas party.

On Saturday mornings we used to return to Beirut in pursuit of
pleasures to which the ancients themselves were no strangers. Together
with the officer who, like me, had been attracted by two Greek girls
from Athens, I used to put up at the St George Hotel, where they
continued to stay. We saw nothing of the city. Once or twice we all
four lunched together at a restaurant perched on the cliff overlooking
some impressive offshore stacks called the Grottes des Pigeons.
Another time we went to the mountains and stayed in a village. For
the rest of the time we sunbathed with them on the hotel beach, swam,
made love, drank, sunbathed, swam, made love, ordered up club sandwiches and so on until at dawn on Monday morning, I used to board
our vehicle to cries of 'Oh, do hurry up, sir!' and roar away for Ras
Shamrah, Tartus or wherever we happened to be making our maps.
We were completely exhausted, unlike our partners who, unknown to
us, had other bedfellows of a more senior, stay-at-home kind during
the week. We had met our match, we both agreed, in these girls, who,
for us at least, did everything for love.

After this extraordinary, almost dream-like interlude in our military
careers, we all returned to the fields of action from which that fickle
goddess Fortune had fancifully removed us. However, before doing
so, we delivered to the DCO by way of the NOIC the final instalments
of our labours which, altogether, were of almost encyclopaedic proportions.

This mass of material, flavoured with a surprising amount of newly-
acquired culture – the reports of the cultivated and gallant sergeant
made particularly good reading – had an extremely short life. Consigned to the most secret archives, the whole lot was used a few months
after we delivered the final sections to stoke the already huge funeral
pyres of documents that were on no account to fall into enemy hands
– although what use they would be to the Germans with Egypt already
in their hands it was difficult to imagine – pyres which created a dense
pall of smoke over Cairo in that summer of 1942, when it seemed more
than probable that Rommel would arrive in the city in person.

## OPERATION WHYNOT

We were captured off the east coast of Sicily on the morning of the twelfth of August, 1942, about four miles out in the Bay of Catania. It was a beautiful morning. As the sun rose I could see Etna, a truncated cone with a plume of smoke over it like the quill of a pen stuck in a pewter inkpot, rising out of the haze to the north of where I was treading water.

There were five of us. Originally there had been seven, but one, a marine, had had to be left behind on the submarine and another, Sergeant Dunbar of the Argylls was missing, killed, wounded or captured, we none of us knew, lost among the coast defences in the dunes. We were all that remained of M Detachment of the Special Boat Section. Three officers, of whom I was one, Corporal Butler of the South Lancashire Regiment and Guardsman Duffy of the Coldstream, one of the smallest sub-units in the British Army, now about to be wiped out completely.

About eight o'clock we were picked up by some Sicilian fishermen who hauled us into their boat like a lot of half-dead fish. They were surprised. We were thankful, although we knew that we would now never make the rendezvous off Capo Campolato which had been fixed for the following night if we failed to reach the submarine by one o'clock on the morning of the twelfth.

I remember lying among the freshly caught fish in the bottom of the boat, some of them exotic, all displaying considerably greater liveliness than we did, and discussing with the others the possibility of taking it over and forcing the fishermen to head for Malta, 120 miles to the south, for the boat had a sail, as well as an engine. And if we had been in a war film made twenty years later this is what we undoubtedly would have done, but we had been in the water for nearly five hours and were very cold and could hardly stand.

Besides, the fishermen were kindly men. They thought that we were survivors from a torpedoed ship and they gave us what little wine and bread they had with them which amounted to a mouthful each. To them the war, as they made clear by various unequivocal gestures, was a misfortune which had brought misery to everyone and, as far as they were concerned, had seriously restricted their fishing. The idea of using violence against such people was unthinkable. And even if we had decided to try and take over the boat it would have been impossible to get away. It was one of a fleet of a dozen or so whose crews now brought them alongside so that they, too, could view this extraordinary haul. We were prisoners without, as yet, having admitted the fact to ourselves. It was too soon. Everything had happened too quickly.

On the afternoon of the tenth, immediately before we sailed from Malta, we had been given the bare, gruesome bones of what had been christened *Operation Whynot*. For the flesh we would have to rely on some last-minute aerial photographs of the target which were still in the darkroom and which we would have to study when we were submerged.

We were told that we were going to attack a German bomber airfield four miles south of Catania in Sicily which was expected to have between fifty and sixty JU 88s on it on the night of the eleventh, and destroy as many of them as we could so that they would be out of action on the twelfth and thirteenth when a British convoy essential to Malta's survival would be within a hundred miles of the island but still beyond effective fighter cover from it. There would be no time for a preliminary reconnaissance. We had to land and go straight in and come out if we could. The beach was heavily defended and there was a lot of wire. It was not known if it was mined but it was thought highly probable. The whole thing sounded awful but at least it seemed important and worth doing. Irregular forces such as ours were not always employed in such ostensibly useful roles.

We travelled to Sicily in *Una*, one of the smaller submarines. Her commander, Pat Norman, was a charming and cheerful lieutenant of our own age.

I was already in the conning tower and we were just about to sail when a steward came running down the mole brandishing a piece of paper which, after having received permission to climb into the conning tower, he presented to me. It was a bill for an infinitesimal sum for drinks which I had ordered in the wardroom (our hosts, the Tenth Submarine Flotilla were so generous that it was almost impossible to buy them any). Apparently the others had already been presented with theirs while I was elsewhere. Actually, I had been attempting to dig down to my kit which had been buried when a large bomb had fallen that morning on the great impregnable-looking Vaubanesque fort in which we were billeted and destroyed my room.

No one, including Norman, had any money on them. Like me, none of them had thought that they might conceivably need money underwater.

'I'll pay you when I get back,' I said, airily. 'There's nothing to worry about. I'm attached to the Tenth Submarine Flotilla.'

'That's what they all say, sir,' he said, gloomily. 'Military officers attached to the Tenth Submarine Flotilla. And then we never see them again, more often than not. I'm afraid I must ask you to give me a cheque, sir.'

I told him with some relish that, if he wanted a cheque from me, he would have to shift some tons of masonry in order to find one.

'No need for that, sir,' he said. 'I've brought you a blank cheque. All you have to do is fill in the name and address of your bank and sign it.'

Even then it seemed an evil omen.

It would be tedious to relate the details of the voyage. They were the same as any other for passengers in a submarine. The wardroom was so minute that apart from the times when I emerged to eat and discuss our plans, such as they were, and pore over the aerial photographs which had been taken from such an altitude that they needed an expert to interpret them and we soon gave up trying to do so, I spent the rest of the time lying on a mattress under the wardroom table, a place to which I had been relegated as the most junior officer of the party. I shared this humble couch with Socks, a dachshund, the property of Desmond Buchanan, an officer in the Grenadiers who was one of our party and who had persuaded Pat Norman to allow him to bring her with him because of the noise of the air-raids on Malta which were practically continuous. ('I wouldn't dream of leaving my little girl here. Her nerves are going to pieces.') From time to time Socks went off to other parts of the submarine, from which she returned bloated with food and with her low-slung chassis covered with oil, a good deal of which she imparted to me. But on the whole it was a cheerful journey and we laughed a lot, although most of it was the laughter of bravado. We all knew that we were embarked on the worst possible kind of operation, one that had been hastily conceived by

someone a long way from the target, and one which we had not had
the opportunity to think out in detail for ourselves. I felt like one of
those rather ludicrous, ill-briefed agents who had been landed by night
on Romney Marsh in the summer of 1940, all of whom had been
captured and shot.

By four o'clock in the afternoon of the eleventh we were in the Bay
of Catania, about a mile offshore, and Pat brought *Una* up to periscope
depth so that we could have a look at the coast.

He got a bit of a shock when he did. He had come up in the midst
of a fleet of Sicilian fishing boats and they swam into the eye of the
periscope like oversize fish in an aquarium. Raising the periscope he
was lucky not to have impaled one of them on the end of it. Nevertheless, with what I thought an excess of zeal, he insisted on giving each
of us an opportunity to look at the coast which we did, hastily, before
causing *Una* to sink to the bottom where she remained for the next
five hours with everything shut off that might produce a detectable
noise. It had not been a very successful reconnaissance; but there had
been nothing to see anyway. With an immense sun glaring at us from
behind a low-lying coast, the shore had appeared as nothing more than
a thin, tremulous black line with a shimmering sea in front of it.

We surfaced at nine o'clock and the four folboats were brought up on
to the casing through the torpedo hatch without their midship frames in
position, the only way we could get them through it, and we then
carried out the final assembly.

It was not a very dark night, but after thirty-six hours in artificial
light underwater it seemed terribly black until we became accustomed
to it, when it seemed altogether too bright. To the north we could see
the lights of Catania and to the west the landing lights of the airfield.
Planes were coming in to land a couple of hundred feet above our
heads, and when they were directly above us the noise was deafening.
The wind was on-shore and there was a nasty swell running which
made the launching of the canoes over the bulges difficult with the
tanks blown, and the loading of them once they were in the water even
more so. One canoe was so badly damaged getting it into the water
that it had to be left behind, together with the marine who was going
to travel in it. He was very disappointed at the time. How fortunate
he was.

'Rather you than me, mate, but good luck anyway,' were the last words addressed to me by a rating as he threw me the stern line; then we set off in arrowhead formation towards the shore, if three canoes can be said to constitute an arrowhead.

The water was extraordinarily phosphorescent. We might have been in a tropical sea and as we dipped the blades of the paddles it exploded into brilliant green and blue fire and as we lifted them out of it they shed what looked like drops of molten metal which vanished when they fell back into the water. At any other time these effects would have seemed beautiful; now they seemed an additional hazard. Surely to the sentries patrolling the beach it must look as if there was a fire out at sea, and surely the crews of the bombers which were still coming in to land over our heads from dead astern must see it, just as surely as they must have already seen the submarine. Together with Corporal Butler of the South Lancashire Regiment, my companion at bow who was no doubt sharing these gloomy thoughts, I paddled towards the shore, trying to hearten myself with the prospect of the bacon and eggs which we had been promised if and when we returned on board.

After a few minutes we heard the boom of surf and soon we were on the outer edge of it. It was not very heavy, but we got out of the canoes as we knew how to without capsizing them, and swam in with them until our feet touched bottom and we could stand. It is better to arrive sopping wet on two feet on a hostile shore than to be capsized or thrown up on it dry but immobile in a sitting position, unless you are a secret agent who must immediately enter the market place and mingle with the crowds.

The beach, with the wind blowing over it and the surf beating on it, seemed the loneliest place in the world. The wire began about fifty feet from the water's edge. We carried the canoes up over the sand and put them down close to the entanglements without being blown to pieces. At least this part of the beach did not seem to be mined with anything that a man's weight would set off, or perhaps we were lucky, there was no way of knowing.

Now we attached the time pencils to the bombs, which were a mixture of plastic and thermite. (With the white cordtex fuses they looked like big black conkers on strings.) This was something that could not safely be done on board a submarine costing a mint of money,

because time pencils were rather erratic, and I always hoped that the
workers in the factory in which they had been made had not got all
mixed up and substituted a thin, thirty-second delay wire for a thicker,
thirty-minute one, or simply painted the outside casing with the wrong
colour paint, which was one of the methods of identifying them,
mistakes that could quite easily happen after a pre-Christmas factory
beano.

When the bombs were ready we buried the canoes upside down in
the sand and obliterated our footprints, working upwards from the
water's edge.

The wire entanglements were about twenty yards wide and they
stretched away along the shore north and south as far as the eye could
see. Behind them, there were two blockhouses about 150 yards apart.
We had landed exactly half way between them. I felt as if I had survived
the first round in a game of Russian roulette.

Now we began to cut a narrow swathe through the wire at a place
where there appeared to be none of the more visible sorts of anti-
personnel mines with which we were acquainted. Nevertheless, it was
a disagreeable sensation. Only God and the enemy knew what was
buried underfoot.

By the time we got to the other side it was ten o'clock. An hour
had passed since we had left the submarine. We were already late, but
it was difficult to see how we could have been any quicker. The earliest
possible time at which we could arrive back at the submarine had been
estimated to be eleven o'clock. The latest possible time, providing that
*Una* had not been discovered, in which case she would have to
submerge and leave us anyway, was one o'clock in the morning.
If all went well it still seemed that we might make it by midnight, or
earlier.

On the far side of the wire at the edge of the dunes, we came to a
track which ran parallel with the shore and presumably linked all the
blockhouses on this stretch of coast. Fortunately, it was deserted and
we pressed on across it and pushed our way through a hedge of some
kind of coarse vegetation which had probably been planted to stop the
sand drifting inland. For the first time in my life I was in Europe.

Beyond the beach there was a high stone wall which, like the wire
entanglements, seemed endless, and we pushed one of our number up

on to the top of it so that we could see what was on the other side, but all that he could report was that the lights on the airfield had been put out. No more planes were coming in and everything seemed quiet.

He hauled us up one by one and we dropped down into what proved to be a farmyard full of dogs. The thump of our great boots as we landed on the cobbles brought them to life, and they came at us barking and yelping. But in spite of the din they were making no windows or doors were flung open and we made a dash for the far side of the yard where there was a gate. It opened on to a lane which eventually led to the edge of the airfield.

On it we encountered a body of Italians and Germans, one of whom opened fire on us and one of our party returned it, firing a single round from a machine pistol.

The effect of these shots was positively magical. Immediately the airfield was brightly lit by searchlights which were disposed around the perimeter – as if the man who had fired at us had his hand on the switches – and then pandemonium broke loose: vehicles started up; Very lights rose; the air was filled with the ghastly sounds of commands being issued in Italian and German; and there was, to me, the equally terrifying noise made by men in boots running in step on a hard surface. It was difficult to repress the thought that we were expected. I had never seen so many JU 88s in my life, all guarded by sentries.

We took refuge in a small wood. 'What I think we should do,' our CO said, 'is . . .'

'Fuck off,' said a readily recognizable voice which was not that of an officer. 'That's what we ought to do, fuck off while there's still time.'

And we did: back to the beach, through the wire, encountering an enemy patrol, the members of which were too frightened to shoot; putting to sea in the only two canoes still undamaged; going out beyond the submarine in the darkness and eventually spending eight hours in the water before being picked up by some Sicilian fishermen who took us to Catania, where we narrowly escaped being shot as saboteurs.

Then to Rome.

Of the fourteen merchant ships which took part in *Operation Pedestal*, five reached Malta, including the tanker *Ohio*, which was enough to

save the island from having to capitulate. At least four of them were
sunk by JU 88s operating from Sicily.

In Rome we were ~~housed~~ in barracks occupied by the *Cavalleria di
Genova*, a regiment in Italy of similar status at that time to one or other
of the regiments of the Household Cavalry in Britain. They still had
their horses and the few officers and men who were about looked like
ardent royalists. Although they were not allowed to speak to us, their
demeanour was friendly. They sent us magazines and newspapers and
the food, which was provided by the officers' mess and brought to us
by a white-jacketed mess waiter who had the air of a family retainer,
was of an excellence to which none of us were accustomed in our own
regiments, although there was not much of it.

Once a day, but never together, we were let out to exercise on the
pathway which surrounded the *manège*. Here 'by chance', we met other
'prisoners', an extraordinarily sleazy collection of renegades and trai-
tors, most of them South African or Irish, dressed in various British
uniforms, some in civilian clothes, who called us 'old boy' and offered
to fix us up with nights on the town and escape routes into the Vatican
in exchange for information.

I enjoyed being alone. It was so long since I had been. From my
room, high up under the eaves of the barracks, I used to watch a
solitary, elegant officer taking a succession of chargers around the tan.
He was a wonderful horseman, even I could tell this without knowing
anything about horses. The days were poignantly beautiful. The leaves
on the plane trees were golden. Here, in Rome, in late August, it was
already autumn. I was nearly twenty-three and this was my first visit
to Europe. Locked up, isolated in the centre of the city, I felt like
the traitor Baillie-Stewart, 'the Officer in the Tower', or, even less
romantically, someone awaiting court martial for conduct scandalous
and unbecoming, looking out across the Park in the years before
the war.

After a few days we were dispersed, the officers to one camp, our
men to another. We all survived the war and so did Socks the dachsund.
Pat, in accordance with Desmond's last wish, took her to Beirut where
she took up residence with Princess Aly Khan.

## A PRISONER IN ITALY

On the seventh of September, 1943, the day before Italy went out of the war, I was taken to the prison hospital with a broken ankle, the result of an absurd accident in which I had fallen down an entire flight of the marble staircase which extended from the top of the building to the basement. The prison camp was on the outskirts of a large village in the Pianura Padana, the great plain through which the river Po flows on its way from the Cottian Alps to the sea. The nearest city was Parma on the Via Emilia, the Roman road which runs through the plain in an almost straight line from Milan to the Adriatic.

'That's right, knock the bloody place down,' someone said, unsympathetically, as it shuddered under the impact. The doctor, who examined my ankle, who was also a prisoner, took much the same view. He couldn't do much, anyway, because he hadn't got any plaster of paris. It was, however, he said, 'on order' and for the time being he did it up with some adhesive plaster which was a rather wobbly arrangement.

The only other occupant of the hospital was another officer who was suffering from a boil on his behind. He was the one who had proposed that we should dig a tunnel, the most dreary and unimaginative way of getting out of any prison, on which a number of us had been working for some months, and which we had only recently abandoned because events seemed to have rendered it unnecessary. The head of the shaft of this tunnel was in a bedroom on the *piano nobile* of the building, practically in mid-air, and the shaft went down through the middle of one of the solid brick piers which supported it and down into the cellars. When we reached mother earth, somewhere below the floor of the cellar, if ever, he had planned to construct a chamber, in which the spoil could be put into sacks and hauled to the surface, and from it the tunnel would be driven outwards under the wire. The shaft had a false lid, designed and made by a South African mining engineer. It was a marvellous piece of work – a great block of cement with tiles set in it that was so thick that when the *carabinieri* tapped the floor of the bedroom with hammers, which they sometimes did, the lid gave off the same sound as the rest of it. This lid was so heavy that special tools had had to be devised to lift it.

There were a lot of attempts at escape, some successful, some of them funny. One prisoner hid himself in a basket of dirty linen, destined for the nuns' laundry over the wall. We wondered what would have happened if they had actually unpacked him inside the convent. Some were very ingenious – two people had had themselves buried in the exercise field which was outside the main perimeter wire and was not guarded at night. They nearly got to Switzerland.

No one from our camp ever reached Switzerland before the Italian Armistice in 1943, up to which time only two British prisoners of war had succeeded in getting there.* It was very difficult to get out of a prison camp in Italy. Italian soldiers might be figures of fun to us, but some of them were extraordinarily observant and very suspicious and far better at guarding prisoners than the Germans were. It was also very difficult to travel in Italy if you did get out. The Italians are fascinated by minutiae of dress and the behaviour of their fellow men, perhaps to a greater degree than almost any other race in Europe, and the ingenious subterfuges and disguises which escaping prisoners of war habitually resorted to and which were often enough to take in the Germans: the documents, train tickets and ration cards, lovingly fabricated by the camp's staff of expert forgers; the suits made from dyed blankets; the desert boots cut down to look like shoes, and the carefully bleached army shirts were hardly ever sufficiently genuine-looking to fool even the most myopic Italian ticket collector and get the owner past the barrier, let alone survive the scrutiny of the occupants of a compartment on an Italian train. The kind of going over to which an escaping Anglo-Saxon was subjected by other travellers was usually enough to finish him off unless he was a professional actor or spoke fluent Italian. And in Italy, before the Armistice, there were no members of the Resistance or railway employees of the Left, as there were in France, to help escaping prisoners out of the country along an organized route.

The building in which we were housed had originally been built as an *orfanotrofio*, an orphanage, with the help of money contributed by pilgrims to the shrine of the miraculous *Madonna del Rosario* who, in

---

* One of them was Captain Anthony, later Major-General, Dean Drummond, CB, DSO, MC and Bar, captured in North Africa in 1941 and escaped in 1942.

1628, had performed the first of a succession of miracles when, in answer to his prayers, she raised a man called Giovanni Pietro Ugalotti from his death bed.

The foundations had been laid back in 1928, but the work had proceeded so slowly that the war began before it could be completed, and it remained empty until the spring of 1943 when it became a prisoner of war camp for officers and a few other ranks who acted as orderlies.

It was a large, three-storeyed building with a sham classical façade, so unstable that if anyone jumped up and down on one of the upper floors, or even got out of bed heavily, it appeared to wobble like a jelly. To those of us who were lodged on one of these upper floors, it seemed so unstable that we were convinced that if any bombs fell in the immediate neighbourhood it would collapse.

Next door to the *orfanotrofio* was the *santuario* in which the miraculous *Madonna del Rosario* was enshrined, and on its walls there were large quantities of ex-votos contributed by those who had been cured of some bodily affliction or saved from disaster by divine intervention – crutches, pale wax replicas of various parts of the human body that had been restored to health, primitive paintings of ships sinking, houses and barns on fire, or being struck by lightning, motor cars and aeroplanes crashing and farm carts being overturned, from all of which, and many other more fantastic mishaps, the occupants were depicted as emerging or being ejected relatively unscathed.

Behind the *santuario*, and joined to it, there was a convent in which a body of nuns resided in complete seclusion from which they never emerged except in case of grave illness or when they were being conveyed to another house of their order. Otherwise, their nearest approach to contact with the outer world was when they participated in the masses celebrated in the *santuario*, at which times they could look out on the congregation in the body of the church unseen, hidden from view behind an iron grille.

All the laundry for the prisoners was done in the convent and from time to time we discovered little notes wrapped up in our clean sheets or tucked inside our shirts, which said that those who had washed them were praying for us and were calling down the blessings of the *Madonna del Rosario* on our unworthy heads.

Although we never saw them most of us liked having the nuns next door, and the *santuario*, too. The clanging of its bells broke the monotony of the long days, making the campanile sway with their violence and frightening the swallows, making them sweep in panic to the sky, until some prisoners who had migraine, or were atheists, or simply disliked bells or noise generally, used to put their heads out of the windows and scream, at the top of their voices, 'I SAY, WOULD YOU MIND TERRIBLY TURNING IT IN?' And if by chance the bells did stop at that particular moment, 'THANK YOU SO MUCH!' Or, if they knew a little Italian, '*GRAZIE TANTO!*'

In the centre of the village, which was called Fontanellato, out of sight of the prisoners in the camp, was the Rocca Sanvitale, a splendid fifteenth-century castle, isolated behind a water-filled moat. In the castle had lived the *Conte Giovanni*, the last of the Sanvitales, one of the most ancient and illustrious families in Italy, which, today, is extinct. The buildings which faced the castle had deep, shadowy arcades under which there were shops and cafés where farmers used to congregate on Saturday, which was market day; and in the street which led to the *santuario* and the *orfanotrofio*, there was a war memorial of the First World War, which for Italy had been much more bloody than the one she was at present engaged in, with a long list of dead on a plaque at the foot of it. This was more or less all we knew about Fontanellato. Apart from a senior officer who had been taken on a tour of the village for some reason, none of us had ever seen it. What I have written is the sum total of what he told us when he returned. It was rather like listening to a lecture by some medieval traveller and hearing him say, as he pointed to the map, 'Here be dragons.'

But here, at Fontanellato, for the first time since I had been captured, there was a regular supply of Red Cross parcels and instead of the parcels being issued complete for us to make what we would of the contents, as had been done in other places, here all the cookable food was removed and prepared in the kitchens. This was much more civilized than keeping a lot of open tins under one's bed, as some of us had previously done (the Italians never allowed us to have unopened tins in case we hoarded them for an escape) and risking death by eating the contents of a tin of disgusting meat loaf that had been open for two or three days or, even worse, spending ages on all fours blowing away at a stove made from old tin cans, stoked up with bits of cardboard or, *in extremis*, pieces of bed board from the bottom of our bunks, as many had done in the past.

Drink and supplementary food were bought on the black market, which was even more extensive and better organized than it was in Britain, and a special float of Red Cross cigarettes was kept for this purpose and for the general corruption of the Italian camp staff, by responsible members of the British administration, ex-bank managers mostly, to whom this sort of thing was second nature.

Officially, we were allowed one tot of vermouth and one of wine each day by our administration, which was all that could be allowed if, in theory, everyone took their ration; but you could always buy other people's ration tickets with cigarettes or chocolate if you preferred drinking to smoking.

The wines were strange, dark and repulsive with various chemical additives, what the Italians call *vini lavorati*, worked on, primitive harbingers of the more sophisticated, doctored wines which made the Italian wine industry the byword that it became after the war; but like meths drinkers we enjoyed them better than no alcohol at all.

There was even a bar in which these concoctions were served, high up in a sort of minstrels' gallery above the chapel, which was used by the more staid prisoners to play bridge, and on Sundays for church services. We were forbidden by the Italians to look out of the windows of the bar which faced the road to the village, and if we did, the sentries in the watchtowers beyond the wire used to fire shots at us, some of which used to come whistling through the windows – the glass had been blown out long ago – and bury themselves in the walls and ceiling of the bar which had the same ecclesiastical decor as the chapel below. These bullet-holes gave the place a raffish appearance, like a middle-western saloon built by some renegade, gun-toting priest.

But in spite of these fusillades we still continued to risk our lives by putting our heads out of the windows, in order to be able to look at the girls of Fontanellato who, every evening when the weather was fine, used to promenade along the road in front of the *orfanotrofio*.

Some of my fellow prisoners had not spoken to a girl since they had been captured in 1940. Old or new prisoners, few of us had set eyes on girls like these for years and years. They were all shapes and sizes and colours and as they went past they laughed, as if enjoying some private joke, and tossed their heads impertinently in our direction. They all had long hair, short skirts and brown, bare legs and, as they swayed along the road, the high-heeled wooden sandals, which they all wore because there was very little shoe leather in Italy, clacked on the hard surface of the road. Some of them walked arm in arm with other girls carefully chosen for their inferior looks; some were so sure of themselves that they walked with girls who were their equals; others wobbled past in little flocks on bicycles, so slowly that they sometimes fell off uttering squeals of alarm – none was ever injured.

Although they were outnumbered by officers drawn from the middle and lower classes who had had to be commissioned, just as they had been in the First War, because there were not enough members of the upper class to go round, it was the upper class which set the style in the *orfanotrofio*, just as they had done in the pre-war world outside; the sons and younger brothers of peers and Highland lairds, young merchant bankers, wine shippers and gentlemen jockeys who had ridden in the National, most of them concentrated in cavalry regiments, rifle regiments, one or two Highland regiments and the Brigade of Guards. These amateur soldiers, for they were mostly amateurs, and any professional soldiers who had the same sort of background (any others were soon made into figures of fun), made up the coteries of OK people who exercised power.

These people were very reluctant to consort with outsiders, but as the *orfanotrofio* was very overcrowded and it was almost impossible to summon up a coterie large enough to take over one of the bigger rooms which contained anything up to twenty-seven beds, and because these rooms were the most desirable because they were on the side of the building which faced away from the afternoon sun, and because not all coteries found other coteries agreeable to them for innumerable reasons which there is no space to go into here, the members always tried to ensure that the rest of the beds were occupied with what they regarded as more or less acceptable ballast, that is to say, or as they would have said if they had actually said it out loud, marginally OK people, the sort of people they were prepared to talk to and drink with while the war was on, and then would never see again. And this included a number of people whom they regarded as being downright common but who had the saving grace of being funny; and they took these comics on to the strength in much the same way as their ancestors had employed jesters and dwarfs, to while away the tedious hours between breakfast, lunch and dinner. Everyone else they ignored completely, unless they owned something worth buying, or had some skill which they could make use of to increase their comfort. It was not that they consigned these unfortunates to outer darkness; they simply never invited them in out of it.

If I had not had marginally OK friends who had not abandoned me when we moved to the *orfanotrofio* from the camp in which we had previously been imprisoned I, too, would have become a dweller in darkness, which I did not want to be. I wanted the opportunity to observe the OK people at close quarters and some inner voice told me, quite correctly for once, that this might be my last chance to do so for most of my life.

Before the war I had rarely spoken to OK people, let alone known any well enough to talk to. Even at Sandhurst in 1940 OK people had been rarities. They were accommodated in the hideous New Buildings, which were not really new at all but were newer than the old ones; or else they were members of something called The Royal Armoured Wing – I now forget where they lived – which had to do with armoured fighting vehicles and therefore with what was still called the Cavalry, which was nothing to do with the Royal Tank Regiment and still isn't, all these years later.

When I was very young I sometimes used to see what I immediately recognised as midget versions of OK people in Children's Hairdressing on the first floor at Harrods, to which my mother, who had been a model girl at the store and had a nostalgia for the place, used to take me from Barnes to get my hair cut. There they exercised themselves on the rocking horses while waiting to be given the treatment and never let me have a go. I used to see them, too, wearing hand-made overcoats with velvet collars and long gaiters with hundreds of buttons down the sides, the sort of outfit which would have caused any un-OK

child to have a fit of apoplexy in the mild spring weather in which
they were dressed like this, being pushed up Sloane Street in huge,
glossy machines known as Victoria carriages, which were short-
wheelbase prams with curled up fronts, like seashells. They travelled
sitting more or less upright with their backs to whoever was pushing
them and, usually, with a dark blue blanket clipped over the front with
their initials, or their parents' initials, embroidered on them, on their
way to the Dell, a charming grassy depression on the far side of Rotten
Row, in the Park. They were still being conveyed about in these carriages at an age when I had long forgotten what it was like to be in a
push-chair.

The nurses who had the pushing of these little OK boys who sat, as
it were, with their backs to the engines, were invariably bad-tempered
looking and absolutely hideous. They wore pork-pie hats with badges
on them, long, drab overcoats of putty-coloured gabardine or grey
flannel, with lisle stockings to match, and clumpy great shoes; not like
my very sexy suburban nanny who wore a uniform bought for her by
my mother – who had not been a model girl for nothing – a blue denim
dress in summertime with stiff white collar and cuffs and black silk
stockings and high-heeled shoes, and whose head was swathed in some
sort of dark blue veiling when she took me out for an airing. Often it
was to have assignations with what looked to me like very old men
but were probably quite young ones, in a graveyard, not in fashionable
S.W.1 but in S.W.13, keeping me quiet while she did whatever she
did with them by giving me handfuls of Carrara marble chippings from
the tombs to play with. (She was fired when my mother found me
still playing with them in the bath.) If this nanny, of whom photographs still exist in an album, which enables me to remember more
clearly than I would otherwise have been able to do what she looked
like, had taken me to the Dell, the other nannies would have ignored
her, not only because she was far too good-looking to be a nanny, but
because I was not an OK child.

Whatever else I may have envied them I certainly did not envy these
little OK boys their nannies.

'Why is the sky blue, Nanny?' I heard one ask in the bell-like
upperclass voice which I envied and always wished that I could emulate
– mine sounded as if it emanated from my boots. To which he got the

reply, 'Ask no questions and you'll be told no lies, little Mr Inquisitive.'

And later when we were all a bit older, and I was on my way to or from the dentist, also in S.W.1, with my mother's 'Help', I sometimes used to see a shambling crocodile of them, all wearing the strange-looking, tomato-coloured caps of a smart pre-prep school, which looked like the sort of caps that some Irish peasants still wear, being shepherded along the road by a number of brisk grown-ups, all wearing no-nonsense-from-you expressions.

'Well-born they may be, Master Eric,' the 'Help' said stoutly, when they had shuffled past, 'but most of them look half-barmy to me.' And when the war came and I was on embarkation leave I saw them again in Harrods, in various splendid uniforms with their mothers and sisters and girl friends who all wore miniature replicas of their regimental badges picked out in diamonds, and again listened with awe to their loud, self-confident voices, usually as we were ascending or descending together in one of the lifts, slightly cracked versions of the bell-like tones I had listened to with envy on the way to the Dell sixteen years before. But this was the first opportunity I had had to consort with them and study them at leisure and *en masse*.

In the camp the members of the coteries moved easily in a mysterious, almost Edwardian world and when they addressed one another they used nicknames, just as the Edwardians had been so fond of doing, which were completely unintelligible to anyone else, and they knew who was who so far down the scale of the aristocracy to a point at which one would have thought that any blue blood corpuscles would have been non-existent. They alone knew that 'Bolo' Bastonby was the nephew of the Earl of Crake, that 'Jamie' Stuart Ogilvie-Keir-Gordon was the youngest brother of the Master of Dunreeking and that 'Feathers' Farthingdale was the third son of the Marquis of Stale by his second wife. No one outside these coteries had even heard of the holders of the titles, let alone 'Bolo' Bastonby, 'Jamie' Stuart Ogilvie-Keir-Gordon or 'Feathers' Farthingdale.

The *orfanotrofio* was more like a public school than any other prison camp I was ever in. If anybody can be said to have suffered in this place it was those people who had never been subjected to the hell of English preparatory and public school life; because although there was no bullying in the physical sense – canes had been taken away for the duration, and the twisting of arms was forbidden by the Geneva Convention – there was still plenty of scope for mental torment; and although the senior officer thought he ran the camp it was really run by people elected by the coteries, just like Pop at Eton, where so many of them had been.

When one of the prisoners was found to be stealing food, a most awful crime in a prison camp where everyone started off with exactly the same amount however much more they managed to acquire by exchanging tobacco and cigarettes for it, and the problem arose of punishing him without the added and unthinkable indignity of handing him over to the Italians to keep in their cells, the *colonello* offered our colonel a small Italian infantry bivouac tent and a piece of parched ground in what was normally a zone that was out of bounds to us on which the sun shone all day, so that the offender could expiate his crime in solitary confinement and on a diet of bread and water provided by the British, from their rations, not by the Italians.

Some of the prisoners were very old prisoners indeed, not in age or seniority but because of the number of years they had been locked up. Most of the 'old' prisoners had wonderful clothes which no one who had been captured later in the war could possibly emulate, things that had been sent to them before the Italians had instituted rigid sumptuary laws for prisoners of war in order to prevent anyone having anything which vaguely resembled civilian clothes. By some technicality those who already had these clothes were allowed to keep them, providing that the larger items bore the large red patches which were sewn on to everything we wore. They had pig's-whisker pullovers, scarves and stocks from the Burlington Arcade secured with gold pins, made-to-measure Viyella shirts, and corduroy trousers, and one who was a member of a cavalry regiment called the Cherry-Pickers, wore cherry-red trousers. Some of this gear had reached them by way of the Red Cross and neutral embassies, but not all of it. One officer had an elegant hacking coat which had been made for him while he was a prisoner, out of a horse blanket which he had rescued from his armoured car when it went up in flames near Sollum, and which he paid the Italian tailor for with cigarettes.

The one thing which united the prisoners in the *orfanotrofio* and which gave them, as it were, a 'team spirit', was their attitude towards the 'Itis'. 'Itis' in the abstract, because it was difficult for any but the most hidebound to actively dislike our 'Itis', apart from one or two horrors who would have been horrors whatever their nationality, and we all loved the 'Iti' girls – soldiers always make an exception for the women of the enemy, for otherwise they would feel themselves completely alone.

The *colonello* was generally conceded to be 'all right', a 'good chap' in spite of being an 'Iti'; and most people liked one of the Italian officers, a *capitano*, because he smoked a pipe and was more English than many of the English. For most of the others and the wretched soldiery who guarded us, the privates and the NCOs, with their miserable uniforms, ersatz boots, unmilitary behaviour and stupid bugle calls, we felt nothing but derision. What boobs they were, we thought. We used to talk about how we could have turned them into decent soldiers if only we were given the opportunity.

How arrogant we were. Most of us were in the *orfanotrofio* because we were military failures who had chosen not to hold out to the last round and the last man, or, at the last gasp, had been thankful to grasp the hand of a Sicilian fisherman and be hauled from the sea, as I had been. We were arrogant because this was the only way we could vent our spleen at being captured and, at the same time, keep up our spirits which were really very low. Deep down in all of us, prisoners isolated from the outside world and Italian *soldati*, far from home, subjected to a twentieth-century Temptation of St Anthony and without the money to gratify it, firing volleys at us in fury because we laughed at them in front of girls who by rights should have been their girls, tormenting us all, reminding us constantly of something for which we felt that we would give up everything we had for one more chance to experience, something we ourselves talked about all the time, was the passionate desire to be free; but what did we mean by freedom? I thought I knew, and so did everyone else; but it meant so many different things to so many of us.

We were, in fact, as near to being really free as anyone can be. We were relieved of almost every sort of mundane pre-occupation that had afflicted us in the outside world. We had no money and were relieved of the necessity of making any. We had no decisions to make about anything, even about what we ate. We were certainly much more free than many of us would ever be again, either during the war or after it. And as prisoners we did not even suffer the disapprobation of society as we would have done if we had been locked up in our own country. To our own people we appeared as objects worthy of sympathy.

On the evening of the 8th September news of an armistice came through. The following morning we left the camp *en masse* to avoid being sent to Germany. It was a close thing; the Germans arrived shortly afterwards. Because of my damaged ankle I left the camp on a horse. That night I was given shelter in the hayloft of a neighbouring farm.

## ESCAPE

The next morning, the 10th September, after a slow start, things began to happen with increased rapidity. It was as if a piece of an old film in which the actors emerge from vehicles, zoom into buildings with incredible speed, and miraculously appear at a window sixteen storeys up within seconds, had been interpolated in a modern one in which the characters move at a normal rate.

Around eleven o'clock an Italian doctor arrived in a Fiat 500. He was an enormous, shambling man with grizzled hair, like a bear and one of the ugliest men I had seen for a long time.

He examined my ankle, which was rather painful after the strains to which it had been subjected, raised his shoulders, made a noise which sounded like *urgh* and went off to have a conference with the *capitano*, who had joined the prisoners when they broke out of the camp.

'The doctor says you must go to hospital,' the *capitano* said, when they emerged from their conclave.

'But that means I shall be captured again,' I said.

'You'll be taken anyway if you don't. Apparently things are not going too well at Salerno and we're six hundred kilometres north of it. Everything's going to break up here, anyway. Unless you can walk you won't stand a chance. The doctor can get you into a hospital in Fontanellato. No one will think of looking for you there.'

While he was speaking, the forerunners of an army of women, girls and small boys began to arrive at the farm on foot and on bicycles; the same girls, or the same sort of girls I had seen on the road outside the camp, except that now they were wearing their working clothes. I felt more timid now that we were at close quarters and there was no wire between us, and so did they, and all we managed were some nervous smiles.

They all carried baskets and panniers filled with civilian clothing, wine, bread, cheese, fruit, eggs and tinned food and cigarettes which they had saved from the *orfanotrofio* after the Germans had left. All at once the farm became a depot for the prisoners who had taken refuge from the Germans behind an embankment.

I found myself a mechanic's jacket and a pair of dark blue cotton trousers and a shirt, filled my pack with the food and cigarettes that were being pressed upon me from every side, and climbed the ladder to the loft where I changed into them, chucking my uniform down from the window into the yard from which it was instantly taken away.

While I was doing this I noticed a bold, good-looking girl. She was different from the others. They were all brown or black haired; but she was an ash blonde with blue eyes and she was very slim which made her seem taller than she was. She looked more like a Scandinavian than an Italian to me, but with more fire. Whatever she was she smiled at me.

Then the doctor arrived. For the last time I descended the ladder and said goodbye to the farmer and his wife who cried. They were the first people in the whole district to take the risk of helping us. Then I hopped across the yard to the Fiat.

As I was getting into it the girl came up and leant over the top of the open door.

'I vill com to see you in the *ospedale*,' she said, in fractured English. She had a deep middle-European voice. 'Wonce I have seen you in the *orfanotrofio* and you vaved and the *soldati* went pom pom. Ve vill have lessons in languages,' she said. 'Your language and my language.' And she smiled again. Then someone shut the door and we drove away.

'If iu uont tu enter dhe steiscen iu mast haev e plaetfom tikit,' Wanda said. '*Se vuole entrare nella stazione deve avere un biglietto.*'

I was lying in a bed in the *Ospedale Peracchi* on the outskirts of Fontanellato, only a few hundred yards from the *orfanotrofio*. I had now been free for three days. It seemed much longer. Wanda was seated on a chair which one of the *suore*, the nuns who were also expert nurses, had placed in a corner of the room, as far away from me as possible. Equally discreetly, the door had been left wide open. Both of us were armed with phrase books, she with a large Italian/English version, I with the English/Italian booklet which I had salvaged on my way out of the *orfanotrofio*. With their help we were making heavy weather of one another's languages, and it was not fair of her to change subjects like this.

Up to now we had been reading useful phrases to one another from the chapters on 'Trams and Buses'. 'Last stop. *Ool ghet aut!*' '*Kwah-lee ow-toh-bus vann-oh ah Toh-reen-oh?* Which buses go to Turin?' I ruffled through the pages of my book which was so small that it looked as if it had been printed for a midget, until I found a section headed 'At the Station – *Alla Stazione*', and said, '*Oh per-soh eel mee-oh beel-yet-oh.* I have lost my ticket.' To which she replied, severely, 'Iu haev misleid iur tikit. Iu caant continiu iur geerni anless iu ricaver it. *Lei ha smarrito il suo biglietto. Non può proseguire il suo viaggio se non lo trova.*'

'*Nohn vawr-ray-ee cohn-teen-u-ar loh.* I don't want to continue it,' I said. I enunciated this, and all the other phrases, with such painstaking slowness that I sounded like a run-down gramophone.

'Iu hev mist dhe train. *È partito il treno,*' she said, triumphantly, like one of the OK people in the orphanage with a royal flush poker.

'*Grahts-ee-ay. Lay ay stah-toh jehn-tee-lay.* Thank you very much. Most kind of you.'

'Rieli nathing,' she said, airily. 'Ai em ounli tu glaed if ai kaen help iu. *Proprio nulla, per me è un vero piacere poterla aiutare.*'

She shut her book and looked at me with an air of despair which, to me, was very beautiful.

'Hurrock,' she said (this is what my name sounded like on her lips).

'You will never learn *italiano* like this. You spik and then you forget. First you must learn *la grammatica*. I have learned English *grammatica*, so also must you learn Italian. And you must learn *presto*, queekly,

queekly. Here, you see, I have written for you a *grammatica* with *aggettivi, come se dice*? Adjectives! Adjectives! *Che lingua!* Also auxiliary verbs and verbs, *regolari* and *irregolari*. You will learn all these, please, by tomorrow.'

'I can't learn all this by tomorrow.'

'You *vill*,' she said, 'or I shall not kom more. I shall teach to someonels. The *superiora* says I can kom ven I vish. If you vont me to kom you must vork.'

She consulted her book. 'Hueer dheers e uil dheers e ui. *Proverbio. Dove c'è la volonta c'è la via.*'

'Where there's a will there's a way,' I said. 'That's a proverb. I want you to come to see me more than anything.'

'Then learn your *grammatica*,' she said, consulting her superior phrase book. '*Far presto!* Luk slipi!'

*               *               *

Every afternoon Wanda visited me in the *ospedale*. We sat together in the back garden, hidden from the outside world by one of the projecting wings of the building and a hedge, under the benevolent but constant chaperonage of the *superiora* and her attendant *suore* who were never far away. Centuries of invasion of their country by foreign soldiery, and the concomitant outrages which had been inflicted on them had made the members of female religious orders particularly adept in protecting not only their own virtues, but that of those temporarily committed to their charge.

She used to tell me the latest news about my friends. How some people had already set off towards the line; others were thinking of going to Switzerland; how one officer whose identity I never discovered had been hidden in the *castello* of a local *principessa* who had been so impressed by his girlish face that she had the brilliant idea of dressing him as a young woman of fashion and putting him on a train to Switzerland. This she had done but, unfortunately, he had looked so desirable on the train that some soldiers had 'interfered' with him, as the *News of the World* used to put it, and discovered the truth, although one of them got punched hard on the nose in the process of doing so.

Wanda herself was in favour of my going to Switzerland – she had none of my optimism about the Allies' capacity to advance rapidly up Italy – crossing from somewhere near the head of the Val d'Aosta with a party which was being organized by the pipe-smoking interpreter; but I hated the idea of going to Switzerland and perhaps spending the winter not imprisoned but interned which seemed to me the same thing, perhaps locked up in a hotel on the shores of some drab Swiss lake, watching the rain beating down into it. Her other plan, which seemed more cheerful and sensible than going to Switzerland, was that I should become gardener's boy at the castle of that same *principessa* who had sent the transvestite officer on his last journey.

In the garden we worked away, teaching one another our respective languages. After our initial, disastrous, but diverting attempt to do it with phrase books, we went back to the beginnings. Wanda made me start at the bottom, conjugating verbs and struggling with pronouns. Fortunately for me she already had a sound knowledge of grammar and was far ahead.

I concentrated on teaching her new words, the way to pronounce the ones she already knew and some colloquial expressions. But as the days went by, listening to her, I found myself increasingly reluctant to destroy her rich, inimitable idiom, and her strangely melancholy accent which to me was a triple distillation of the essence of middle Europe. It seemed monstrous to graft on to this vigorous stem my own diluted version of English, originally learned in a London suburb and further watered down by school teachers and the BBC.

'*Questo è un sasso*. Dis is a ston,' she would say, picking up a piece of gravel from one of the paths. 'I strait it avay,' throwing it over her shoulder. She also employed a remarkable word of her own invention 'to squitch'. This could be used to describe any kind of operation from corking a bottle of wine to mending a piece of complicated machinery. 'You just squitch it in,' she said, as I tried to replace the winder which had come off her dilapidated wrist-watch.

It would have been tedious if we had confined ourselves to studying one another's languages; but, as well, we had long, rambling conversations about our lives. She told me about her family. They were Yugoslavs, Slovenes from the Carso, the great, windswept limestone plateau which extends inland from the Gulf of Trieste at the head of the Adriatic towards Ljubljana, territory which had been ceded to Italy after the dismemberment of the Austro-Hungarian Empire in 1919. Her father had been a schoolmaster in a Slovene village in the Carso called Stanjel until the provisions of the peace treaty moved the Italian frontier with Slovenia twenty-five miles inland from the Adriatic, when it was re-named San Daniele del Carso by the Italians. Much later, in the early thirties, Mussolini decided to break down the strong national-istic spirit which still existed in those parts of Slovenia which had been ceded to Italy. He forbade the use of the Slovene language and Slovenian teachers were deported to Italy. Among them was Wanda's father. He was of the same age as the *colonello* at the *orfanotrofio* but his background was entirely different. He scarcely knew any Italian at all, his second language being German, the official language of the Empire (he had served in the Austrian Army in the First World War) but now he was sent to Fontanellato to teach in the school there where, for some years knowing little of the language, he experienced great difficulty in correcting his pupils' essays. He was a liberal of the old sort and detested Fascists and Fascism. Wanda told me that her family had never been allowed to return to their country and that her mother cried very often when she thought of her home, although the local people at Fontanellato, who had originally called them *Tedeschi*, Germans, were now very friendly. She herself was an accountant and she worked in the *Banca d'Agricoltura* in the village.

When Wanda was not at the *ospedale* she was either working at the bank or else taking supplies to the other prisoners in the surrounding country. Fortunately, the weather was still good. Meanwhile, I got on with the 'prep' which she had set me; but without her I found the garden a rather creepy, shut-away place. Occasionally a low-flying German aircraft roared overhead; almost equally loud were the roars of out-patients who were having their teeth extracted without the aid of painkillers, by Giulio, a local man who not only acted as *infirmiere* but also stood in as a dental surgeon in urgent cases in the absence of the real dentist who only visited Fontanellato once a week.

Every day the news got worse. On the twelfth of September Radio Roma broadcast the news that Mussolini had been rescued by German parachutists. The station was now in the hands of the Germans, and temporarily at least, it seemed more reliable and less euphoric than the BBC which, according to Wanda who had heard it, had actually broadcast on the same day the sound of the bells of St Paul's ringing out in rejoicing at the invasion of Italy.

On the thirteenth and fourteenth the news from Salerno was really awful. Rome announced that the Germans were launching massive counter-attacks on the beachhead, and this was confirmed by the BBC. By the sixteenth the news was better. The counter-attack seemed to have lost its steam; but on that day an order was broadcast that all Italian officers, NCOs and men were to present themselves forthwith in uniforms at the nearest German headquarters. No one but a lunatic would have obeyed such an order, and, in fact scarcely anyone did; but what was more serious was another announcement to the effect that anyone sheltering or feeding prisoners of war would be dealt with under martial law, and I had visions of the *superiora* going before a firing squad as Nurse Cavell had done. It was obvious that I could not stay in the *ospedale* any longer and, for the first time I realized what Wanda had been trying to din into me, that a knowledge of Italian was going to be essential if I was to avoid being recaptured.

On or about the sixteenth the *Gazzetta di Parma*, Italy's oldest newspaper, which had enjoyed a very brief period of editorial freedom after the Armistice, before once again being muzzled, published a statement by the Commandant of the SS in Parma. Full of gruesome bonhomie, he conveyed his felicitations to the population and especially to members of the Fascist organisations, and then went on to speak of a new period of prosperity in store for the Italian people. Next to this absolutely crazy announcement there was a notice to the effect that a curfew was imposed on the inhabitants of the entire Province from ten p.m. onwards, and that anyone who disregarded it was liable to be shot.

The next day, the seventeenth of September, while we were having what was to be our last language lesson together, I told Wanda that I must leave the *ospedale*.

'You are right,' she said. 'If you had not suggested it yourself I was going to tell you. I am worried for you but I am much more worried for the *superiora*. There are Germans everywhere now. But it will have to be tomorrow. My father and the doctor will arrange something. They are great friends.'

I was worried for everyone who was helping me. All I had to lose was my freedom; their lives were in danger. I was particularly worried about Wanda and all the other women and girls quartering the country round about on their bicycles bringing food every day to the prisoners who were still hiding among the vines wondering, like me, what was the best thing to do.

Our relationship had changed a great deal since we had first met. It had progressed far beyond the stage of giving one another language lessons. I had begun by thinking her a very good-looking girl and being flattered that she should take any notice of me. Then I had begun to admire her courage and determination; now I was in love with her.

These feelings were not entirely one-sided. Now, when we were alone together, we sat as close as we dared to one another on the seat in the garden, knowing that we were under observation by one or other of the *suore* but on several occasions I managed to kiss Wanda in one of the dark corridors on the way back to my room.

With my lunch, which was brought to me on a tray by one of the more forbidding-looking *suore*, who had been specially selected for this dangerous mission by the *superiora* in order to discourage the *carabinieri* from rooting amongst its contents, came a message, hidden under an almost redhot dish. It was unsigned but I recognized the style. 'Get out!' it read, in English. 'Tonight, 22.00, if not Germany tomorrow, 06.00. Go east 500 *metri* across fields until you reach a very little street, then torn right and go on 500 *metri* until you reach a bigger street. Wait there! Don't worry about clothes.'

These were less ambiguous orders than most of those which I had been accustomed to receive during the last few years and, what was best, they left the method of executing the escape to the discretion of the person who was going to carry them out. They had, in fact, been drafted by Wanda's father who had not been an officer in the Austrian Army for nothing, and she had rendered them into English.

They were not difficult to carry out. At 21.57, after having eaten a formidable last dinner at 19.30, I opened the door of my room for the tenth time that afternoon and uttered the magic words, *Ho mal di stomaco* to the solitary *carabiniere* on duty. They no longer stirred him to mirth, or his companion either, when he was on duty. After a few hours spent in a dark corridor sitting on a pair of chairs of a hardness which only

the Roman Catholic church could devise, outside a labour ward from
which awful sounds came from time to time, they had decided to each
do stints of two hours on guard, while the one off duty sat below in
the entrance hall. Whichever one of them was on duty now ignored
me completely.

As soon as I had hopped into the *gabinetto* I locked the door, and
after a short interval began to make various groaning and grunting
noises which I hoped were appropriate, having practised them already
that afternoon on nine previous visits, at the same time hoisting myself
with some difficulty through the high, narrow window which I had
already opened, and slid with surprising ease, down a convenient drain-
pipe, bootless and in my pyjamas, like someone leaving a burning
house in an early Keystone film, to land with a great clonk on my
plastered foot on the path below.

There was no need to worry about making a noise. The croaking of
innumerable frogs, and the chirping of crickets were deafening; but I
was no less apprehensive for that. Wishing that I had with me the
crutches I had used in the *ospedale*, I rushed across the path and crashed
through a hedge into a large field of stubble, over which an enormous
moon was just rising. It was horribly bright and, as I began to cross
it, I heard violent banging noises from the interior of the *ospedale*,
which must have been the *carabiniere* hammering on the door of the
*gabinetto*. I set off across the stubble at a terrific rate, which was extraordinarily painful with one bare foot, like walking on nails, so fast that
I failed to see a large, concealed ditch, into which I plunged up to my
waist in black slime. The 500 metres to the very little street where I
was to 'torn' to the right seemed longer than I had imagined they
would, but eventually I reached a rutted track which led away to the
north, and there was no doubt that this was it.

I followed it for a quarter of a mile or so, past a farmhouse with a
yard full of savage, barking dogs, until I reached a place where three
roads met. There, at the junction, I found a motor car with two men
hovering impatiently about it. One of them was the doctor, the other
was someone whom I had never met before, a man with grey hair *en
brosse*, whom the doctor addressed as *Maestro*. It was Wanda's father.

'You are late,' he said in Italian with more than a hint of severity,
just as I imagined he did to the boys and girls in his class. He had the

On the way to the Hindu Kush. Hugh Carless sitting for a pilgrim photograph in Meshed, the holy city in north-eastern Iran.

*Above:* Not feeling so good in Nuristan, 1956

*Opposite top and bottom:* Tajik villagers in the Panjshir valley on the way to Nuristan.

*Left:* Hazards of travel by rail at Kasganj Junction.

*Below:* Calcutta: disembarking at the Armenian ghat downstream of the Howrah Bridge after descending the Ganges from Hardwar.

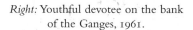
*Above:* Football match at Banaras.

*Right:* Youthful devotee on the bank
of the Ganges, 1961.

*Overleaf:* Hindu pilgrims wading
ashore at Sagar Island, where the
Ganges reaches the sea in the
Bay of Bengal.

Pilgrim encampment on Sagar Island.

same high forehead and the same stubborn expression which I had seen on her face when she had been trying to make me work harder at my Italian, except that he looked as if he wore it permanently. I would have liked to have asked him how his daughter was but this was not the right moment, exposed in the moonlight at a treeless crossroads, with a hue and cry beginning less than half a mile away.

'I'm sorry,' I said. It sounded feeble and for a moment I thought of adding some flippant, mock-heroic remark about having had to go to the lavatory on the way, but I was not yet sufficiently good at the language, and if I had I would probably have found myself being bent over the bonnet of the Fiat and being given 'six of the best' with a Slovene cane for impertinence.

'Well, get in!' said the doctor. 'Don't stand there!' He sounded just like a doctor who has been called out in the middle of the night to minister to some trivial complaint which, in effect, he had. Neither of them commented on my extraordinary appearance, wearing nothing but pyjamas and covered in filth. Fortunately they had somehow contrived to get my boots and clothes from the *ospedale*.

As I got into the back of the car I noticed for the first time that the door panel had a Red Cross painted on it. This at least partly explained how the Doctor was able to drive about the countryside during the curfew without being riddled with bullets. But now, if we were stopped and I was found travelling with these rather severe-looking middle-aged men who addressed one another formally as *maestro* and *dottore*, who, as Wanda had told me, first became friends because of their longstanding mutual distaste for Fascism, there was little doubt that they would be shot.

Before I left for the mountains I had one last encounter with Wanda. She brought disastrous news, having cycled twenty kilometres to a wood in which I had spent the night to do so.

Early that morning before it was light and while everyone was still in bed, a mixed force of Germans and Fascists had descended on the neighbourhood of Fontanellato and surrounded the house of a farmer called Baruffini in which they found several prisoners. Then they beat the surrounding fields in which a number of others were sleeping under the vines. Altogether their total bag was thirteen. But worst of all one of the prisoners had been mad enough to keep a day-to-day journal of all his doings in clear, which gave the names of a number of people who had helped him and which he had not even had the presence of mind to hide or destroy when he was taken. As a result of this, further arrests had been made and more were thought to be imminent.*

The other news was not good but it was less tragic. At the same time as all this was going on, the Germans had requisitioned the *castello*, in which Wanda had succeeded in arranging that I should be taken on as the gardener's boy, in order to turn it into a military headquarters, it was said, for Field-Marshal Kesselring. I was lucky to have got out of the *ospedale* when I did. Once the castle became a headquarters for someone as important as Kesselring, all the roads for miles around would have blocks on them.

'Pity you didn't go there before,' Wanda said. 'No one would think the gardener's boy in a German headquarters could be English.' It would certainly have been a joke if I had already been installed in the *castello* and had been taken over by the Germans, with the rest of the staff, to help look after the Field-Marshal.

The last piece of information she brought concerned the *carabinieri* at the hospital. They had been saved from severe punishment by an extraordinary circumstance. On the night that I escaped from it another British prisoner had been brought to it suffering from some serious complaint and they had simply substituted him for me.

'I know you never wanted to, but you won't be able to go to Switzerland now, perhaps you never will,' she said. She spoke in Italian. 'And none of us may be able to help you any more. We may not be here to do so. No one, except the people who have got it now, know how many names that stupid wrote down in his little book. The doctor could be in it and so could my father.'

And so could she. My blood ran cold at the thought of it.

'Look,' I said in English. This was no time for language lessons. 'You must give up trying to help me, all of you. If I'm caught all that will happen is that I'll be sent to Germany and be put in another camp; but if any of you are caught helping me you're quite likely to be shot.

---

* Some of these unfortunate people were taken to Germany, including Signor Baruffini, who died in Buchenwald, and other members of his family.

It just isn't worth it. I'm protected by the Geneva Convention. They won't shoot me. And my ankle's fine now. I can look after myself.'

'I don't know anything about your Geneva Convention,' she said, 'but I know more about Fascists than you do and if they take you and send you to Germany, you may be there for years and years the way things are going and you may never come back. What we're going to try and do is get you to the mountains tomorrow, and when things have quietened down a bit I'll try and take you down closer to the line myself.'

I tried to argue with her and for the first time since I had known her she became very angry.

'You're a stupid young man,' she said, 'almost as stupid as the one who kept a little book with all his stupid thoughts in it and all those names, and if we'd known he was doing that he would have been killed I can tell you. It's a pity we didn't know. Do you really think the doctor and my father are helping you just because they like the colour of your eyes? It's because this is the only way at the moment in which they can do anything against the Fascists. They really hate them, those two old men. Much more than I do.'

'And what about you?' I said. 'Is that the only reason why you've done what you have?'

She took my hands in the darkness and held them. 'Oh, Hurruck,' she said, 'when I said that you were stupid I didn't really meant it. Stupid in Italian, *stupido*, is a very rude word which gives great offence, as I told you when you were in the *ospedale* and a word that you just never use to an Italian; but it is an expression that I have learned from you who always tell me that to call someone stupid, "don't be so stupid", is what you always say to one another in England, is just another expression like "*luk slipi*"; but now you really are being Italian stupid to say such a thing to me.' By now she was crying with vexation.

'I'm sorry,' I said. 'It was a silly thing to say.' She let go of my hands.

'Sorry! That's all you English ever are. Sorry to have troubled you! Even,' she said, 'if they go through a door in front of you that's all they say. Sorry! Why do they go through it first if they know they're going to be sorry afterwards? It's a word like stupid. It doesn't mean anything. When you and your friends say "sorry" I feel like hitting you!' And she began to cry even harder.

There was nothing I could say and if I did say anything it would be all wrong. I put my arms round her and held her close to me among the tall maize for a long time until I had to go back to my hiding place.

'I must go now,' she said, 'because of the curfew; but wherever you go, whatever happens, I'll see you again. Never forget it.'

*             *             *

After some time spent hidden in the woods, Wanda told me that the doctor was going to take me to the mountains. He proposed to drive me down the Via Emilia, the main German line of communication with the battlefront, a hazardous business.

'Get in!' the doctor said as soon as I reached it, which were about the only words he ever seemed to address to me. 'We can talk later!'

'I don't think you ought to be . . .' I began to say, but he cut me short.

'IN THE NAME OF GOD, GET IN!' he said. 'This place is swarming with Germans. It's like Potsdam.' I got in. There was nothing else to do.

I was not the only passenger. In the back seat of the little car there was a very small, toothless old man, wrapped in a moth-eaten cloak, a garment which is called a *tabar* in this part of the world, and with an equally moth-eaten hat to match. Both had once been black, now they were green with age. What he was, guide, someone whom the doctor had recruited to lend versimilitude to the outing, or simply an old man of the mountains on the way back to them from a black-market expedition I was unable to discover because, during the entire journey, he never uttered a word. He simply sat there in the back with a heavily laden rucksack on his knees, either completely ignoring the doctor when he addressed some remark to him in his dialect, or else uttering what was either a mindless chuckle or something provoked by the workings of a powerful and possibly diabolical intelligence.

Eventually we arrived at the junction of the minor road, on which we had been travelling, with the Via Emilia. Blocking the entrance to it there was a German soldier, probably a military policeman, on a motor cycle. He had his back to us and was watching the main road on which a convoy was moving south towards the front. Knowing what sort of man the doctor was, I was afraid that he might hoot imperiously at him to get out of the way but fortunately he simply switched off the engine and waited for the man to go, which presently he did when a gap occurred in the interminable procession of vehicles, roaring away on his machine in pursuit of them, and we followed him.

'Sixteenth Panzer Division,' the doctor said. 'Reinforcements.' How he could know this I could not imagine. There were no insignia on the vehicles to proclaim that they were part of Sixteenth Panzer Division, but he said it with such authority that I wouldn't have dreamed of questioning what he said. He was not a man given to making idle remarks.

I was paralysed by the thought of what would happen if he was stopped, if only for having the impertinence to pass part of a German Panzer Division on the move when all other civilian vehicles had been halted in order to allow it to monopolize the road; and I was temporarily hypnotized by the sheer proximity of the enemy in such strength and numbers. I had only to stretch out my right hand through the open window as we went sedately past them to touch their tanks, which were of a sort and size that I had not even seen in diagrams; their self-propelled guns which I recognized; their half-tracked vehicles with anti-aircraft guns at the ready which looked a little like great chariots; and the lorries full of tough-looking Panzer Grenadiers, all ready to peel out of them if the convoy was attacked from the air, who looked down at our tiny vehicle with the red crosses painted on the sides and on the roof, which were making this journey possible, with a complete lack of curiosity, just as our own soldiers would have done in similar circumstances, which I found extremely comforting. Less disinterested were a lot of grumpy-looking officers up in front in a large, open Mercedes, one of them wearing the red tabs of a general on the lapels of his leather coat, who all glared at us as they probably would have done if we had passed them in a Fiat 500, a Mercedes-load of important businessmen, on the autobahn between Ulm and Stuttgart in the years before the war, and, just as I would have then, I had an insane temptation to thumb my nose at them.

Soon, mercifully, we outdistanced the convoy, passed a castle among
trees, crossed a wide river with more shingle than water in it by a long
bridge, the approaches to which were flanked by allegorical statuary,
and after crossing another, shorter bridge, entered the city of Parma,
in the centre of which, or what looked like the centre to me, the doctor's
motor car broke down under the eyes of Garibaldi, a large statue of
whom stood in the *piazza*.

Fortunately it was half past one in the afternoon, according to a
large, elaborate clock on the face of a building in the square and the
city was in the grip of the siesta. Apart from a couple of German
*feldgendarmen* with metal plaques on their chests who were obviously
there to direct the convoy on its way when it arrived, and whose
presence in the *piazza* was probably enough to cause its depopulation,
the place was deserted.

Quite soon the reinforcements for Sixteenth Panzer Division, or
whatever they were, began to rumble through it and once again I felt
myself the cynosure; while the doctor fiddled with the engine which
was fuelled with methane gas, I pretended to help him with my head
buried in the engine – as far as anyone can bury his head in the engine
of a Fiat 500 – and an old man who was the other passenger sat in the
back cackling with laughter as if he was enjoying some private and
incommunicable joke. 'Heh! Heh! Heh!'

Eventually the engine started and the rest of the journey to the mountains was without incident.

## IN THE MOUNTAINS

'The Baruffas will look after you,' the doctor said, 'until we can find
a place deeper in the mountains. This is a safe house, although it's on
the road, but stay away from the windows and don't go outside. I'll
be back in a few days,' he said, 'and if you want me to I'll bring
Wanda.' And he smiled one of his rare smiles.

'I do want you to,' I said.

We shook hands. I heard him reverse the Fiat out of the farmyard

on to the road and drive off. Two days later the Fascists came for him
while he was asleep in his bed.

Apart from the slow ticking of a longcase clock, it was very quiet
in the kitchen now and sad after all the joking and drinking. The fire
which had been stirred up when we arrived had died down.

'You must go,' Signor Baruffa said as soon as the doctor's car was
out of earshot. He was not smiling anymore. His wife was not smiling
either. She began washing the glasses from which we had been drinking
strong, dark wine.

I couldn't believe him.

'Why? You said . . .'

'I'm afraid. *Ho paura.*' Literally what he said was, 'I have fear.' In
the three weeks since Italy had collapsed it was an expression I had
already heard many times.

'Of what are you afraid?'

In the *pianura*, the great plain of the Po, which was alive with enemies
of all sorts, everyone had *paura* and with good reason. Here, in the
heart of the Apennines on the road to nowhere, it seemed absurd.

'I am afraid of the Germans. I am afraid of the Fascists. I am afraid
of spies. I am afraid of my neighbours, and I am afraid of having my
house burned over my head and of being shot if you are found here.
My wife is also afraid. Now go!'

'But where shall I go?'

'I cannot tell you where to go. Only go!'

'You *must* tell me!'

'Then go to Zanoni!' It sounded like an imprecation. 'Zanoni is poor.
He has nothing to lose. His house is not like this, by the road. It is up
the valley, above the mill. It will only take you an hour. Now go, and
do not tell Zanoni that I sent you!'

I went. There was nothing else to do. Neither of them came to the
door. As I crossed the threshold there was a long rumble of thunder
immediately overhead, a blinding flash of lightning, an apocalyptic
wind bent the trees in the yard, and it began to rain heavily. In all my
life I had never felt so utterly abandoned and alone.

There was no difficulty in finding the way. The valley was narrow
and a stream ran down through it and under a bridge on the road where
the Baruffas' farm was, and from the house a path climbed high along

the right side of the valley past abandoned terrace fields with mounds of pale stones standing in them, paler still under the lightning, which the people who had cultivated the land had weeded from the earth by hand.

Soon, both the stream and the far side of the valley were invisible, blotted out by the rain which was clouting down, while the thunder boomed and rolled overhead and long barbs of lightning plunged earthwards. There was nowhere to shelter from them but mercifully after a while they ceased and were replaced by sheet lightning which I hoped was less dangerous.

The path was surfaced with long cobbles and the stones were spattered with the dung of sheep and cows and what was more likely to be the dung of mules than horses in such a mountainous place. Some of it was fresh, all of it was now being washed away by the torrents of water which had turned the steeper parts of the path, which were in steps, into a series of waterfalls in which I slipped and fell on all fours, swearing monotonously. Although I did not know it then, this path was the main road to two villages higher up the mountainside, and at any other time I would have almost certainly have met other people on it. I was, in fact, lucky without appreciating my luck. This was the last occasion while I was in Italy that I ever used such a public path. From now on, whenever I travelled anywhere, unguided, it was always by more unfrequented tracks or through the woods.

After I had been climbing for about three-quarters of an hour, the path descended the side of the valley to the place where the mill was. The stream was in full spate. It came boiling down over the rocks and under a little hump-backed bridge and surged against the draw-gate which shut off the water from the leat. The mill-house was a tall, narrow building with a steep-pitched roof and it had rusty iron shutters clamped tight over the windows as if for ever, and a rusty iron door. Looking at this sinister building it was difficult to know on such an evening whether it was inhabited or not; but no smoke came from the chimney and no dog barked. The only sounds that could be heard above the thunder, the howling of the wind and the roar of the water, were the furious rattling of a loose paddle on the mill-wheel and the clanking and groaning of the wheel itself as it moved a little, backwards and forwards on its bearings.

By now, although it was only five o'clock it was almost dark. To the right of the bridge a steep track led away uphill towards a clump of trees beyond which I could just make out some low buildings. This I thought must be *casa* Zanoni and I squelched up the track towards it.

The house itself was more like an Irish dun than a house, a stone fort built against a rock on the hillside. It was so small that the cowshed, which had a hay loft over it, seemed bigger than the house itself and the cowshed was not large. Every few seconds the house and its out-buildings were illuminated by the lightning so that they looked as if they were coated with silver.

They were roofed with stone slabs and down towards the eaves these great tiles had rocks on top of them, rocks to stop the wind ripping them off. Smoke and sparks were streaming from the chimney of the house which had a cowl on it made from four little piles of stones with a flat piece laid on top of them, so that it looked like a shrine on a mountain with an offering burning in it. Apart from the smoke and sparks the house was as shut up and uninhabited-looking as the mill, but when I got closer I could hear, deep inside it,. the sound of a dog barking.

The door of the cowshed was closed but through cracks and holes in it, faint pinpricks of light shone out into the yard in which the mire was boiling under the weight of the rain. I stood on the threshold and said, '*Permesso, non c'è nessuno?*' – 'Excuse me, is there not no one?' – using one of the useful, colloquial, ungrammatical phrases which Wanda had taught me, the sort that everyone used in this part of Italy, and which were so important to me now, and a voice said, '*Avanti!*'

I pushed open the door and went in. There was a sweet warm smell of fodder and cows and the light of a lantern was casting huge, distorted shadows of the animals, which I could not yet see, on the whitewashed wall in front of me. It was like Plato's Myth of the Cave. There was the sound of milk spurting into a pail; and now that the door had closed behind me, much more faintly, there was the noise of the storm.

Then the milking stopped and I heard a stool being pulled back over the stone floor and a small man appeared from behind one of the great, looming beasts which were to the left of the doorway. He had a small, dark moustache, wispy hair all over the place, a week's bristle on his face and although, as he told me later, he was only thirty-two, to me, ten years younger, he looked almost old enough to be my father.

He was wearing a suit of what had originally been thick brown corduroy, but it had been repaired so many times with so many different sorts of stuff, old pieces of woollen and cotton cloth in faded reds and blues and greens, and bits of ancient printed material, the kind of thing you see in museums, that it was more like a patchwork quilt with a little bit of corduroy sewn on to it here and there. But how I envied him his suit at this moment. It might be decayed but at least it was warm and dry. In the Sunday best black and white striped trousers, a cotton shirt and the thin black jacket that Wanda's father had given me, all soaked through, I felt as if I had just been fished out of an icy river.

'Signor Zanoni?' I said.

'Yes, I am Zanoni. Who are you?'

'My name is Enrico.' This was the nearest anyone in the country had so far been able to get to my Christian name. My surname was beyond them. Nevertheless, I gave it and then spelt it out phonetically in Italian. 'Newby – ENNE A DOPPIO V BER IPSILON.'

'NEVBU,' he said, 'Che nome strano!' He raised the lantern above his head and shone the light into my face. 'And what are you, Signor Nevbu, a Tedesco?'

He took me for a German deserter from the Wehrmacht of whom there were now said to be a considerable number who had prematurely left their units at the Armistice under the mistaken impression that the war was practically over. What an appropriate word for a German Tedesco was. It made me think of some great creature with an armoured shell, a sort of semi-human tank of which the carapace was a living part, the sort of machine that Hieronymus Bosch might have produced if he had been asked to design a fighting vehicle. What I was probably thinking of was a testudo.

I told him what I was and where I had come from.

'Now tell me who sent you here,' he said, as soon as I had finished.

I told him this, too. I didn't feel that I owed the Baruffas anything; but I didn't tell him why they had sent me to him. There was no need.

'I know why,' he said. 'It's because old Baruffa has paura; but that's all very well, I have paura, too.'

I wanted to make an end of it one way or the other.

'Signor Zanoni,' I said, using one of my small store of stock phrases, *'Posso dormire nel vostro fienile?'* 'Can I sleep in your hayloft?'

'Did anyone see you on the road coming here?' he said.

I told him that I had seen no one and that I was as sure as I could be that no one had seen me.

There was a long pause before he answered, which seemed an age. 'No,' he said, finally, 'you can't.'

I knew now that I was done for. I had no food and very little money to buy any, about 100 lire which, at that time, was something like thirty shillings, and I was in no position to go shopping. The only clothes I had, apart from a pullover in the sack which I was carrying, were the ones I stood up in and everything in the sack, including my sleeping-bag was sopping wet, too. Even if I could find another house in the darkness it would be dangerous to knock on the door without knowing who the occupants were. Yet a night on the mountainside in this sort of weather would probably finish me off.

'No, you can't sleep in my hay,' he said after another equally long pause. 'You might set it on fire and where would I be then? But you can sleep in my house in a bed, and you will, too, but before we go in I have to finish with Bella.' And he went back to milking her.

I shall never forget the moment when Signor Zanoni led me through the boiling slush in the yard and into the kitchen. It was more like a cavern than any room I had ever been in. One wall of it was part of the mountain, a great, smooth, shiny protruding rock which had been partly hollowed out to form the fireplace, itself a cave within a cave, as black as the outside of the copper pot which was suspended over the fire on a long chain, and the other three walls were made of rough blocks of undressed stone, some of them boulders, which heightened the illusion that this was an excavation rather than a room. In it the hot embers of the fire gave everything a reddish tinge and lamps hung on hooks on the walls which were nothing more than iron dishes filled with oil in which the wicks floated, the sort of lamps the Etruscans might have used while digging their tombs.

On one side of the fireplace there was a niche in the rock with a seat in it which was occupied by the oldest woman I had ever seen. Everything about her was black, except for her face which was so wrinkled – and the wrinkles were so regular and so close together – that they

were like the contours of a steep-sided valley on a large-scale map. She
wore black felt shoes, thick black stockings, some kind of long black
garment the sleeves of which concealed her hands, and a sort of black
coif or hood which hid her hair from view, if indeed she had any. And
when I was taken forward to be introduced to her, which was the first
thing that was done, I found that even her eyes were invisible, hidden
behind a pair of thick pebble glasses in wire frames which pressed
against her eyeballs, so that the water in them turned to steam in the
heat of the fire. I spoke to her and her lips moved but no sound came
from them. It might have been a welcome that she was trying to utter,
or it could have been a prayer.

Then I was made to take off my wet clothes behind a high-backed
wooden settee and I was given a big brown blanket to wrap myself
in. Signora Zanoni made me sit down at a table and I was given *gnocchi*
to eat, *pasta* made with potatoes and flavoured with tomatoes, and
some rough red wine to drink, and she encouraged me to eat more,
while three small children peeped out at me from behind her skirt like
mice, and I was made to drink more wine by her husband. Later I was
taken up a staircase that was like a ladder to a bedroom on the upper
floor of the house where I exchanged the blanket for a long, hand-
knitted vest which smelt of sheep and reached down below my knees.

The bed was high and white and ghostly-looking in the light of the
single candle, and there was a great lump in the middle of it that looked
very strange to me.

'It's the priest (the *prete*),' said Signor Zanoni. 'You'll be warm
enough when he gets out of it.' What he said sounded almost obscene
on the lips of a man like this, but then his wife peeled back the sheet
and blankets for a moment, long enough to remove from it a strange
contrivance, something that I had never seen before, or even heard of
– an iron pot full of hot coals from the fire on a wooden base with a
framework of laths over it to stop the bedding coming in contact with
the pot and catching fire. This was the priest, a dangerous apparatus
which, in its time they told me later, had burned down many
houses.

Then they went away and I climbed up into the bed and burrowed
down into it between the rough, white sheets. It was the best bed I
have ever slept in before or since. It was as warm and soft as a woman

and almost equally alive. I was almost tempted to talk to it but instead I fell asleep laughing with sheer joy while the thunder rolled and the rain beat down on the roof overhead. At this moment, about seven o'clock on the night of the twenty fifth of September, 1943, there could have been few people in the whole of Fortress Europe more contented or fortunate than I was.

*          *          *

It was unsafe to remain in Signor Zanoni's house because it was too near the track and he decided to take me to the house of a farmer who lived at a lonely place called Pian del Sotto.

## TO THE PIAN DEL SOTTO

I picked up my pack, the contents of which were now dry, having been by the fire for two nights, and followed Signor Zanoni out of the orchard and down to the left bank of the stream by a path that was so overgrown and overhung by bushes that it would have been invisible to me, where we crossed it by four big stepping stones. Then we scrambled up the bank through the undergrowth, and after he had made sure that there was no one about we crossed the track which led up from the hump-backed bridge and entered the wood, the one from which the cuckoo had called but which was now silent.

He was wearing his old patchwork suit and from a metal clip on the belt under his jacket he took a billhook and began to cut a way up through the brambles between the trees. They were mostly oaks and some sort of thorn-bearing tree which I had never seen before. The oaks were not like English oaks. The trunks were mostly small enough to encircle with two hands and few of them were more than twenty feet high. Perhaps if they had been thinned they would have done better, or perhaps they were just small by nature.

'*Colle del Santo*,' Signor Zanoni said. 'It's not far now, only about twenty minutes from here if you use the track. It'll take us a bit longer.'

We were on a little pass, the meeting place of two tracks which crossed one another diagonally and we were between the two lower arms of the crossing. The track on the right was the one from the mill which we had by-passed by coming up through the forest. It continued over the pass and downhill into the head of another valley on our left and then through meadows to a small village of stone houses, larger versions of Signor Zanoni's, huddled together on the mountainside below a wooded ridge from which long, bare screes poured down towards it. Along this track a man was urging two heavily laden pack-mules towards the village under a sky that was now cold and threatening.

The other track wound up around the edge of the wood to our left and continued straight up the mountain beyond the crossing between two long hedgerows of bramble, and this was the one we took. In spite of being near a village this windswept pass with a splintered, dying chestnut tree on one side of it and a little shrine with a worn carving of some saint on the other, from which it took its name, had a very remote feeling about it.

We went up the outside of one of the hedges which was high enough and thick enough to hide us from anyone who might be using the path itself and after forcing our way up through another wood we came out on the edge of it, in a little promontory of trees, the only part of it which had been able to raise itself above the relative shelter of the slope on which it grew. We were on the edge of an inclined plateau about half a mile long and between three and four hundred yards wide, in which the fields swept down at a crazy angle to a cliff formed by an enormous landslide which appeared to be still going on. Apart from some root crops there was nothing growing. The harvest had already taken place and the rest of the fields were nothing but expanses of stubble and stones, although some of the less rocky ones had been ploughed. Some looked as if they had never been cultivated at all. Towards the northern end of the plateau, which was completely exposed to all the winds of heaven, except those from the west from which it was sheltered by the bulk of the mountain which was covered with forest and which soared above it, stood a great, bleak farmhouse, faced with grey cement and with so many storeys under its red-tiled roof that it looked like some rural skyscraper.

'Pian del Sotto,' Signor Zanoni said. 'We're nearly a thousand metres here.'

He went on alone towards the house, where I heard him being welcomed by a furious dog, while I stood at the edge of the wood with the wind moaning through the trees, waiting for whatever was going to happen next. It was certainly a lonely place. Far below, beyond the end of the landslip, were the fields full of grass and clover that I had seen from the Colle del Santo and I could just see the stone roofs of the houses in the village. Here, we were almost as high as the ridge under which it stood and now, for the first time, I could see part of the main ridge of the Apennines running down along the borders of Tuscany, with long slanting lines of rain in the sky above it as if someone had been scribbling with a black pencil on a sheet of grey paper.

I was becoming cold now and I was more tired than I had expected to be after such a comparatively short journey. I was not as fit as my occasional bursts of activity in the *orfanotrofio* had led me to believe but my ankle seemed completely mended. At least I could run if necessary.

I heard a window open somewhere in the house and then an awful scream as if someone was being murdered, 'ARMAAAHNDOOOO!' was what it sounded like, sufficient in a place such as this to make my blood, already chilled by the keening wind, turn to ice. What on earth was going on inside this forbidding-looking building? Had the occupants done away with Signor Zanoni? Perhaps they were all in-bred and mad as hatters.

Almost immediately afterwards Signor Zanoni appeared in front of the house and signalled me to come and as I got to the door where he was waiting, a huge brute of a dog tethered to a running wire which gave it more scope for attacking intruders than it would have had on a chain alone, leapt out at me from where it had been lying in wait, snapping and snarling, longing for nothing better than to be at my throat.

'What was that noise I heard after you went to the house?' I said as soon as we were out of range of it. 'It wasn't the dog.'

'Noise?' he said. 'Oh, that was Agata, Luigi's wife, calling Armando, the boy who works for them. She's a good woman Agata, but she's got a terribly strong voice.

'It's not going to be easy,' he went on. 'They've just heard that anyone who helps prisoners of war will be sentenced to death.'

'I never heard that. Is it true?' I said.

'I told them. I had to. It would not have been right to do otherwise.'

'Then you knew?'

'It was announced four days ago. I heard it down in the village. Luigi has a radio but it doesn't work very well. None of them up here go anywhere, except on Sundays, and yesterday it was raining so much that they all stayed at home.'

'Did your wife know?'

'Yes, she knew.'

If they knew then the doctor must have known and Wanda and her father must have known, and the Baruffas and all the other people who had helped me. All of a sudden everything seemed much less simple than it had done.

'Mind you,' he said, 'I don't think they would dare do it, shoot people I mean, and neither do any of these people here. The Government, or what is supposed to be the Government, would have to shoot hundreds, perhaps thousands, I don't know how many, but, all the same it's making them think. It's making me think; that's why the people here haven't decided about you yet. They want to see you first.'

I said that I didn't think it was right to ask them to take me now that I knew about the death penalty.

'Then there's only one thing you can do, Enrico,' he said, 'and that's come back with me. It's quite simple, really.'

'Let's go in,' I said.

There were five people in the kitchen, two men and three women: the farmer, a tallish, erect, thin man who, to me, looked exactly like Company Sergeant-Major Clegg of the Grenadier Guards, the one who used to scream at us outside the Old Buildings at Sandhurst; his wife, who was about the same age as he was, fiftyish, who had a pale face with a front tooth misssing; and two young women, one with short, black hair, who was obviously the daughter, thin and slight like her mother, the other a big, powerful girl, an Amazon with long auburn hair to her shoulders. The other man was a stocky, muscular youth with dark, greasy hair, carefully combed. All of them were wearing working clothes and big mountain boots. The girls were washing up in a stone sink, the signora was stirring up the fire which had only recently been lit, and her husband was sitting at the table on which there was a bottle of wine and two half-charged glasses. There was a feeling in the air as if a lot of talking had been done. The farmer had his hat on, as did Signor Zanoni.

I was introduced to the company in a general way, no names were exchanged, and there was a good deal of rather remote *buon giorno*ing, and when this was over I was invited to sit down at the table and I was given a glass of wine, which was extraordinarily acid, and some very good bread and some slices of sausage. Then they began to talk, or rather Signor Zanoni and the farmer began to talk, in a dialect that was so deep that I could make nothing of it, with the wife throwing in an occasional sentence, or a word, from the fireplace where she stood with her arms folded tightly across the place where her bosom would have been if she had had one. Up to now the only time I had heard the mountain dialect had been a muffled version of it, coming up through the floor of Signor Zanoni's bedroom. Hearing it unfiltered and close to I found it equally incomprehensible.

As no one in the room took the slightest notice of me while my fate was being decided, I was able to look around me. It was long and high and the walls and ceiling, which had once been white, were now the colour of old ivory. At the far end of it a window looked out over the plateau to the ridge above the village. There was a fireplace with a high shelf over it, crowded with the sort of objects which end up over fireplaces, in this case a cast-iron coffee grinder, some dried bulbs, a piece of palm leaf left over from some bygone Sunday, a number of curled-up picture postcards and a book with the title *Lunario Barba-Nera* in archaic type.

On the right of the fireplace was the sink at which the girls were working; close to it there was a cast-iron stove with a silver-painted stovepipe rising from it which vanished into the wall just under the ceiling, and behind me, where I sat facing the fireplace there was a tall, dark cupboard and a chest on short legs with a removable table-top, a piece of furniture known as a *madia*, in which the flour which was used to make the *pasta* was kept, a piece of furniture which every house I had been to in the *pianura* and the mountains possessed. And on a box under the window there was a dilapidated radio set with wires sprouting from it, which must have been the one that had not given the information about people who helped prisoners of war being shot.

After what seemed an eternity the conversation rumbled noisily to a close, rather like a train of goods wagons coming to rest in a marshalling yard. It was the signora who was responsible for these effects, with her deafening interjections. Pound for pound she was the noisiest woman I had ever met. It was she who had uttered the bloodcurdling call to the boy Armando, to bring him in from whatever he was doing, to attend the family council.

Now her husband was filling Signor Zanoni's glass from a fresh bottle, at the same time looking at me as he poured it, with the air of someone who was about to acquire a slave. Watching him performing this difficult feat, I felt that something had been concluded.

'Luigi is of the opinion that if you want to stay here it is all right,' Signor Zanoni said at last. 'And so is Signora Agata, as long as things stay as quiet as they are. There's a lot of work to be done in the fields and they will be glad to have you, but they can't pay you anything. They'll give you your food and a bed. When you're working outside you will have to keep away from the path to the house, always. You're sure to be seen by someone wherever you're working, but if anyone asks who you are they'll say that you're someone from Genoa, a fisherman who's been bombed, and isn't quite right in the head. If anyone does speak to you act as if you're stupid and pretend that you're deaf and dumb. You'll have to keep your sack of stuff up in the woods above the house in the daytime, in case you have to run for it. Dig a hole and cover it up so that when it rains it won't get wet. If you have to escape at night there's a way out over the roof of the *stalla* from the second floor. They'll show it to you. If you need me at any time, one of them will bring me a message. And I'll arrange with the Baruffas so that when your friends come for you they'll send them to me. Now they'll show you where your room is and they'll give you some clothes to work in. The ones you have won't last more than a day or two in the fields and they don't look right.'

The room to which Agata's daughter, Rita, the thinner of the two girls, escorted me was high up under the eaves of the building and we climbed up to it by a series of steep and flimsy staircases. In it there was a window at floor level which faced north and by kneeling down it was possible to look out along the track which led to the farm. I found this out while I was helping her to make the bed up. It was a very dilapidated bed but the bedding was very clean. And I was glad when she provided me with a *vaso da notte*, which may seem an unimportant detail, but released me from the necessity of descending all those stairs in the middle of the night and having to face that revolting dog in the yard.

When I got back to the kitchen Armando, the black-haired boy, and Dolores, the big girl, had disappeared and Signor Zanoni was about to leave. I had changed into the working clothes which Agata had given me and they looked a hundred years old. Signor Zanoni's working suit was composed of shreds and patches; but, at least, it covered his nakedness completely. Luigi's was made up of dozens and dozens of holes connected by pieces of black velveteen that was so tough that I wondered how the holes had appeared in it in the first place. It looked like a nineteenth-century poacher's suit in which the occupant had been caught in the cross fire from several gamekeepers' shot-guns. Nevertheless, I was delighted with it. Wearing it I felt that I was part of the scenery.

I accompanied Signor Zanoni to the door and as soon as we got to it the dog began baying for blood.

'That's a brute of a dog,' Signor Zanoni said (*Un cane proprio brutto*, was how he actually described it). 'Keep out of its way, it's starving. I'd shoot it if it was mine, or else I'd feed it. Everything's kept very short here; but I've told them that if they want you to work they must give you enough to eat. They're not mean, but they're all used to doing without much. And I've told them that it's no good them speaking *dialetto* to you because you won't understand.

'Don't forget us,' he said. 'We won't forget you.'

I shook his hand and watched this small, kindly, resourceful man as he walked along the path that led down to the Colle del Santo.

## LIFE AT THE PIAN DEL SOTTO

'Come with me,' a voice said. It was Luigi. It was the first time he had spoken to me, apart from wishing me *buon giorno*. I followed him round to the back of the house where the fields swept uphill to the edge of the woods in all their stoniness. Many of them could scarcely be called stones. They were rocks and boulders which had come rolling down off the mountain. It was like looking out on a parable.

'I want those fields cleared of stones,' he said, quite casually. 'All of them. I should start with that one up there. The others will help you with the big ones, when they've finished what they're doing, in a week or two. There's a cart over there,' he indicated a vehicle with solid wooden wheels and sides made from the plaited stems of osiers. It looked like a primitive chariot.

'What shall I do with them,' I said, 'when I've put them in the cart, the stones?'

'You can do what you like with them,' he said, 'as long as they don't stop on my land.'

Then he looked at me, and seeing that I was genuinely puzzled, he gave me the same kind of foxy grin that Sergeant-Major Clegg used to when he announced to us that there would be no weekend leave.

'You can throw them over the cliff,' he said. 'You can start now.'

And he went back into the house.

One Sunday, when I was out on the mountainside, I had a strange encounter. The sun was hot and soon I took off my shirt and then my boots and socks. The air was filled with the humming of bees and the buzzing of insects and from somewhere further up the mountain there came the clanking of sheep bells, carried on a gentle breeze that was blowing from that direction. Then a single bell began to toll in the valley, and other more distant bells echoed it, but they soon ceased and I looked across to the distant peaks which previously had been so clearly delineated but were now beginning to shimmer and become indistinct in the haze that was enveloping them. And quite soon I fell asleep.

I woke to find a German soldier standing over me. At first, with the sun behind him he was as indistinct as the peaks had become, but then he swam into focus. He was an officer and he was wearing summer battledress and a soft cap with a long narrow peak. He had a pistol but it was still in its holster on his belt and he seemed to have forgotten that he was armed because he made no effort to draw it. Across one shoulder and hanging down over one hip in a very unmilitary way he wore a large old-fashioned civilian haversack, as if he was a member of a weekend rambling club, rather than a soldier, and in one hand he held a large, professional-looking butterfly net. He was a tall, thin, pale young man of about twenty-five with mild eyes and he appeared as surprised to see me as I was to see him, but much less alarmed than I was, virtually immobilized, lying on my back without my boots and socks on.

'Bon giorno,' he said, courteously. His accent sounded rather like mine must, I thought. 'Che bella giornata.'

At least up to now he seemed to have assumed that I was an Italian, but as soon as I opened my mouth he would know I wasn't. Perhaps I ought to try and push him over the cliff, after all he was standing with his back to it; but I knew that I wouldn't. It seemed awful even to think of murdering someone who had simply wished me good day and remarked on what a beautiful one it was, let alone actually doing it. If ever there was going to be an appropriate time to go on stage in the part of the mute from Genoa which I had often rehearsed but never played, this was it. I didn't answer.

'Da dove viene, lei?' he asked.

I just continued to look at him. I suppose I should have been making strangled noises and pointing down my throat to emphasize my muteness, but just as I couldn't bring myself to assail him, I couldn't do this either. It seemed too ridiculous. But he was not to be put off. He removed his haversack, put down his butterfly net, sat down opposite me in the hollow and said:

'Lei, non è Italiano.'

It was not a question. It was a statement of fact which did not require an answer. I decided to abandon my absurd act.

'Si, sono Italiano.'

He looked at me, studying me carefully, my face, my clothes and my boots which, after my accent, were my biggest giveaway, although they were very battered now.

'I think that you are English,' he said, finally, in English. 'English, or from one of your colonies. You cannot be an English deserter; you are on the wrong side of the battle front. You do not look like a parachutist or a saboteur. You must be a prisoner of war. That is so, is it not?'

I said nothing.

'Do not be afraid,' he went on. 'I will not tell anyone that I have met you, I have no intention of spoiling such a splendid day either for you or for myself. They are too rare. I have only this one day of free time and it was extremely difficult to organize the transport to get here. I am anxious to collect specimens, but specimens with wings. I give you my word that no one will ever hear from me that I have seen you or your companions if you have any.'

In the face of such courtesy it was useless to dissemble and it would have been downright uncouth to do so.

'Yes, I am English,' I said, but it was a sacrifice to admit it. I felt as if I was pledging my freedom.

He offered me his hand. He was close enough to do so without moving. It felt strangely soft when I grasped it in my own calloused and roughened one and it looked unnaturally clean when he withdrew it.

'*Oberleutnant* Frick. Education Officer. And may I have the pleasure of your name, also?'

'Eric Newby,' I said. 'I'm a lieutenent in the infantry, or rather I was until I was put in the bag.' I could see no point in telling him that I had been in SBS, not that he was likely to have heard of it. In fact I was expressly forbidden, as all prisoners were, to give anything but my name, rank and number to the enemy.

'Excuse me? In the bag?'

'Until I was captured. It's an expression.'

He laughed slightly pedantically, but it was quite a pleasant sound. I expected him to ask me when and where I had been captured and was prepared to say Sicily, 1943, rather than 1942, which would have led to all sorts of complications; but he was more interested in the expression I had used.

'Excellent. In the bag, you say. I shall remember that. I have little opportunity now to learn coloquial English. With me it would be more appropriate to say "in the net", or, "in the bottle", but, at least no one has put you in a poison bottle, which is what I have to do with my captives.'

Although I don't think he intended it to be, I found this rather creepy, but then I was not a butterfly hunter. His English was very good, if perhaps a little stilted. I only wished that I sould speak Italian a quarter as well.

He must have noticed the look of slight distaste on my face because the next thing he said was, 'Don't worry, the poison is only crushed laurel leaves, a very old way, nothing modern from I.G. Farben.'

Now he began delving in his haversack and brought out two bottles wrapped in brown paper which, at first, I thought must contain the laurel which he used to knock out his butterflies when he caught them; but, in fact, they contained beer, and he offered me one of them.

'It is really excellent beer,' he said. 'Or, at least, I find it so. To my taste Italian beer is not at all good. This is from Munich. Not easy to get now unfortunately. Permit me to open it for you.'

It was cool and delicious. I asked him where he had come from.

'From Salsomaggiore, in the foothills,' he said. 'It is a spa and like all spas it is very melancholy, or at least I find them so, although we Germans are supposed to like melancholy places. It is the feeling that no one who has ever visited them has been quite well, and never will again, that I find disagreeable. Now it is a headquarters. My job there is to give lectures on Italian culture, particularly the culture of the Renaissance, to groups of officers and any of the men who are interested. It is scarcely arduous because so few of them are.'

'I must confess,' he went on, 'that there are some aspects of my countrymen's character that I cannot pretend to understand. I do not speak disloyally to make you feel more friendly to me because, no doubt, you, also, do not always understand your own people, but surely only Germany would employ a professor of entomology from Göttingen with only one lung, whose only interest is *lepidoptera*, to give lectures on Renaissance painting and architecture to soldiers who are engaged in destroying these things as hard as they are able. Do you not think it strange?'

'I wouldn't say that,' I said, 'I'm sure we do the same sort of thing and, if we don't, I'm sure the Americans do.'

'Really,' he said. 'You surprise me. You would not say that it is strange?'

'The intention is, of course,' he continued, 'to make us popular with the inhabitants, but that is something we can never be. For instance, I came to that village down there by car, I suggested to the driver that he might like to accompany me up here; but he is not interested in the countryside or *lepidoptera*. Besides he told me that there is a regulation against leaving military vehicles unattended. I did not ask him to accompany me because I wanted his company but because I knew that he would not enjoy himself in that village, or any other. When we arrived at it no one would speak to us. There was scarcely anyone to speak to anyway, which was very strange because it is a Sunday. They must have thought I had come to make some kind of investigation. It might have been better if we had not been wearing guns; but it is a regulation.

I could visualize the state of panic the village must have been thrown into by their arrival, with young men running from the house and the *stalle* and up the mountainsides, like hunted hares.

'It is not pleasant to be disliked,' he said, 'and it is very unpleasant to be German and to know that one is hated, because one *is* German and, because, collectively, we are wrong in what we are doing. That is why I hate this war, or one of the reasons. And of course, because of this, we shall lose it. We must. We have to.'

'It's going to take you a long time to lose it at this rate,' I said. 'Everything seems to be going very slowly.'

'It may seem so to you,' he said. 'But it won't be here, in Italy, that we shall be beaten. We shall hold you here, at least through this winter and perhaps we could hold you through next summer, but I do not think there will be a next summer. What is going on in Russia is more than flesh and blood can stand. We are on the retreat from Smolensk; we are retreating to the Dnieper. According to people who have just come from there we are losing more men every day than we have lost here in the Italian peninsula in an entire month. And what are you doing?' he asked.

I told him that I was on my way south towards the front. There seemed no point in telling him that I was living here. Also I was ashamed.

'If you take the advice of an enemy,' he said, 'you will try to pass the winter here, in these mountains. By the time you get to the battle front it will be very, very cold and very, very difficult to pass through it. Until a few days ago we all thought we would be retiring beyond the Po; but now the winter line is going to be far south of Rome. It has already been given a name. They call it the *Winterstellung*.'

'Tell me one thing,' I said. 'Where have we got to now. I never hear any news.'

'You have Termoli and Foggia on the east coast, which means that you will now be able to use bombers in close-support and you have Naples; but take my advice and wait for the spring.'

I asked him where he had learned his English. He told me that he had spent several summer vacations in England before the war.

'I liked England,' he said. 'And the English. You do not work hard but you have the good sense not to be interested in politics. I liked very much your way of life.'

He got to his feet.

'Lieutenant,' he said, 'it has given me great pleasure to have met you. Good luck to you and, perhaps, though I do not think it probable, we shall meet again after the war at Göttingen, or London.'

'Or Philippi,' I felt like saying, but didn't.

'Now if you would be so kind,' he said, 'please give me the empty bottle as I cannot obtain more of this beer without handing the bottles back. Bottles are in short supply.'

The last I saw of him was running across the open downs with his net unfurled, in the direction from which I had come, making curious little sweeps and lunges as he pursued his prey, a tall, thin, rather ungainly figure with only one lung. I was sorry to see him go.

When I got back to the Pian del Sotto that evening everybody had already returned, except Armando, and the sole subject of conversation was the arrival at the village in the valley of *Oberleutnant* Frick and his driver and their subsequent departure from it. The bush-telegraph was working well – it was a pity that it operated in two directions, outwards as well as inwards.

As I imagined it would, the panic created by their arrival had sent all the men of military age in the area rushing off to the woods and in the time that it took someone who had a kinsman in our village to climb up by some secret path over the cliff and down to it, the *paura* had begun there and with similar results – even Armando had skedaddled – and it had been communicated to the occupants of every other village within walking distance. It was as if a stone had been thrown into a pond and the splash it had made became ripples moving outwards in concentric circles, one behind the other, as more messengers had gone out bringing the latest reports on the situation, what in our army were called 'sitreps'.

In the village in the valley the *paura* had begun to diminish as soon as the *Oberleutnant* had assembled his butterfly net and had begun to move out of the village on what he imagined was the way up the mountain. Officers were known to be addicted to outdoor sports, it was the one thing that officers were known to have in common, whatever their nationality, and this one was obviously a fisherman, though what he hoped to land with such a flimsy net and no rod in a river which had hardly any water in it at this season, no one knew and no one dared to ask. None of them had ever heard of butterfly hunting, or laid eyes on a German officer.

It was now the middle of October. I always knew what day of the week it was but I was never sure of the date and no one in the house seemed to know either. Agata knew that the preceding Sunday, the second one in succession on which I had gone out for the day, but without this time meeting anyone or collecting any fungi, was the seventeenth after Pentecost, but no one else did, not even her daughter. The only calendar in the house was contained in the almanack over the fireplace, *Barba-Nera Lunario dell' Astronomo degli Appennini*, to which I had recourse on wet days but I discovered when I first opened it that it was already four years old and was no good for movable feasts, and was all wrong about the moon which had been full on the preceding Wednesday, which was my second one at the Pian del Sotto, and was also, according to the book, the day of *S. Eduardo re d'Inghilterra confes.*, which I would have been tempted to celebrate if I had noticed it at the time.

The following day was a Friday and in the afternoon I was left alone on the plateau to carry on with the work of *zappatura*, breaking up clods with a *zappa*, a hoe. Because it was a fine, warm day Rita had been taken off by her mother to help with the enormous operation which involved changing all the sheets and pillow cases in the house, and washing the dirty ones at the spring at the top end of the plateau where there was a large open cistern of water. There they walloped the linen on a sort of stone washboard. This was done every week and when the washing was finished it was hung on long lines at the edge of the cliff where it became incredibly white in the sun and wind. On this particular afternoon Dolores was not helping with the washing which she usually did; she was somewhere out of sight, working either in the house or in one of the outbuildings; Armando was ploughing, and soon after the midday meal Luigi had gone away up into the woods to decide on what trees they would cut that autumn.

Late in the afternoon, while I was hacking away with my *zappa*, I was consumed with an urgent need to visit the *gabinetto* which was a great bore, not only because it involved a longish walk but principally because it brought me within biting range of the odious Nero who seemed to bear even more murderous feelings towards me than he did to the rest of the family – and they were evil enough – probably because I was something foreign which smelled nasty to him and certainly because I used to throw the contents of the *vaso da notte* at him, which I would not have dreamt of doing if he had been nice to me in the first place. As it was, in order to reach the *gabinetto*, I always used to arm myself with a couple of carefully selected stones, one for the inward run, the other for the run-out of the yard, except when there were other members of the family present in which case they used to take over the defensive duties. Getting past Nero into the yard always reminded me of *Operation Pedestal*, I being one of the practically defenceless merchant ships, Nero a dive bomber.

On this occasion I did what I always did, pretended to make for the door of the house and as he made a rush to intercept me, foaming at the mouth (he was much too enraged to bark), I altered course to port and rushed through what was the equivalent of the Sicilian Channel, the narrows between the house and a pigsty, jumping over his chain as I did so, at the same time raising one of the stones above my head in a threatening manner and roaring at him at the top of my voice, which sufficiently impressed him with my murderous intentions to halt him long enough to let me get through and out of biting distance. And as usual, I succeeded.

When I emerged from the *gabinetto*, still prudently clasping my stones, I was more or less at peace with the world. Nero was not. As always, he was furious at having been thwarted in his desire to tear me to pieces, and this time his rage lent him a supernatural strength. I was about thirty yards from him when, practically at the full length of his chain, he executed a fantastic leap in the air very similar to the capriole, one of the most difficult of all the evolutions performed by the horses in the Spanish Riding School in Vienna, of which I had seen photographs in a book in the *orfanotrofio*.

In doing so, he broke the running wire to which his chain was shackled and which gave him so much mobility. It parted with a twang like a breaking harp string and he landed on his stomach, unlike the horses in the Riding School, from which position he immediately regained his feet and streaked at me, as much like a rocket as a powerful mongrel dog trailing twenty feet of chain behind it could manage to be; and I took to my heels and fled in the direction from which I had come.

Yet terrified as I was of him, I was damned if I was going to take refuge in that awful *gabinetto*, and wait for him to break through the flimsy outer walls and eat me up inside it.

Having rejected it I had very little of refuge. I might have tried for the *stalle* but all the doors were shut. My best chance of survival seemed to lie in reaching a barn about thirty yards away in which hay was stored. This barn had a sort of lean-to construction outside it in which the hay was piled until it could be transported to the upper floor. I was doing well with Nero about fifteen yards behind me when I tripped over some large piece of disused agricultural machinery which was concealed in the grass, hurting myself dreadfully, and by the time I got up the bloody dog was almost on me; but fortunately his chain became entangled in the thing and this gave me sufficient time to reach the lean-to under which the hay rose up in a solid, sheer, unscalable wall above me.

I was just about to turn and make a last desperate stand with the one stone which remained to me (I had dropped the other when I fell over) and with my boots as a last resource, when Dolores appeared like a

chatelaine on top of it, knelt down, extended a brawny arm and hauled
me up with Nero holding on to one of the turn-ups of my decrepit
trousers which came away in his fangs and left him below, roaring
with vexation. Although Dolores was a fantastically strong girl the
effort she made threw her on her back in the hay and as I came shooting
over the top with our hands locked I fell beside her, not on top of her
as I would have done in a film about bucolic peasant life.

For a moment she lay there, with tears of laughter rolling down her
cheeks. Then, still laughing, she turned towards me, enfolded me in
her arms like a great baby and kissed me passionately.

It was an unforgettable experience, like being swallowed alive, or
sucked into a vortex. It was not just one kiss, it went on and on. I felt
myself going.

It was entirely spontaneous. She was obviously not expecting visitors, certainly not me, and because it was a warm evening and much
hotter up in the barn where she had been working, she had taken off
the tight sweater which she usually wore and was now dressed in
nothing but a faded, sleeveless, navy blue vest which displayed
her really superb upper works to great advantage, a short skirt and
boots.

This was not the first time I had seen her in this outfit. I saw her
like this almost every evening when it was fine, washing herself at the
trough, together with Rita, before going inside for the evening meal,
but I had always endeavoured to put her out of my mind.

This had not been as difficult as the reader might imagine. Apart from
the fact that my thoughts were with Wanda, my unofficial *fidanzata*, I
would not have allowed myself to even try to do what I was
undoubtedly engaged in doing at this moment, if for no other reason
than it would have been a gross abuse of hospitality which was being
offered to me at tremendous risk and which, if it was discovered by
my host and hostess and the facts were broadcast, could have a disastrous effect on the whole relationship between prisoners of war and
those who were helping them. I had not even had to work this out for
myself. Even before we left the *orfanotrofio* the colonel had gone to
great pains to impress on us all that we must behave with the utmost
punctiliousness in any dealings we had with the civilian population,
and, indeed, after the prisoners made their first contact with them in

the yard of the farmhouse near Fontanellato where the food and clothing depot was set up, his warning seemed superfluous. Anyone who
did otherwise would have had to be possessed of a heart of stone. I
myself was probably on terms of greater intimacy with Wanda than
any of the other prisoners were with the girls of Fontanellato, but they
were such that not even the *superiora* or her *suore* could possibly take
exception to them, although I had kissed her; but even they did not
know this. And at the Pian del Sotto my relationship with Rita and
Dolores had been equally formal until they had begun to tease me
about my '*fidanzata*', as they insisted on calling her, and it was not
only the previous day when they had begun to ask me which of them
I was going to take to the dance that for a few moments I felt the
atmosphere between us as we *zappa*'d away, to be charged with
sexuality.

'Kiss me,' she said.

I thought I had been doing so.

With all these thoughts whirling through my mind, and out again,
I really kissed Dolores.

'More,' she said.

She turned over until she was more or less lying on top of me which,
unless I had had something like seven feet of hay under me would
probably have done me an injury. Now I was drowning in long auburn
hair. She smelled delicious, better than the girls in Alexandria I used
to take out with their seemingly inexhaustible supply of expensive
scent, a compound of herself, honest out-door sweat, which was nothing like the awful body odours of urban civilization, wood smoke,
creamy milk and clean byres, and over everything hung the sweet
smell of hay and I didn't even have hay fever. The season was over.
Somewhere, far off, I could hear Nero howling. What an escape I had
had. Out of the frying pan into the fire.

'More,' she said again. She was a great girl. In another age, when
big girls were appreciated as they deserved to be, she would have been
plucked from the fields to be the mistress of a king. This was the kind
of girl in search of whom Saracenic pirates had put landing parties
ashore and, having taken her, would have stowed her away under
hatches in their galleys intact and undamaged, or more or less, to be
auctioned in a Near Eastern market place and to become the principal

ornament in a harem of a pasha, or even a sultan who recognized quantity and quality when he set eyes on it.

'Touch me,' she said. It seemed superfluous. To me we appeared to be touching at all the points at which human beings could possibly be in contact with one another. What marvellous, strong legs she had.

'Let's go into the barn,' she said, after a while. It seemed unnecessary when we were invisible to every other living thing, except for a few spiders and the doves which had come back under the eaves of the lean-to from which they had scattered in alarm and where they were now cooing sensuously, providing a sort of background music for us, where none was necessary, sunk in a couch of hay as ample and probably much more comfortable than the Great Bed of Ware.

I was spared the necessity of deciding where the next round would take place, although there was little doubt what the outcome would be, by the gong, as it were, which saved us both – in this case Agata, who had returned to the house together with Rita, burdened with washing, to find that Nero was on the loose. She, I was glad to hear, was as frightened as I had been and was now announcing the fact from within the safety of its four walls:

'AHMAANDO! EEENRICCO! DOLLORESSS! E SCAPPATO NERO!'

Although what she expected me to do about it, except take to the trees, was not clear. Even Dolores dared not turn a deaf ear to Agata. She gave me one more kiss and then sat up, hitching her vest, which had got a bit disarranged, up on her shoulders. 'Never mind,' she said, throwing her magnificent hair back in a way which could only be described as pert, and looking like something in *La Vie Parisienne*, 'you can bring me home tomorrow night, after the *ballo*. Rita *will* be angry.' And she went down over the edge of the hay like a commando scrambling on the side of an assault ship and into a landing craft, leaving me to follow and compose whatever sort of alibi I pleased.

The *ballo*, a country dance, took place at the Pian del Sotto. It was rudely interrupted by a mixed band of Fascists and Germans who descended on the village, and I was lucky to escape. This meant that I could no longer continue to work at the farm and no longer had a roof over my head. And it was at this moment that I received a summons to meet the village elders and hear what they proposed.

There were a number of wine bottles on the table and each man had a charged glass in front of him. I was motioned to take a seat and a glass of wine was poured for me. There was no small talk. The Chairman of the Board, for that was obviously what he was, said carefully and very slowly so that I could understand, 'We have been talking about you among ourselves for some days. Many of the people in this village and in the farms round about have sons and relatives who are being hunted by the Germans. Three of them were taken the other day. Some of them have sons in Russia of whom, so far, there is no news and who may never return. They feel that you are in a similar condition to that of their sons who, they hope, are being given help wherever they are, and they think that it is their duty to help you through the coming winter, which otherwise you will not survive. I speak for them because my father was born here, and they have asked me to do so. And as it has now become too dangerous to shelter you in their houses, they have decided to build you a hiding place which no one except the people assembled in this room, our families and one other person, and he is a kinsman, will ever hear about. The work will begin at dawn tomorrow.'

## A CAVE OF ONE'S OWN

We left the house singly at half past four the following morning, after drinking acorn coffee with *grappa* in it. I had a terrible hang-over. After a marvellous dinner prepared by the elegant wife of the mysterious chairman, during which I had complimented her on the excellent mud she had produced, confusing the word for mushroom *fungo* with *fango*, which had put everyone in high good humour, the five of them had settled down to a carouse, in which I had been invited to join, as a result of which I had slept soundly in a *stalla*.

We met at the foot of the scree where I was sick and then felt better. Each of us was carrying one or more of the implements that would be needed, picks, spades, a saw, a felling axe. A mule carried the rest of the heavy gear lashed on either side of a pack saddle; crowbars, a sledgehammer, provisions, and the most impossible thing of all for human beings to carry through a forest, two pieces of corrugated iron which had been specially bought in one of the bigger villages down in the valley.

The mule made light of the weight it was carrying, perhaps because it was a small load for a mule. Full of energy at this awful hour, it went up the screes and slabs at a good three miles an hour. Reluctantly, the Chairman of the Board had remained behind. It was obvious that he was not a fit man and would have to content himself with spinning the webs in which we were all enmeshed and contemplating the results of having spun them, just like a real chairman, behind an uncluttered desk.

By the time we reached the ridge the cocks in the village were beginning to crow and soon first light began to seep through the trees. It was a melancholy morning with a soft, penetrating rain falling. The route we followed was more or less the same one that the small boy, Pierino, had used when he had brought me down the mountain from the bothy in which I had been sheltering with a shepherd called Abramo the previous evening, but in reverse: except that these men knew it better than he did and avoided some of the more difficult obstacles; and quite soon we reached the place where there were some small cliffs, and here we halted and I was left alone with the mule while the others went off in various directions to look for a suitable site.

Finally, one of them beckoned to the others who joined him and they stood together for some time pointing and talking until, at last, they summoned me to join them too.

'This is the place where it will be,' the man who had chosen it said. He was a tall, lean, handsome man with long white hair, a nose like an eagle's beak and quick, unstudied movements, very much like those of the small boy, Pierino. It was obvious that he was the one who was in overall command of the operations in the field. His name was Francesco.

The place which had been agreed on was in one of the clefts between the cliffs and it was a good one for the purpose. No one in their senses would try to force a way through it, and if they did they would get nowhere. It was a cul-de-sac filled with trees. The only thing I could

see against it was that once the leaves were gone any sort of hut standing
in it would be conspicuous; but I had not taken into consideration the
ingenuity of these mountain men.

First they dug out a number of trees by the roots from the bottom
of the ditch. When I say 'they' I have to include myself in a minor way
because I, too, was allowed to work under supervision. Then they dug
a trench, piling up the spoil about ten feet away from the innermost
cliff and parallel to it, except at the ends where it curved in to meet it.
This took much longer than they thought because while they were
digging it they uncovered a perfectly enormous rock, much bigger
than anything I had ever met with on the Pian del Sotto. They had a
long discussion about this rock, whether or not they should abandon
the site and start again somewhere else, but they decided to continue
as it would be impossible to cover up the traces of their work. So they
dug around it until it was almost free and then the most vigorous of
them hit it with a sledgehammer many times without any result, and
then they had a *merenda*, during which we ate bread and sausage and
drank wine with the soft, very wetting rain falling on us. Listening to
them I gathered that they had more or less decided to light a fire over
it and try to split it with cold water; but they seemed to be waiting
for someone else to arrive whose opinion they respected.

Then, as if he had been waiting for his cue, an old man appeared on
the cliff above us and looked down rather critically on the party
assembled below. He carried a long-barrelled hammer-gun, similar to
Abramo's, although it was now strictly forbidden to possess any kind
of firearms, and he held a green umbrella over his head. He was accompanied by a long, lean, good-looking dog which had a coat which
looked like tortoise-shell, and after he had drunk some wine they
showed him the rock. His name was Bartolomeo.

He went over it with his hands, very slowly, almost lovingly. It
must have weighed half a ton. Then, when he had finished caressing
it, he called for a sledgehammer and hit it deliberately but not particularly hard and it broke into two almost equal halves. It was like magic
and I would not have been surprised if a toad had emerged from it and
turned into a beautiful princess who had been asleep for a million years.
Even the others were impressed. There was no need to ask what this
old man's profession had been. Although he looked like a man of the

woods he must have spent some part of his life either working in a quarry, or as a stone-mason.

The rest was easy. He gave the two immense halves a few more light taps and they broke into movable pieces. Then he produced a smaller hammer from a bag and for the remainder of the time he was with us, except when he was making a chimney for the hut which he did by cutting a deep groove in the face of the cliff, he knapped these pieces into small blocks which he used to build a dry-stone wall on the inner side of the earthwork which had been made with the spoil from the trench.

While he was working away the rest of the party got on with their own tasks. Using the trunks of the trees which they had cut down, two of them made an immensely strong framework to support the roof. To me it seemed unnecessarily robust; but at this stage I still thought that they were building a conventional hut. Then, before they put it on, they waited for the other two to finish their jobs. One was making a couple of beds inside the hut, the other was stacking a big mule-load of firewood inside it. When the beds were finished and the fuel was in they put the framework of the roof on: the upper end was embedded in the cliff, the lower end rested on the wall Bartolomeo had made on the inner side of the rampart and when this was done they wired the corrugated iron on to it and covered the whole thing with a thick layer of earth and stones and moss all the way down from the cliff to the ground so that, when it was finished, it looked from any angle like an old overgrown rock fall and it was so well-covered that when we jumped down on to it from the top of the cliff it gave off a solid sound and was completely immovable. The entrance was hidden under the roots of a beech tree which grew out of the side of the cliff, and when a piece of old sacking was draped over it, because of the angle of the wall it was completely invisible.

Late in the afternoon, when the work was almost finished, the wives of three of the men who had been building the hut arrived. On their backs they carried pack-baskets of plaited willow loaded with rice, which was priceless and had been bought on the black market, salt, cheese, bread, acorn coffee and cooking and eating utensils, enough for two persons.

'In case you want to get married, that's why they've made two beds,' one of them said, and the three of them had a good laugh at this.

When all this stuff had been stowed away inside the hut the men lit a fire in the new fireplace and when he saw that it drew well and didn't smoke Bartolomeo went off with his dog without saying a word to anyone.

Then they showed me how to work the fire so that it wouldn't smoke me out, and they told me that I shouldn't light it in the daylight until the weather got really cold, except to make coffee in the early morning. They showed me how to conceal the hole at the top of the chimney with a special stone when the fire wasn't alight and they showed me where I could get water, by going through the labyrinth and then down over the cliff edge a hundred and fifty feet or so, to a place where a little spring issued from the rocks, which, they said, no one used anymore. And they told me how important it was to cover my tracks when returning to the hut – the last thing that they themselves did was to pick up every chip of wood – every small piece of wire that had been left over from the building operations, and all the match sticks they had dropped. No one threw away cigarette ends at this stage of the war.

Then we all went into the cave, for that is what I had decided to call it, and they blew up the fire and we drank some wine together. And then they told me that only they themselves or their parents or their children would visit me with supplies, and that so that I would know that they were members of one or other of these two families, they would give us a password and this would be *Brindisi*. In this way, Francesco, the man with the eagle nose, said they hoped to prevent the news that I was still in the neighbourhood from spreading. '*Ma!*' someone said doubtfully. '*Speriamo*,' they all said and the women crossed themselves.

Owls were beginning to hoot in the forest now. They picked up their instruments, the mule was already loaded, and then they wished me good luck and told me not to stay in the hut all day or I would become *triste* but to take care; and then they went away together down the mountain and I was left alone in the dwelling in which I was to pass the winter – the final refuge, and the triumphal artefact, of the men of the mountains. Some time later, I was joined in it by a great friend called James, and we remained together until we were recaptured.

After reaching the mountains I only saw Wanda once more when she made a hazardous journey to meet me at the Colle del Santo. In the interval her father was arrested and imprisoned in Parma. By the exercise of considerable ingenuity she succeeded in securing his release.

Later she and her parents were all three arrested and it was only by a miracle that they were saved from being sent to Germany.

James and I were recaptured in January 1944 and sent to a prison camp in Czechoslovakia, and later to Brunswick in Germany where we were liberated by the Americans in April 1945.

That winter I flew back to Italy, borrowed a jeep from an ex-POW, who was now ADC to a general, and drove to Fontanellato where I found Wanda. We were married in Florence at Santa Croce in the spring of 1946, and returned to England later that year.

It was then that I became a member of the rag trade – a business in which I was to spend the next ten years without any conspicuous success.

# Rag Trade

'IT'S ALL VERY WELL your father telling you to stay in the showroom, Mr Eric,' said Miss Stallybrass. 'But it's difficult to know what to give you to do. You'd better sit over there.' She indicated a small piece of furniture that was more like a prie-dieu than a desk. 'At least you'll see what happens. Miss Axhead from Manchester is coming in at ten to put down her season's order. But I warn you she takes a long time to make up her mind.'

On the first stroke of ten Miss Axhead arrived. She was a powerful-looking woman of about fifty dressed in what I was later to recognize as a buyer's cold-weather uniform; a Persian lamb jacket that was almost completely square; sheepskin boots worn over patent-leather shoes and an incredible hat with bits of Persian lamb on it, the left-overs from the sacrifice that had produced the coat, and a 'little' black dress. Escorted by Miss Stallybrass she sank down on a sofa and, with a good deal of puffing and blowing, proceeded to take off her over-boots. I was introduced by Miss Stallybrass. I then hid myself as best I could behind my inadequate prie-dieu.

'That's a pretty brooch,' Miss Stallybrass said, by way of opening gambit, admiring a hideous marcasite ornament in the form of a sealy-ham's head that Miss Axhead had pinned to her little black dress.

'That's my little Boy-Boy,' said Miss Axhead, betraying a depth of emotion that would have been difficult to deduce from her appearance.

An hour later Miss Axhead was still sitting on the settee. During this time she had discussed with Miss Stallybrass the Government and Sir Stafford Cripps; the sealyham which, by the sound of it, was ripe for destruction; the play to which she had been taken the previous evening by one of her suppliers, a rather gentle intellectual who, before the purges, had been a professor at Göttingen University, which she had not enjoyed; Christian Science; *The Robe*, which she was reading in bed and was thoroughly enjoying; several unpleasant ailments from which her friends were suffering; the discomfort of the hotel in which she always stayed when she came to London; and the iniquity of the Dress Buyer, her lifelong friend, who was cutting in on her territory by buying dresses with jackets and with whom she was no longer on speaking terms. Apart from the Dress Buyer there was no mention of business at all.

It was now eleven o'clock. Mrs Smithers appeared with tea and biscuits. She had already produced a snifter for Miss Axhead when she arrived, which had kept her going until the main supplies were brought up. Mr Wilkins, the senior traveller, emerged from his fox-hole to pay his respects to Miss Axhead. Adroitly, he asked a number of questions to which he already knew the answers, having been privy to the entire conversation. 'Delighted to see you, Miss Axhead,' he said, and withdrew with the air of a trusted counsellor.

My father arrived. He also discussed the political situation, going over the ground that had already been covered by Miss Stallybrass, but with more conviction, and told her one of his little jokes which made Miss Axhead laugh. He was followed by the head of the Costume Department, who had been hovering anxiously at the door under the impression that Miss Axhead might escape her. Miss Axhead was also the suit buyer. During this time other coat buyers who arrived unannounced, without appointments, were siphoned off into Gowns and Costumes and Rosie and Julie, our model girls, made long and circuitous journeys backwards and forwards between the Coat Stockroom and Costumes, by-passing Mantles completely so that Miss Axhead should not be disturbed.

At twelve-thirty Miss Axhead was offered a gin and tonic, which she accepted gratefully, and at a quarter to one she went upstairs 'to make herself comfortable' before going out to lunch with Miss Stallybrass.

Miss Stallybrass was dressed to the nines in a suit with a very pronounced stripe and a large fur cape. The effect was a little top-heavy and when she went to collect some petty cash from the Counting House to pay for the lunch, the head of it, Miss Gatling, asked her if she was 'bombed out'.

'I always enjoy coming to Lane & Newby,' Miss Axhead said as they were leaving. 'It has such a homely atmosphere. I feel I can really let my hair down.'

At two-thirty they returned. I thought Miss Stallybrass looked a little tired, but she was still game and her laugh was as hearty as ever. Miss Axhead was full of beans and described her summer holiday at Torquay in some detail. At three o'clock Mrs Smithers arrived with more tea and Dundee cake and at three-thirty Miss Axhead telephoned to another supplier, who had been waiting for her since two, to say that she was 'held up'.

She now began to talk about her 'specials'. These were customers who were either so rich that nothing sufficiently splendid could be found for them amongst Miss Axhead's stock of 'models' or else were so misshapen that they needed something that was made-to-measure. All the details of these difficult customers were written down on several crumpled sheets of paper and from time to time Miss Axhead looked at them despairingly.

It was obvious that unless Miss Axhead saw the collection very soon she would become bogged down among her specials and we should never get an order at all. Miss Stallybrass sensed it too.

'I think it would be better if we showed you the collection and then we can put down the specials afterwards,' she said in her fruitiest voice.

It was a tense moment. I knew that if Miss Axhead decided to deal with her specials first we were doomed.

'All right,' she said, finally, after a long pause. 'Only I must do my specials and time's getting on.'

We showed the collection. Occasionally Miss Axhead spotted something that would do for a special and the proceedings ground to a halt while Miss Stallybrass hunted for suitable patterns. At the same time Miss Axhead was suggesting alterations.

'If you could use the collar of "Dawn" and the back of "Snowdrop" that would be just right for Mrs Bean. Then you can do it the other way round for Mrs Woodcock. They can't have the same style, their husbands belong to the same golf club. You remember Mrs Bean. She's the one who . . .' Miss Axhead's voice sank to a whisper as she launched into blood-curdling details of the private life of the Beans.

'Special order "Bean",' Miss Stallybrass wrote in her flowing hand.

'Velour 477 Colour Ruby. Collar as Dawn. Back as Snowdrop. What size did you say Mrs Bean is, Miss Axhead?'

'Ooh, she's a size!' said Miss Axhead, with relish. 'I'll have to send you the measures. You'd better send me a sketch for Mrs Bean and for Mrs Woodcock, she's an awkward shape too. We like our pudding in the North.' 'Send sketches,' Miss Stallybrass wrote. I wondered how she was going to cope with this one. 'Dawn' and 'Snowdrop' were made by different tailors who detested one another.

At five o'clock the workrooms shut. There was a sound like an avalanche as the girls thundered down the staircase to the cellars where they kept their coats. The model girls left, ostensibly to catch a train.

With maddening slowness the order was written down. When it was complete it amounted to two thousand five hundred pounds, but it was so peppered with codicils inserted by Miss Axhead, all of which necessitated complex modifications of the original models, that it was doubtful if it could ever be executed and still show a profit. A large part of it was conditional on the dozens of 'specials' being acceptable to the Beans and the Woodcocks, most of whom appeared to pass their time in playing a grown-up version of 'I spy with my little eye' whilst their husbands were on the golf course.

At six-forty-five Miss Axhead was taken into the office for a final little drink with my parents. 'It will be nice to have a chat,' she remarked as she rose from the settee, which groaned as if in thankfulness at her departure. 'I don't think any of my girls realize what a hard job we have of it.'

'I entirely agree,' said Miss Stallybrass. As always it was impossible to tell what she was agreeing with.

'Are all our customers like Miss Axhead?' I asked Miss Stallybrass when finally she had been taken away.

'Some of them are a damn sight worse,' she replied unexpectedly. 'Poor old Mary Axhead. As well as that dear little dog she's got a sister who's not very well.'

'I didn't know you liked dogs,' I said.

'Me!' she said. 'I loathe 'em!'

# WILD CALEDONIA

My first visit to Scotland with the 'Gown Collection' was as a commercial traveller in the company of Mr Wilkins.

A porter from the hotel was on the platform to meet us.

'You're in Number Five, Mr Willukins. Your usual,' he said, touching his cap. 'I'll look after the skips.'

The way to the Station Hotel led through a maze of grubby passages, flanked by large chocolate-coloured photographs of Scottish scenery, all of which looked as if they had been exposed in a steady drizzle. Soon we found ourselves in a part of the hotel not normally seen by the public where we met scullions from the kitchens on errands with covered buckets.

We were welcomed by a senior porter with an air of authority and shiny, quick eyes, like a bird's.

'You're in Number Five, Mr Willukins,' he said – and to me: 'How is Mr Newby – I haven't seen him since the war – and Mrs Newby? I remember they used to have a big sitting-room upstairs. Times change. He was a fine man, Mr Newby.' He made it sound like a dirge.

In spite of the warmth of the welcome it was difficult to be enraptured by the room to which we were now escorted.

Stockroom Number Five was a tall, narrow room illuminated by a fifty-watt bulb. The decorations had once been beige but the efforts to clean them had resulted in the walls becoming one great smear. The only furniture was a number of cane chairs and two trestle tables which were covered with white sheets that had been neatly patched. The effect was of a mortuary or a place where members of the Reformed Church might pray together before proceeding to England by train.

In addition to these rudimentary furnishings there was a telephone that had once been black and which was now the colour of old bones, and a dog-eared telephone book on which a succession of commercial travellers, made desperate by the inadequacies of the telephone system, had doodled frenziedly as they waited for calls to Kilmarnock and Galashiels that never came through. The view from the window, which was surprisingly clean, took in the roof of Waverley Station and one span of the North Bridge. At intervals the entire prospect was blotted out by clouds of smoke.

'I thought we were having a sitting-room,' I said. I felt too wretched to show any spirit.

'All the sitting-rooms were booked,' said Mr Wilkins. 'Let's have breakfast.'

'What about a bath and shave?'

'Time's getting on.' He took a gold watch from his pocket. 'Half past eight. Our first appointment's at nine-thirty and we have to unpack.'

In spite of not having shaved his face was as smooth as butter. Mine resembled a gooseberry.

Breakfast was like a slow-motion film of a ritual. At intervals waitresses brought food, but with none of the supporting things that make breakfast possible. Butter arrived without toast; porridge without milk; tea without sugar. In obedience to some defunct regulation there was only one bowl of sugar to four tables, every few minutes it disappeared completely. Other commercials seemed better served – they munched lugubriously, immersed in their *Expresses* and *Daily Mails* – a few like ourselves gazed in the direction of the kitchens or half-rose in their seats in an extremity of despair.

By the time we had finished breakfast it was ten past nine. In twenty minutes the first customer was due to arrive.

There was no time to wash or shave. We raced to the Stockroom. To me it seemed inconceivable that one night in a cabin trunk could have wreaked such havoc upon dresses that had been packed with such care. Mrs Ribble's crêpes looked as though they had been used for the purpose of garrotting someone. Even the woollen dresses looked as though they had been trampled underfoot as I hung them on the rails which had been provided by the stockroom porter. Only Mr Wilkins' coats and suits, heavy, tailored garments, had escaped unscathed. By this time I was used to Mr Wilkins' monopoly of good fortune. He seemed to bear a charmed life.

'Now, Mr Eric,' said Mr Wilkins, 'this is the programme for today.'

It was now nine-twenty-seven. He handed me a sheet of hotel writing paper, part of a large supply which he had filched on the way to breakfast, on which he had drawn up a time-table:

9-30    Mrs McHaggart, Robertsons, Edinburgh
10-30   Mrs McHavers, Lookies, Dundee
11-00   Miss McTush, Campbells, Edinburgh
11-45   Mrs McRobbie, Alexander McGregor, Edinburgh
2-30    Miss Wilkie, McNoons of Perth
4-30    Miss Reekie, Madame Vera, Edinburgh

To me it seemed more like a gathering of the clans in some rainswept glen than an assignation to buy dresses in the sub-basement of a Railway Hotel.

In the three minutes that remained to us before the arrival of Mrs McHaggart, Mr Wilkins briefed me on their idiosyncrasies. Just as a last-minute revision outside the examination hall is useless so Mr Wilkins' brilliant summing-up only increased my confusion.

'Mrs McHaggart is a good Buyer but she doesn't like us to serve any of the other stores in Princes Street. Of course we do – it wouldn't be worth coming here otherwise – and she knows it. The women here know everything,' he said, gloomily. 'You can't keep anything from them. They all have friends and relatives in one another's shops.

'What we have to do is to get Mrs McHaggart's order down on paper. If it's good enough then we don't show the things she's chosen to Miss McTush. They're enemies. If we get a poor order from Mrs McHaggart then we show everything to Miss McTush and change the styles. Miss McTush knows we do this so we can't change them very much. Mrs McRobbie is the same as Mrs McHaggart and Miss McTush. She's in Princes Street too. The important thing is to keep the three of them from meeting. If they do at least one of them won't give us an order; that's why I've put in Mrs McHavers between Mrs McHaggart and Miss McTush, because she comes from Dundee. Miss McTush doesn't really mind what Mrs McHaggart and Mrs McRobbie buy as long as she gets her delivery before they do. In fact we deliver to them all at the same time – we don't dare do otherwise – so Miss McTush is just as difficult as the others. Mrs McHaggart only buys Coats and Suits and two-pieces. She's not supposed to buy two-pieces but she does. That's why we don't see Miss Cameron, the Dress Buyer. Miss McTush buys everything. Mrs McRobbie buys everything. Miss Reekie can buy anything but usually she buys nothing. She's a most difficult woman. I call her "The Old Stinker",' said Mr Wilkins, 'on account of her name being Reekie. I usually take Miss McTush and Mrs McHavers out to lunch together because Mrs McHavers comes from Dundee. On Tuesday I take Mrs McHaggart. First thing on Tuesday morning I call on the ones who haven't given us an appointment. With luck we see some of them in the afternoon or on Wednesday morning. We usually manage to get off to Glasgow on Wednesday afternoon for an appointment in the evening.'

'Don't you give Mrs McRobbie lunch?'

'She's got an ulcer. She never eats lunch. I like Mrs McRobbie,' said Mr Wilkins.

'What about the evenings?'

'If you want to take Buyers out in the evening, Mr Eric, that's your affair,' said Mr Wilkins. 'Personally I drink beer.'

As he said this there was a murmuring sound outside the door and Mrs McHaggart appeared. We were off.

I spent the next seven years tottering up the backstairs of stores with armfuls of samples or stock which I was anxious to get rid of. For hours and sometimes days I waited with my feet sinking deeper and deeper into the carpet for Buyers who had just gone on holiday, were just going, were in London, Paris, Berlin, Stockholm, Rome, Zurich or the ladies' powder room; had a cold, had been dismissed or had not yet been appointed; were having coffee, an affair with the Managing Director, a baby (so rare an excuse that even I was satisfied); had not yet started to buy, had finished buying, had over-bought; didn't want anything until after the Budget, Christmas, Easter, The Funeral (in the better end of the trade the decease of Royalty was always unseasonable); thought the clothes too expensive, too old-fashioned, too smart for the provinces or just didn't like them. Hemmed in by subterfuge I almost grew to love the ones who didn't like them and said so. It is not a business renowned for candour. I called on the Buyer of one London Store for five years without seeing anything but her feet protruding from under a screen.

Wherever I went in England, Ireland, Scotland or Wales I was dogged by the wicker baskets which I inherited from Mr Wilkins when he gave up travelling. At least twice a day, I packed and unpacked them,

standing waist-deep in tissue paper. Although I counted them incessantly, like a warder with a working party, sometimes one would go
missing, temporarily, perhaps because by nature I was less careful than
Mr Wilkins. On two occasions they vanished completely. Standing on
the platform at York, having just alighted from the London train I saw
them stacked in the guard's van of an express that was steaming out
of the station bound for the south. Another time I saw them all sink
into the Mersey when the hook came off the crane that was loading
them into the Irish Packet. I was delighted, business was difficult, I
was selling stock and the contents were adequately insured.

To reach my customers, besides trains and ships, I used motor-cars,
taxis, buses and once, during a strike which paralysed the entire island,
a bicycle. Air travel was normally too expensive with such a weight
of luggage but once I went to Belfast by plane five days after having
had my appendix out and conducted my business propped up against
the wall of a stockroom in the Grand Central Hotel. Like Mr Wilkins
before me I too reached Inverness only to find that it was an early-
closing day. I also spent Shrove Tuesday, 1949, marooned in Scar-
borough because for some unfathomable reason the inhabitants were
all on the beach having a tug-of-war.

Fortunately for me, however absurd it may seem in retrospect, I had
a private dream to sustain me.

In prison I had consorted with numbers of amateur explorers: Hima-
layan mountaineers; men who had spent months on end in airless South
American forests (one had contracted a loathsome disease in the Matto
Grosso which made him yearn to eat earth); Frenchmen who had
burrowed deep into the Sahara in Citroen motor-cars; and others,
mostly officers of the Indian Army who had spent their leaves before
the war travelling, generally without official blessing, in High Asia.

Talking with them about the wind-swept places they had visited was
an agreeable form of escapism from the confined circumstances in
which we found ourselves. In this cloud-cuckoo atmosphere extravagant plans were laid for vast journeys which we were to carry out
together when we were finally liberated. I found myself being invited
to cross Sinkiang in the opposite direction to that taken by Peter Flem-
ing; to set off in search of a curious tribe who were reputed to live in
nests in trees somewhere in the East; and to join a semi-private army

called the Tochi Scouts which spent its peacetime existence skirmishing vigorously on the North-West Frontier of India.

It is a measure of my eccentricity that when I returned from Germany one of the first things I did was to prepare myself carefully for the sort of Buchanesque existence I had imagined in prison, and which I expected to begin as soon as I had 'found my feet'.

I ordered a formidable pair of boots from a firm that had been making the same sort of article at the time when Whymper climbed the Matter-horn. In fact, I first saw their advertisement in Murray's *Guide to Switzerland*, 1878, and was agreeably surprised to find that they were still in existence.

I also expended a large number of clothing coupons on a stout knickerbocker suit made from a strong-smelling tweed, the product of a peasant industry that folded up in 1946. This together with some hairy pullovers and some stout stockings from the Outer Hebrides set me up sartorially.

Realizing that it was not enough to have the proper clothes I joined a Learned Society and attended the annual dinner at which I sat between a Central European savant who spoke no English and a Rear-Admiral who turned out to be stone-deaf. I was ready for anything – but nothing happened. The men I had known in prison had returned whence they came. I felt a little hurt and very much alone.

But although this came as a shock to my pride I was determined to use up some of the excess energy and imagination I had accumulated and I took to packing my knickerbocker suit and my great boots at the bottom of one of the wicker baskets whenever I was doomed to spend the week-end away from home. So that on Friday evening if I found myself in Newcastle I used to put my baskets in the Left Luggage at the station, change into my grotesque outfit and set off for the lonely country beyond the Roman Wall.

In Glasgow I used to leave the collection hanging up in the sitting-room at the hotel. During working hours I used to hide my boots in a wicker basket and my hairy suit hung on one of the rails with the other suits in the collection as far away as possible from the things I hoped to sell. In spite of this it was actually ordered on one occasion by the owner of a small business in Galashiels who was under the impression that it formed part of the collection.

'Now that's the sort of jacket our ladies like, Mr Newby. It's a great
pity you haven't anything else like that. I should have ordered it. But
you know what Galashiels is. I can only have one of a style.'

Glasgow was my real stepping-off place. On Friday evenings I used
to leave for the hills, returning by an early train on Monday morning
covered in mire. In this way I made solitary and to me impressive
excursions into the wild country about Ben Ime and Ben Vorlich; once
I crossed the Moor of Rannoch in a snowstorm.

The only persons who knew anything about these journeys were
Wanda and the Hall Porter at the Station Hotel. It was his job to look
up the trains and work out the connections that would get me back to
Glasgow on Monday morning. He regarded it as a piece of amiable
lunacy, less demanding than some of the requests made to him by
commercials stranded in his hotel for the week-end.

If I had to take a model girl with me on the journey these arrangements became even more complicated. I usually managed to avoid
this by showing the dresses 'in the hand' but with some of the more
sophisticated evening dresses which I was trying to foist on the customers it was commercial suicide to show them on a hanger and I had
to take a model girl. It was a depressing business; either they were the
victims of long-standing engagements and were saving up for three-
piece suites or else they suffered from weak ankles. Only one insisted
that she was an outdoor girl and set off to accompany me to the summit
of Arthur's Seat, an eminence in the outskirts of Edinburgh, in high
heels – the only shoes she had with her. She made it but although it
was a remarkable tour-de-force the experiment was never repeated.

In spite of my enthusiasm, after two years I cancelled my subscription
to the Learned Society. The reports in the Journal of 'A New Route
Through the Pamirs' or 'Some Notes On A Visit To The Nomads of
Central Afghanistan' had for me a mocking quality in the way of life
in which I found myself. Even the tickets for the monthly lectures
went unused, except as firelighters.

It was not until 1956 when Lane and Newby's as I knew it was no
more that someone suggested that I should go on an expedition with
him to a range of mountains called the Hindu Kush.

At that time I was working for Worth-Paquin, a couture house in
Grosvenor Street.

## DEATH OF A SALESMAN

With all the lights on and the door shut to protect us from the hellish draught that blew up the backstairs, the fitting-room was like an oven fitted with mirrors. There were four of us jammed in it: Hyde-Clarke, the designer; Milly, a very contemporary model girl with none of the normal protuberances; the sour-looking fitter in whose workroom the dress was being made; and Newby.

Things were not going well. It was the week before the showing of the 1956 Spring Collection, a time when the *vendeuses* crouched behind their little cream and gold desks, doodling furiously, and the Directors swooped through the vast empty showrooms switching off lights in a frenzy of economy, plunging whole wings into darkness. It was a time of endless fittings, the girls in the workrooms working late. The corset-makers, embroiderers, furriers, milliners, tailors, skirt-makers and matchers all involved in disasters and overcoming them – but by now slightly insane.

This particular dress was a disaster that no one was going to over-come. Its real name, the one on the progress board on the wall of the fitting-room, pinned up with a little flag and a cutting of the material, was *Royal Yacht*, but by general consent we all called it *Grand Guignol*.

I held a docket on which all the components used in its construction were written down as they were called up from the stockroom. The list already covered an entire sheet. It was not only a hideous dress; it was soaking up money like a sponge.

'How very odd. According to the docket *Grand Guignol*'s got nine zips in it. Surely there must be some mistake.'

Hyde-Clarke was squatting on his haunches ramming pins into *Grand Guignol* like a riveter.

'This dress is DOOMED. I know it's doomed. BOTHER, I've swal-lowed a pin! Pins, quickly, pins.'

The fitter, a thin woman like a wardress at the Old Bailey and with the same look of indifference to human suffering, extended a bony wrist with a velvet pin-cushion strapped to it like a watch. He took three and jabbed them malevolently into the material; Milly swore fearfully.

'Mind where you're putting those . . . pins. What d'you think I am – a bloody yoga?'

'You MUST stand still, dear; undulation will get you nowhere,' Hyde-Clarke said.

He stood up breathing heavily and lit a cigarette. There was a long silence broken only by the fitter who was grinding her teeth.

'What do you think of it now, Mr Newby?' he said. 'It's *you* who have to sell it.'

'Much worse, Mr Hyde-Clarke.' (We took a certain ironic pleasure in calling one another Mister.) 'Like one of those flag-poles they put up in the Mall when the Queen comes home.'

'I don't agree. I think she looks like a Druid in it; one of those terribly runny-nosed old men dressed in sheets at an *Eisteddfod*. How much has it cost up to now?'

I told him.

'Breathe OUT, dear. Perhaps you'll look better without any air. I must say there's nothing more gruesome than white jersey when it goes wrong.' 'Dear' breathed out and the dress fell down to her ankles. She folded her arms across her shoulders and gazed despairingly at the ceiling so that the whites of her eyes showed.

'There's no need to behave like a SLUT,' said Hyde-Clarke. He was already putting on his covert coat. 'We'll try again at two. I am going to luncheon.' He turned to me. 'Are you coming?' he said.

We went to 'luncheon'. In speech Hyde-Clarke was a stickler in the use of certain Edwardianisms, so that beer and sandwiches in a pub became 'luncheon' and a journey in his dilapidated sports car 'travel by motor'.

Today was a sandwich day. As we battled our way up Mount Street through a blizzard, I screeched in his ear that I was abandoning the fashion industry.

'I saw the directors this morning.'

'Oh, what did they say?'

'That they were keeping me on for the time being but that they make no promises for the future.'

'What did you say?'

'That I had just had a book accepted for publication and that I am staying on for the time being but I make no promises for the future.'

'It isn't true, is it? I can hardly visualize you *writing* anything.'

'That's what the publishers said, originally. Now I want to go on an expedition.'

'Aren't you rather old?'

'I'm just as old here as on an expedition. You can't imagine anything more rigorous than this, can you? In another couple of years I'll be dyeing my hair.'

'In another couple of years you won't have any to dye,' said Hyde-Clarke.

On the way back from 'luncheon', while Hyde-Clarke bought some Scotch ribs in a fashionable butcher's shop, I went into the Post Office in Mount Street and sent a cable to Hugh Carless, a friend of mine at the British Embassy, Rio de Janeiro.

CAN YOU TRAVEL NURISTAN JUNE?

It had taken me ten years to discover what everyone connected with it had been telling me all along, that the Fashion Industry was not for me.

The answer came back: OF COURSE, HUGH.

Nuristan, in the Hindu Kush, was a region that I had long wanted to explore.

Hugh Carless, who had replied so opportunely to my cable, entered the Foreign Service in 1950. The son of a retired Indian Civil Servant, himself a man of unusual intellectual attainments, he is, like so many Englishmen, in love with Asia. For a time he was posted to the School of Oriental Studies, from which he emerged with a good knowledge of Persian.

His Persian being both fluent and academic, he was lucky to be posted to our Embassy at Kabul where he could actually make use of his talents.

From time to time he wrote me long letters, which came to me by way of the District Postmaster, Peshawar, which I read with envy in the bedrooms of the provincial hotels I stayed in when I 'travelled'. They spoke of long, arduous, and to me fascinating, journeys to the interior, undertaken with horses and mysterious beings called Tajik drivers.

It was early in 1952 that he first mentioned Nuristan.

'An Austrian forestry expert, a Herr von Dückelmann, has recently

dined with me,' he wrote. 'He has been three or four times in Nuristan.
Food there is very scarce, he says, and although he himself is a lean,
hardy man he lost twelve pounds in weight during a ten day trip to
the interior.'

Later in 1952 he wrote again.

> I have just returned from an expedition to the borders of
> Nuristan, *The Country of Light*. This is the place for you. It
> lies in the extreme N.E. of Afghanistan, bordering on Chitral
> and enclosed by the main range of the Hindu-Kush moun-
> tains. Until 1895 it was called Kafiristan, *The Country of the
> Unbelievers*. We didn't get in but we didn't expect to, the
> passes are all over 15,000 feet and we didn't have permission.
> So far as I can discover no Englishman has been there since
> Robertson in 1892. The last Europeans to visit it – von
> Dückelmann apart – were a German expedition in 1935, and
> it's possible that no one has visited the north-west corner at
> all. I went with Bob Dreesen of the American Embassy.

I had heard of Dreesen. He was one of the American party which
escaped from the Chinese Communist advance into Turkestan in 1950,
evacuating the Consulate from Urumchi by lorry to Kashgar and then
crossing the Karakoram Range into India with horses. Hugh went on
to speak of a large mountain, nearly 20,000 feet high, that they had
attempted to climb and of one of his men being hit on the head by a
great stone.

Hugh's telegram was followed by a spate of letters which began to
flow into London from Rio. They were all at least four pages long,
neatly typed in single spacing – sometimes two would arrive in one
day. They showed that he was in a far more advanced state of mental
readiness for the journey than I was. It was as if, by some process of
mental telepathy, he had been able to anticipate the whole thing.

Then, quite suddenly, the tone of the letters changed.

> I don't think we should make known our ambition to go to
> Nuristan. Rather I suggest we ask permission to go on a
> *Climbing Expedition*. There are three very good and un-

climbed peaks of about 20,000 feet, all on the marches of
Nuristan. One of them, Mir Samir (19,880) I attempted in
1952 (*vide* my letter of 20.9.52). We climbed up to some
glaciers and reached a point 3,000 feet below the final pyramid. A minor mishap forced us to return.

He was already deeply involved in the clichés of mountaineering jargon.
I re-read his 1952 letter and found that the 'minor mishap' was an
amendment. At the time he had written, 'one of the party was hit on
the head by a boulder'; he didn't say who.

I was filled with profound misgiving. In cold print 20,000 feet does
not seem very much. Every year more and more expeditions climb
peaks of 25,000 feet, and over. In the Himalayas a mountain of this
size is regarded as an absolute pimple, unworthy of serious consideration. But I had never climbed anything. It was true that I had done
some hill walking and a certain amount of scrambling in the Dolomites
with my wife, but nowhere had we failed to encounter ladies twice
our age armed with umbrellas. I had never been anywhere that a rope
had been remotely necessary.

It was useless to dissemble any longer. I wrote a letter protesting in
the strongest possible terms and received by return a list of equipment
that I was to purchase. Many of the objects I had never even heard of
– two Horeschowsky ice-axes; three dozen Simond rock and ice pitons;
six oval karabiners (2,000 lb. minimum breaking strain); five 100 ft
nylon ropes; six abseil slings; Everest goggles; Grivel, ten point cram-
pons; a high altitude tent; an altimeter; Yukon pack frames – the list
was an endless one. 'You will also need boots. I should see about these
right away. They may need to be made.'

I told Wanda, my wife.

'I think he's insane,' she said, 'just dotty. What will happen if you
say no?'

'I already have but he doesn't take any notice. You see what he says
here, if we don't go as mountaineers we shan't get permission.'

'Have you told the Directors you're leaving?'

'Yes.'

'You *are* in a spot. We're all in a spot. Well, if you're going I'm
going too. I want to see this mountain.'

I wrote to Hugh. Like an echo in a quarry his reply came back, voicing my own thoughts.

> I don't think either of you quite realize what this country is like. The Nuristanis have only recently been converted to Islam; women are less than the dust. *There are no facilities for female tourists*. I refer you to *The Imperial Gazetteer of India*, volume on Afghanistan, page 70, line 37 *et seq*. This is somewhat out of date but the situation must be substantially the same today.

I found the book in a creepy transept of the London Library.

'What does it say?' asked Wanda. 'Read it.'

'"There are several villages in Kafiristan which are places of refuge, where slayers of their fellow tribesmen reside permanently!"'

'It says "fellow tribesmen" and I thought you were going to Nuristan. This says Kafiristan.'

'Don't quibble. It was called Kafiristan until 1895. It goes on; listen to this: "Kafir women are practically slaves, being to all intents and purposes bought and sold as household commodities."'

'I'm practically a slave, married to you.'

'"The young women are mostly immoral. There is little or no ceremony about a Kafir marriage. If a man becomes enamoured of a girl, he sends a friend to her father to ask her price. If the price is agreed upon the man immediately proceeds to the girl's house, where a goat is sacrificed and then they are considered to be married. The dead are disposed of in a peculiar manner."'

'Apart from the goat, it sounds like a London season. Besides he admits it's all out of date. I'm coming as far as I jolly well can.'

'What about the children?'

'The children can stay with my mother in Trieste.'

I was heavily involved on all fronts: with mountaineering outfitters, who oddly enough never fathomed the depths of my ignorance; possibly because they couldn't conceive of anyone acquiring such a collection of equipment without knowing how to use it: with the Consuls of six countries, and with a Bulgarian with whom I formed an indissoluble entente in a pub off Queen's Gate. He was a real prototype Bulgarian with a big moustache and lots of black hair.

With the Autumn Collection. It was now the second week in May. I was leaving in a fortnight. To add to my troubles I now received a letter from Hugh. It was extremely alarming. I read it to Hyde-Clarke.

> 'These three climbs will certainly be a good second-class mountaineering achievement. But we shall almost certainly need with us an experienced climber.'

'I thought you said he was an experienced climber.'
'So I did. Do listen!'
'What about Brown who is now in India as a head of a public school at Begumpet?'

> 'He was head of the Outward Bound Mountaineering School in Eskdale, and has done a good deal of Alpine climbing. He and I were at Trinity Hall together. I have sent him a cable asking him to join us in Kabul by air for a five-week assault on three 20,000 feet peaks but he may be on leave. His address in London is v/c (WRATH)W.C.I.'

'Very appropriate, but what a terrifying cable to receive.'
'That's only the beginning. Listen to this.

> 'It is just possible that he may not be able to come. In which case we must try elsewhere. In my opinion the companion we need should not only have climbing ability and leadership but round out our party's versatility by bringing different qualities, adding them to ours.'

'It sounds like the formula for some deadly gas.'
'Will you listen! This isn't funny to me.

> 'Perhaps he would be a Welsh miner, or a biologist, or a young Scots doctor. Someone from quite another background, bringing another point of view . . .'

'For the first time,' said Hyde-Clarke, 'I'm beginning to be just a little bit jealous. I'd love to listen to you all lying on top of one another in one of those inadequate little tents, seeing one another's points of view.'

'Why don't you come too? I don't see why Hugh should be the only one to invite his friends.

'All proper expeditions seem to have a faithful administrative officer, who toils through the night to get everyone and everything off from London on time and then is forgotten.'

'I like the part about being forgotten.'

'I know how busy you must be but couldn't you find one?'

'With a ginger moustache and a foul pipe . . .'
'Captain Foulenough?'
'Why don't you write to Beachcomber?'
We pursued this fantasy happily for some time.

'Have you approached the Everest Foundation? They are there to assist small parties such as ours.'

'Not quite like yours, I should have thought,' said Hyde-Clarke.

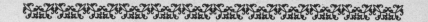

# Birth of an Explorer

WHEN HUGH ARRIVED from New York ten days later I went to meet him at London Airport. Sitting in those sheds on the north side which still, twelve years after the war, gave the incoming traveller the feeling that he was entering a beleaguered fortress, I wondered what surprises he had in store for me.

His first words after we had greeted one another were to ask if there was any news about the third man.

'Not a thing.'

'That's bad,' he said.

'It's not so disastrous. After all, you have done some climbing. I'll soon pick it up. We'll just have to be careful.'

He looked pale. I put it down to the journey. Then he said: 'You know I've never done any *real* climbing.'

It took me some time to assimilate this.

'But all that stuff about the mountain. You and Dreesen . . .'

'Well, that was more or less a reconnaissance.'

'But all this gear. How did you know what to order?'

'I've been doing a lot of reading.'

'But you said you had porters.'

'Not porters - drivers. It's not like the Himalayas. There aren't any "tigers" in Afghanistan. No one knows anything about mountaineering.'

There was a long silence as we drove down the Great West Road.

'Perhaps we should postpone it for a year,' he said.

'Ha-ha. I've just given up my job!'

Hugh stuck out his jaw. Normally a determined-looking man, the effect was almost overwhelming.

'There's nothing for it,' he said. 'We must have some lessons.'

Wanda and I were leaving England for Istanbul on 1 June. Hugh and I had just four days to learn about climbing.

The following night after some brisk telephoning we left for Wales to learn about climbing, in the brand new station wagon Hugh had ordered by post from South America.

We had removed all the furniture from the drawing-room to make room for the equipment and stores. Our three-piece suite was standing in the garden under a tarpaulin. The drawing-room looked like the quartermaster's store of some clandestine force. It was obvious that Hugh was deeply impressed.

'How long have you been living like this?'

'Ever since we can remember. It's not all here yet. There's still the food.'

'What food?' He looked quite alarmed.

'Six cases of Army ration, compo, in fibre boxes. From the SAS. It's arriving tomorrow.'

'We can always leave it in England. I don't know about you but food doesn't interest me. We can always live off the country.'

I remembered von Dückelmann, that hardy Austrian forester without an ounce of spare flesh on him, who had lost twelve pounds in a fortnight in Nuristan.

'Whatever else we leave behind it won't be the food.'

'Well, I suppose we can always give it away.' He sounded almost shocked, as if for the first time he had detected in me a grave moral defect. It was an historic moment.

With unconcealed joy my wife watched us load some of the mountaineering equipment into the machine.

'We'd better not take all of it,' said Hugh. 'They might wonder why we've got so much stuff if we don't know how to use it.'

Over the last weeks the same thought had occurred to me constantly.

'What about the tent?'

The tent had arrived that morning. It had been described to me by the makers as being suitable for what they called 'the final assault'. With its sewn-in ground-sheet, special flaps so that it could be weighed down with boulders, it convinced me, more than any other single item of equipment, that we were going, as the books have it, 'high'. It had been specially constructed for the curious climatic conditions we were likely to encounter in the Hindu Kush.

'I shouldn't take *that*, if I were you,' said my wife with sinister emphasis. 'The children tried to put it up in the garden after lunch. Whoever made it forgot to make holes for the poles.'

'Are you sure?'

'Quite sure. You know it's got those poles shaped like a V, that you slip into a sort of pocket in the material. Well, they haven't made any pockets, so you can't put it up.'

'It's lucky you found out. We should have looked pretty silly on Mir Samir.'

'You're going to look pretty silly at any rate. I shouldn't be surprised if they've done the same thing to your sleeping-bags.'

'Have you telephoned the makers?'

'That's no use. If you send it back to them, you'll never see it again. I've sent for the woman who makes my dresses. She's coming tomorrow morning.'

It was nearly midnight when we left London. Our destination was an inn situated in the wilds of Caernarvonshire. Hugh had telephoned the proprietor and explained to him the peculiar state of ignorance in which we found ourselves. It was useless to dissemble: Hugh had told him everything. He was not only an experienced mountaineer, but was also the head of the mountain rescue service. It is to his eternal credit that he agreed to help us rather than tell us, as a more conventional man might have done, that his rooms were all booked.

We arrived at six o'clock the following morning, having driven all night, but already a spiral of smoke was issuing from a chimney at the back of the premises.

The first thing that confronted us when we entered the hotel was a door on the left. On it was written EVEREST ROOM. Inside it was a facsimile of an Alpine hut, done out in pine wood, with massive benches round the walls. On every side was evidence of the presence of the great ones of the mountain world. Their belongings in the shape of ropes, rucksacks, favourite jackets and boots were everywhere, ready for the off. It was not a museum. It was more like the Royal Enclosure. Sir John and Sir Edmund might appear at any moment. They were probably on the premises.

'Whatever else we do I don't think we shall spend much time in the *Everest Room*,' said Hugh, as we reverently closed the door. 'For the first time I'm beginning to feel that we really do know damn all.'

'EXACTLY.'

At this moment we were confronted by a remarkably healthy-looking girl.

'Most people have had breakfast but it's still going on,' she said.

The only other occupant of the breakfast room was a compact man of about forty-five. He was wearing a magnificent sweater that was the product of peasant industry. He was obviously a climber. With an hysterical attempt at humour, like soldiers before an attack, we tried to turn him into a figure of fun, speaking in whispers. This proved difficult, as he wasn't at all comic, just plainly competent.

'He looks desperately healthy.' (His face was the colour of old furniture.)

'Everyone looks healthy here, except us.'

'I don't think it's real tan.'

'Perhaps he's making a film about mountain rescue.'

'How very appropriate.'

'Perhaps he'll let us stand-in, as corpses.'

After breakfast the proprietor introduced us to the mystery man. We immediately felt ashamed of ourselves.

'This is Dr Richardson,' he said. 'He's very kindly agreed to take you out and teach you the rudiments of climbing.'

'Have you ever done any?' asked the Doctor.

It seemed no time to bring up my scrambles in the Dolomites, nor even Hugh's adventures at the base of Mir Samir.

'No,' I said firmly, 'neither of us knows the first thing about it.'

We had arrived at six; by nine o'clock we were back in the station wagon, this time bound for the north face of the mountain called Tryfan.

'Stop here,' said the Doctor. Hugh parked the car by a milestone that read 'Bangor X Miles'. Rearing up above the road was a formidable-looking chunk of rock, the *Milestone Buttress*.

'That's what you're going to climb,' said the Doctor. 'It's got practically everything you need at this stage.'

It seemed impossible. In a daze we followed him over a rough wall and into the bracken. A flock of mountain sheep watched us go, making noises that sounded suspiciously like laughter.

That evening, having done a lot of climbing, much of it rather alarming, and after a large, old-fashioned tea at the inn with crumpets and boiled eggs, we were taken off to the *Eckenstein Boulder*. Oscar Eckenstein was a renowned climber at the end of the nineteenth century, whose principal claim to fame was that he had been the first man in this or any other country to study the technique of holds and balance on rock. He had spent his formative years crawling over the boulder that now bore his name. Although it was quite small, about the size of a delivery van, his boulder was said to embody all the fundamental problems that are such a joy to mountaineers and were proving such a nightmare to us.

For this treat we were allowed to wear gym shoes.

Full of boiled egg and crumpet, we clung upside down to the boulder like bluebottles, while the Doctor shouted encouragement to us from a safe distance. Occasionally one of us would fall off and land with a painful thump on the back of his head.

'YOU MUST NOT FALL OFF. Imagine that there is a thousand-foot drop under you.'

'I am imagining it but I still can't stay on.'

Back at the inn we had hot baths, several pints of beer, an enormous dinner and immediately sank into a coma. For more than forty hours we had had hardly any sleep. 'Good training,' was Hugh's last muffled comment.

By this time the waitresses at the inn had become interested in this artificial forcing process. All three of them were experienced climbers who had taken the job in the first place in order to be able to combine business with pleasure. Now they continued our climbing education.

They worked in shifts, morning and afternoon, so that we were climbing all the time. We had never encountered anything quite like them before. At breakfast on the last day, Judith, a splendid girl with auburn hair, told us her father had been on Everest in 1933.

As we were leaving for London, Judith gave me a little pamphlet costing sixpence. It showed, with the aid of pictures, the right and wrong ways of climbing a mountain.

'We haven't been able to teach you anything about snow and ice,' she said, 'but this shows you how to do it. If you find anything on the journey out with snow on it, I should climb it if you get the chance.

'I wish we were coming with you,' she added, 'to keep you out of trouble.'

'So do we,' we said, and we really meant it. Everyone turned out to say goodbye. It was very heart-warming.

'You know that elderly gentleman who lent you a pair of climbing boots,' Hugh said, as we drove through the evening sunshine towards Capel Curig.

'You mean Mr Bartrum?'

'Did you know he's a member of the Alpine Club? He's written a letter about us to the Everest Foundation. He showed it to me.'

I asked him what it said.

'He wrote, "I have formed a high opinion of the character and determination of Carless and Newby and suggest that they should be given a grant towards the cost of their expedition to the Hindu Kush." '

Wanda and I drove to Istanbul in Hugh's Land Rover; and together the three of us drove on to Tehran where Wanda left us to go back to Trieste where she had left our children with her mother. On 5 July we arrived in Kabul having driven 5000 miles. The roads east of Istanbul were fearful then. It had taken a month. Our journey was about to begin.

There is no space for all our subsequent vicissitudes but we failed to climb the mountain although we got within 800 feet of the summit. We could easily have said we got to the top. There were no witnesses. In an insane moment of honesty we subsequently sent a telegram to *The Times* from Kabul telling them of our failure and they printed it!

We found Judith's little book a great help on the glacier while cutting our first steps.

Then, with our three Tajik drivers and their three horses we crossed the 16,000 feet Chamar Pass into Nuristan where we met our first Nuristanis.

We were a hundred yards from an *aylaq*, a bothy, when there was a shout and we saw our first Nuristanis.

They came pouring out of the bothy and raced over the grass towards us at a tremendous pace, dozens of them. It seemed impossible that such a small building could have contained so many men. As they came bounding up they gave an extraordinary impression of being out of the past. They were all extraordinary because they were all different, no two alike. They were tall and short, light-skinned and dark-skinned, brown-eyed and grey-eyed; some, with long straight noses, might have passed for Serbs or Croats; others, with flashing eyes, hooked noses and black hair, might have been Jews. There were men like gypsies with a lock of hair brought forward in ringlets on either side of the forehead. There were men with great bushy beards and moustaches that made them look like Arctic explorers. There were others like early Mormons with a fuzz of beard round their faces but without moustaches. Some of the tallest (well over six feet), broken-nosed, clean-shaven giants, were like guardsmen in a painting by Kennington. Those who were hatless had cropped hair and the younger ones, especially those with rudimentary beards, looked as strange and dated as the existentialists of St Germain des Prés; while those whose beards were still in embryo were as contemporary as the clients of a *Café Espresso* and would have been accepted as such without question almost anywhere in the Western World.

They were extraordinary and their clothes were extraordinary too. All but those who were bare-headed wore the same flat Chitrali cap that Hugh had worn ever since we had left Kabul, only theirs were larger and more floppy, and the colour of porridge. Worn on the back of the head the effect was Chaucerian.

They wore drab brown, collarless shirts, like the Army issue, and over them loose waistcoats or else a sort of surcoat – a waistcoat without buttons. Their trousers were brown home-spun, like baggy unbuckled plus-fours. They reached to the middle of the calf and flapped loosely as their wearers pounded up the meadow. They seemed to wear some kind of loose puttee around the lower leg, and some of the younger men wore coloured scarves knotted loosely around their necks. All were barefooted.

'It's like being back in the Middle Ages.'

It was the only coherent remark Hugh had time for. The next moment they were on us, uttering strange cries. Before we knew what was happening we were being borne towards the *aylaq* with our feet barely touching the ground, each the centre of a mob, like distinguished visitors to a university.

I had a blurred vision of a heap of ibex horns and a row of distended skins hanging on the wall of the bothy (inside out they looked like long-dead dogs), then I received a terrific crack on the head as we hurtled in through the low opening – we were inside.

The floor was bare earth but on it were spread several very old rugs made of something that looked like felt, with a pattern of black and orange diamonds on them, brought up here to end their days at the *aylaq*. In the centre of the floor there was a shallow depression in which a dung fire smouldered. Over it, balanced on two rocks, was a cauldron in which some great mess was seething. There was no chimney or opening of any kind and the walls were blackened with smoke.

We were made to sit on the floor and our hosts (for that was what they turned out to be – up to now it had not been apparent what their attitude was) brought in two round wooden pots full of milk which they set before us, together with a couple of large ladles. The pots held about half a gallon each, and seemed to be made from hollowed-out tree-trunks. They were decorated with the same diamond pattern I had noticed on the rugs. Both vessels and cutlery were of heroic proportions, fit for giants.

We were extremely thirsty. Hugh was already dipping into his pot.

The bothy was crammed to the point of suffocation with people all jabbering an unknown tongue. I wondered if it were Bashguli. It was certainly unlike any other language I had ever heard but there was no way of discovering what it was.

After drinking nearly a quart of icy milk (the pots had just come out of the river), I felt as if I were going to burst. I put down my tree-trunk. Sitting next to me was one of the hairless Espresso boys. He picked up the ladle. 'Biloogh ow,' he grunted (at least that was what it sounded like) and began to forcibly feed me as though I were senile.

Here in the summer months, men of the tribe lived without their women, looking after the flocks and cattle, making curds and butter to store for the winter and for trade with the outside world and every so often sending down some of their number to the valleys far below with the heavy goatskins I had seen hanging outside – a journey of from one to five days according to the destination – a sort of grim compassionate leave.

All the time this recital was going on we were being ransacked. I could feel inquisitive fingers prying about my person, opening button flaps, groping in my pockets for my handkerchief, scrabbling at my watch-strap.

We had already passed round several packets of cigarettes and a fight had developed for the empty packets. It was the silver paper they wanted. But what they really longed for were binoculars. They loved my camera, until they discovered that it was not a pair of binoculars, but they soon found Hugh's telescope and took it outside to try it.

In a world that has lost the capacity for wonderment, I found it very agreeable to meet people to whom it was possible to give pleasure so simply. Thinking to ingratiate myself still further with them, I handed over my watch. It was the pride of my heart (I, too, am easily pleased) – a brand-new Rolex that I had got in Geneva on the way out from England and reputed proof against every kind of ill-treatment.

'Tell the headman,' I said to Hugh, 'that it will work under water.'

'He doesn't believe it.'

'All right. Tell him it will even work in that,' pointing to the cauldron which was giving off steam and gloggling noises.

Hugh told him. The headman said a few words to the young existentialist who had the watch. Before I could stop him he dropped it into the pot.

'He says he doesn't believe you,' said Hugh.

'Well, tell him to take it out! I don't believe it myself.' By now I was hanging over the thing, frantically fishing with the ladle.

'It's no good,' I said. 'They'll have to empty it.'

This time Hugh spoke somewhat more urgently to the headman.

'He says they don't want to. It's their dinner.'

At last somebody hooked it and brought it to the surface, covered with a sort of brown slime. Whatever it was for dinner had an extraordinary nasty appearance. The rescuer held it in the ladle. Though too hot to touch, it was still going. This made an immense impression on everyone, myself included. Unfortunately, it made such an impression on the man himself that he refused to be parted from it and left the bothy.

'Where's he going?'

'He's going to try it in the river.'

*          *          *

When the time came to leave there was no sign of Hugh's telescope or my watch.

'I want my telescope,' Hugh told the headman.

'What about my watch?' I asked, when his telescope was finally produced from somewhere round the corner.

'He says the man who had it has gone away.'

'Well, tell him that he must bring him back.'

There was a further brief parley.

'He says the man wants to keep it.' Somehow Hugh contrived to make this sound a reasonable request.

'WELL, HE CAN'T! GET IT BACK FOR ME! MAKE AN EFFORT!'

'It's *you* who should make the effort. It's really too much having to do your work *all* the time.'

I could have struck him at this moment.

'Damn it, you can hardly understand the man yourself and you speak fluent Persian. How the devil do you expect me to make him understand anything?'

Just then I saw the man who had taken my watch skulking behind one of the walls of the *aylaq*. I went round the building the other way and came up behind him, and took hold of his wrists. Although he was without any apparent muscle, he was immensely strong. He radiated a kind of electric energy.

'*Tok-tok*,' I said. At the same time I looked down at my own wrist and nodded my head violently.

He began to laugh. I looked into his eyes; they were strange and mad. He had about him an air of scarcely controlled violence that I had noticed in some of the others inside the hut. An air of being able to commit the most atrocious crimes and then sit down to a hearty meal without giving them a further thought. The man was a homicidal maniac. Perhaps they were all homicidal maniacs.

I saw that his right hand was clenched and I forced it open. Inside was my beautiful watch. He had washed it in the river. It was still going and it continued to do so.

As we left the *aylaq* three more Nuristanis came running up the valley, moving over the ground in short steps but with unbelievable swiftness. All three had full brown beards, they wore short fringed overcoats of a very dark brown – almost black, perhaps the last vestiges of the glory of the Black-robed Kafirs; on their backs were slung empty pack-frames.

'They have come up from the Ramgul to take the place of those who will go down with butter tomorrow morning,' said Abdul Ghiyas, our Tajik driver.

No one said good-bye to us. Some of the Nuristanis had already gone loping up the mountain-side towards the flocks; the rest had retired into the bothy. It was a characteristic of these people that their interest in strangers was exhausted almost as quickly as it was born.

After a month on the march we finally climbed out of Nuristan by another 16,000 foot pass – the Arayu.

All of us, proprietors and drivers were now ill. For this reason our caravan presented a curiously scattered appearance, as it wound its way up the dreadful slope, exposed to wind and sun and the whistles of the marmots who were out in force among the rocks. As one or the other of us succumbed, a ruthless atmosphere prevailed; no one waited for anyone else and those who had fallen out had to catch up as best they could when they finally emerged, green-faced, from behind the inadequate boulders that covered the lower slopes.

The climb began in earnest at a quarter to ten and took three hours. The last few hundred feet were *moraine* and the way through it was marked by cairns, two stones on top of one another. But it was worth all the suffering. Once again, as on the Chamar, we stood on the great dividing ridge of the whole massif. To the left the ridge plunged down in snow-covered slopes straight into a glacial lake; to the right of the *col* the mountains were smoother, more rounded. Ahead was Mir Samir.

Here on the Arayu, one of the lonely places of the earth with all the winds of Asia droning over it, where the mountains seemed like the bones of the world breaking through, I had the sensation of emerging

from a country that would continue to exist more or less unchanged
whatever disasters overtook the rest of mankind. This was long before
the days of Soviet helicopter gunships.

We went down towards the north, following the cairns and later the
stream from the top of the watershed, with the cold yellow mountains
all about us standing alone, like sentinels.

It was mid-afternoon before we stopped. In spite of everything,
I was mad with hunger. Hugh, having a queasy feeling, was more
finicky.

'It's your turn to cook,' he said. 'I want green tea and two boiled
eggs.'

'Well, I want a damn great meal.'

There was a screaming wind. Boiling water at 15,000 feet or thereabouts is a protracted operation using nothing but solid fuel. Whilst I
was waiting for the egg water to boil, I fried two eggs in thirty seconds
and ate an entire apple pudding, cold.

Hugh looked like death but he was in a fury. At first I thought he
would have some kind of seizure.

'Look at you. Hogging it. You only think of yourself. When are
you going to cook something decent for *me*?'

'You asked for boiled eggs. I can't think of anything more difficult
at this height. You can cook them yourself and anything else you want
in the future.'

I set off over the green grass down the valley alone.

In spite of this ridiculous tiff, rarely in my life had I felt such an
ecstatic feeling of happiness as I did coming down from the Arayu.
The present was bliss beyond belief; the future looked golden. I thought
of my wife and children; I thought of the book that I had already
written; I even thought about the Everest Foundation and the grant
that up here seemed certain to materialize (it didn't – one can hardly
blame them).

I went down past high, cold cliffs already in shadow where the first
tented nomads were, down and down for two hours.

Eventually I came out in a great green meadow with a river running
through it like a curled spring. The sun was just setting, the grass that
had been a vivid green had already lost its colour, the sky was the
colour of pearls.

Under the wall of the mountain on the left there were four rocks, each forty feet high and fifty long; built out from under them were the stone houses and pens of the summer *aylaq*. Women and children dressed in white were standing on the roofs watching the herds come slowly down from the fringes of the mountain. Standing in the river two bullocks were fighting.

Before going to the *aylaq* I waited for Hugh to appear.

'You know I've had the most extraordinary feeling coming down,' were his first words when he appeared. 'As if there was never going to be anything to worry about again.'

'I expect it's the altitude.'

The night was a bitter one. The wind howled over the screes but we dined on rice pudding (the rice was provided by the headman, our own provisions were exhausted) and, although we were blinded by the smoke of the wormwood, *artemisia*, root, we were content to be where we were.

All through the next day we still had the same feeling of extreme happiness. Until late in the afternoon we went down; always with the great bone-coloured mountains on either side and valleys choked with the debris of glaciers, leading to regions of snow and ice and to rocks too sheer for snow to cling to them.

We came to cornfields and a village called Arayu, full of savage dogs and surly-looking Tajiks and mud houses like those of Egyptian *fellahin*.

This patch of cultivation was succeeded by a mighty red-cliffed gorge where there were caves in which we sheltered from the midday sun. But not for long. The path to Parian and Shāhnaiz led up out of it high over the mountain. At the watershed we turned still more to the north going downhill again now and into a final narrow valley where the wind threw the spray from a river in our faces. It was spray from the Parian, the Upper Panjshir. We had made it.

We crossed the river by a bridge, went up through the village of Shāhnaiz and downhill towards the Lower Panjshir.

'Look,' said Hugh, 'it must be Thesiger.'

Coming towards us out of the great gorge where the river thundered was a small caravan like our own. He named an English explorer, a remarkable throwback to the Victorian era, a fluent speaker of Arabic, a very brave man, who has twice crossed the Empty Quarter and, apart from a few weeks every year, has passed his entire life among primitive peoples.

We had been on the march for a month. We were all rather jaded; the horses were galled because the drivers were careless of them, and their ribs stood out because they had been in places only fit for mules and forded innumerable torrents filled with slippery rocks as big as footballs; the drivers had run out of tobacco and were pining for their wives; there was no more sugar to put in the tea, no more jam, no more cigarettes and I was reading *The Hound of the Baskervilles* for the third time; all of us suffered from a persistent dysentery. The ecstatic sensations we had experienced at a higher altitude were beginning to wear off. It was not a particularly gay party.

Thesiger's caravan was abreast of us now, his horses lurching to a standstill on the execrable track. They were deep-loaded with great wooden presses, marked 'British Museum', and black tin trunks (like the ones my solicitors have, marked 'All Bishop of Chichester').

The party consisted of two villainous-looking tribesmen dressed like royal mourners in long overcoats reaching to the ankles; a shivering Tajik cook, to whom some strange mutation had given bright red hair, unsuitably dressed for Central Asia in crippling pointed brown shoes and natty socks supported by suspenders, but no trousers; the interpreter, a gloomy-looking middle-class Afghan in a coma of fatigue, wearing dark glasses, a double-breasted lounge suit and an American hat with stitching all over it; and Thesiger himself, a great, long-striding crag of a man, with an outcrop for a nose and bushy eyebrows, forty-five years old and as hard as nails, in an old tweed jacket of the sort worn by Eton boys, a pair of thin grey cotton trousers, rope-soled Persian slippers and a woollen cap comforter.

'Turn round,' he said, 'you'll stay the night with us. We're going to kill some chickens.'

We tried to explain that we had to get to Kabul, that we wanted our mail, but our men, who professed to understand no English but were reluctant to pass through the gorges at night, had already turned the horses and were making for the collection of miserable hovels that was the nearest village.

Soon we were sitting on a carpet under some mulberry trees, surrounded by the entire population, with all Thesiger's belongings piled up behind us.

'Can't speak a word of the language,' he said cheerfully. 'Know a lot of the Koran by heart but not a word of Persian. Still, it's not really necessary. Here, you,' he shouted at the cook, who had only entered his service the day before and had never seen another Englishman. 'Make some green tea and a lot of chicken and rice – three chickens.

'No good bothering the interpreter,' he went on, 'the poor fellow's got a sty, that's why we only did seventeen miles today. It's no good doing too much at first, especially as he's not feeling well.'

The chickens were produced. They were very old; in the half-light they looked like pterodactyls.

'Are they expensive?'

'The Power of Britain never grows less,' said the headman, lying superbly.

'That means they are very expensive,' said the interpreter, rousing himself.

Soon the cook was back, semaphoring desperately.

'Speak up, can't understand a thing. You want sugar? Why don't you say so?' He produced a large bunch of keys, like a housekeeper in some stately home. All that evening he was opening and shutting boxes so that I had tantalizing glimpses of the contents of an explorer's luggage – a telescope, a string vest, the *Charterhouse of Parma, Du Côté de Chez Swann*, some fish-hooks and the 1/1000000 map of Afghanistan – not like mine, a sodden pulp, but neatly dissected, mounted between marbled boards.

'That cook's going to die,' said Thesiger; 'hasn't got a coat and look at his feet. We're nine thousand feet if we're an inch here. How high's the Chamar Pass?' We told him 16,000 feet. 'Get yourself a coat and boots, do you hear?' he shouted in the direction of the camp fire.

After two hours the chickens arrived; they were like elastic, only the rice and gravy were delicious. Famished, we wrestled with the bones in the darkness.

'England's going to pot,' said Thesiger, as Hugh and I lay smoking the interpreter's King Size cigarettes, the first for a fortnight. 'Look at this shirt, I've only had it three years, now it's splitting. Same with tailors; Gull and Croke made me a pair of whipcord trousers to go to the Atlas Mountains. Sixteen guineas – wore a hole in them in a fort-night. Bought half a dozen shotguns to give to my headmen, well-known make, twenty guineas apiece, absolute rubbish.'

He began to tell me about his Arabs.

'I give them powders for worms and that sort of thing.' I asked him about surgery. 'I take off fingers and there's a lot of surgery to be done; they're frightened of their own doctors because they're not clean.'

'Do you do it? Cutting off fingers?'

'Hundreds of them,' he said dreamily, for it was very late. 'Lord, yes. Why, the other day I took out an eye. I enjoyed that.

'Let's turn in,' he said.

The ground was like iron with sharp rocks sticking up out of it. We started to blow up our air-beds. 'God, you must be a couple of pansies,' said Thesiger.

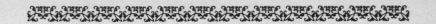

# Ganga Ma: Mother Ganges

IN 1963, HAVING BEEN GIVEN the sack by the John Lewis Partnership who had employed me as a Fashion Buyer, Wanda and I decided to travel down the Ganges to Calcutta from Hardwar in the foothills of the Himalayas, a distance of 1200 miles, most of the way in rowing boats.

I love rivers. I was born on the banks of the Thames and, like my father before me, I had spent a great deal of time both on it and in it. I enjoy visiting their sources: Thames Head, in a green meadow in the Cotswolds; the river Po coming out from under a heap of boulders among the debris left by picnickers by Monte Viso; the Isonzo bubbling up over clean sand in a deep cleft in the rock in the Julian Alps; the Danube (or one of its sources) emerging in baroque splendour in a palace garden at Donaueschingen. I like exploring them. I like the way in which they grow deeper and wider and dirtier but always, however dirty they become, managing to retain some of the beauty with which they were born.

For me the most memorable river of all was the Ganges. I had not seen it for more than twenty years since the time when, as a young officer, I had spent six months on its banks at a remote military station some fifty miles from Kanpur.

## THE FIRST SIGHT OF THE RIVER

Together with Wanda I went out on to one of the platforms of the temple. Upstream towards Rishikesh, the river wound between sand and shingle, sometimes hidden from view amongst groves of trees from which long, horizontal bands of mist were slowly rising. Immediately below was the Har-ki-Pairi Ghat with its ludicrous clock tower and, just upriver from it, the barrage at Bhimgoda that channelled the water from the mainstream into the canal reducing the river below it to a trickle among stones that were the colour of old bones. This attenuated stream was the Ganges, the river that we hoped to travel down until we reached the sea. To the south of the Hardwar Gorge, here, at its narrowest, not more than a mile wide, it wound away, a narrow ribbon, reach after reach of it until it was swallowed up in the haze of the vast plain that stretched through all points of the compass from east of south to the extreme west.

Now, for the first time, I realized the magnitude of the journey that lay before us; but I had none of the feelings of the explorer. This was no uncharted river. Millions lived on its banks, regarding it as an essential adjunct without which their existence would be unthinkable, if not impossible; bathing in it, drinking it; washing their clothes in it; pouring it on to their fields; dying by it; being taken into its bosom by it and being borne away.

We set off down the Ganges at two o'clock in the afternoon. It was 6th December, my forty-fourth birthday. Our immediate destination was the Balawali Bridge, twenty-five miles as the crow flies from Hardwar, a journey which we believed would take two days. The boat, which was twenty-five feet long and built of steel, was deep-loaded, so deeply and with such a quantity of gear that only three of the five oarsmen's benches could be occupied. Besides the six occupants (we had recruited two more boatmen and the Irrigation Engineer had sent one of his own men to ensure that his boat was not misused) there was the now augmented luggage, plus further purchases we had made in the bazaar at Hardwar; sacks of chilli powder and vegetables; namdars – blankets made from a sort of coarse felt; teapots, kettles, hurricane lamps and reed mats. I had even bought an immense bamboo pole from a specialist shop in the bazaar as a defence against dacoits (robbers) whose supposed whereabouts were indicated on some rather depressing maps. Our bills were paid. We had left a hundred rupees for a lorry-man to come to collect the boat downstream. Prudently we had put this into the hands of two men from Shell who by this time were the only people we trusted. We had paid the thirty-two men who had come tottering barefooted across a mile of hot shingle with the boat upside over their heads all the way from the Canal to the Ganges; we had shaken hands with everybody – some, whom we had never seen before, had wept; and for the second time in two days we had advanced money to boatmen for them to buy provisions for the journey (we never saw the first two boatmen again). We were ready to go.

As we crouched low in the boat while the current took us under the bridge, an old bridge-builder who was wearing spectacles as large as the headlamps of a Rolls Royce, dropped sacred sweets on us as a provision for the journey. His tears wetted our heads. The boatmen put their oars in the rowlocks and rowed off smartly. We were off.

Two hundred yards below the bridge and some twelve hundred miles from the Bay of Bengal the boat grounded in sixteen inches of water. This was no shoal. There was no question of being in the wrong channel. At this point the uniform depth of the river was sixteen inches. I looked upstream to the bridge but all those who had been waving and weeping had studiously turned their backs. The boatmen uttered despairing cries for assistance but the men at the bridge bent to their tasks with unwonted diligence. As far as they were concerned we had passed out of their lives. We might never have existed.

We all got out, including Wanda, who was wearing an ingenious Muslim outfit which consisted of peg-top trousers of white lawn and a hieratical-looking shift. She simply took off her trousers and joined us, still apparently fully dressed, in the water.

The bottom of the river was full of rocks the size of twenty-four-pound cannon balls which were covered with a thin slime of green weed. The water was absolutely clear. It frothed and bubbled about our calves. Fifty yards below the place where we had gone aground, the shallows terminated in a waterfall down which the river cascaded. We began to dig a passage towards it with our hands, lifting the great slimy stones and plonking them down on either side of the boat. Under them were more stones of equal size and even greater slipperiness.

It is difficult to describe the emotions that one feels when one is aground on a twelve-hundred-mile boat journey within hailing distance of one's point of departure. It is an experience that has fallen to the lot of some blue-water sailors who have grounded when setting off to sail round the world. But about them there was something of tragedy which derived from the grandeur of the design. To be stranded in a river sixteen inches deep is simply ludicrous.

## DOWN THE GANGES

A list of suggestive articles which are needed on the journey is given here but the pilgrims may have all or some of them as desired and needed.

| Religious | Cloths | Medicines | Utensiles |
|---|---|---|---|
| Japalma | Rugs, Blanket | Amrutanjan | Canvas bucket |
| Agarbattis | Muffler | Smelling Salt | Cooker |
| Camphor | Dhavali or Silk | Vaseline bottle | Oven |
| Dhup Powder | Dhoti | J & J De Chane's | One set of |
| Kumkuma | Dhoties 2 | Medical Service | stainless steel |
| Sandalwood | Shirts 4 | set with its | vessels |
| Powder | Baniyans 2 | guide book | Ladle |
| Wicks soaked in | Uppar clothes 3 | Homeopathic | Spoons–3 |
| ghee and | Towels 3 | Box & a guide | Fraid pan |
| Kundi | Waterproff | Booh | Tiffin Carrier |
| Asanam | cloth (2 yards) | Diarrhoea Pills | Tumbler |
| Bhagavad Gita | Rotten cloth | Dysentery Pills | Glass |
| or any | (pieces 4) | Indigestion Pills | |
| religious book | Coupeens 2 | Malaria Pills | |
| for daily use | Cloth bag for | Boric Powder | |
| Bhajan Songs or | money to keep | Cotton | |
| Namavali | round waist | Cloth (Plaster) | |
| Sri Ramakoti | Bedding | Bandage cloth | |

| Book | Mosquito Curtain | Aspro Tablets Purgative chacklets Tooth powder or paste |
|------|------------------|-------------------------------------------------------|

*Miscellaneous*

Looking Glass and comb
Soaps for bath and wash
Nails of all sizes
Locks 2
Cloth bags for food stuffs
Pen knife
Small gunny bag for coal
Wrist Watch
Umbrella
Hand stick
Visiting Cards
List of departed souls and their Gotras
Hand bags 2
Note book
White Papers
Fountain pen and pencil
Candles
Needles and thread
Railway Guide
Pilgrim's Travel Guide
A small hand axe
Good Camera with flash
Movie (Cene) Camera

Tongue Cleaner
Suit case or hand jip bag
Lock and chain
Pandari bag to carry things on shoulder
Safety pins
Change for Rs. 10-00
Setuvu from Rameswaram
Ganges from Allahabad
Haridwar or Gangottari
Rail and Road Maps
Battery light with spare Batteries
Thermos Flask
Hurricane Lamp
Match box
Calendar both Telugu and English
News Papers
Ink bottles
Postage stamps and cards

from *A Pilgrim's Travel Guide*

# THE GANGES AT ALLAHABAD

In the evening we walked back over the Ganges across the forty spans of the Izzot railway bridge. Upstream to the north long strings of camels and bullock carts were crossing the bridge of boats which carried

the Grand Trunk Road in the direction of Allahabad. The river tore
down under it, tugging at the caissons. From them small boys were
diving into the water and being swept, miraculously, into the shallows
where still smaller children who were making unhappy mooing noises
were bathing with their mothers. The dust hung heavily over the
approaches to the bridge and the smoke rose straight into the air from
the fires at the burning ghats, where even at this late hour wood for
the cremations was still being weighed out on the scales. Inland a green
sea of fields lapped at the wooded banks and stretched away northwards
into the distance. When the rains came there would be a forty-foot rise
in the level of the Ganges and they would be submerged under twenty
feet of water. Downstream the two rivers and the white boats on them
were flooded in an intense golden light; beyond the Jumna mist was
already forming in the rice fields; swifts swooped about the walls of
Akbar's Fort which threw a dark oblong shadow across the sandbank
on which camp fires were now beginning to burgeon. As the sandbank
had dried out and its surface had become hard it had cracked. Now it
was covered with thousands of deep fissures. By day armies of men
were engaged in filling them in. Seen from the height of the bridge it
resembled a huge jig-saw.

Under one of the last of the forty spans of the bridge a lunatic was
sitting out in the stream on a pillar of silt fifteen feet high. This pillar,
which was precariously supported by one of the buttresses of the
bridge, was on the point of collapsing into the water. The lunatic was
gesticulating violently and singing at the top of his voice. He seemed
perfectly happy. How he had got there in the first place was a mystery;
how he was to get back alive was equally incomprehensible. No one
except ourselves took the slightest notice of him. This was India. He
would work out his own salvation. As he sat there a train rumbled
overhead and the vibration caused more chunks to fall off his perch,
reducing still more his chances of survival.

## THE DAY OF MAKARA SANKRANTI

A peculiar fact which has never been satisfactorily
explained is the quick death, in three or five hours,
of the cholera vibrio in the waters of Ganges.
When one remembers sewage by numerous
corpses of natives, often cholera casualties, and
by the bathing of thousands of natives, it seems
remarkable that the belief of the Hindus, that the
water of this river is pure and cannot be defiled
and that they can safely drink it and bathe in it,
should be confirmed by means of modern bac-
teriological research.

> An unnamed Canadian professor,
> said to be of McGill University,
> cited in *Mother Ganges*

On the afternoon of 13th January, we drove up the Grand Trunk Road
to Allahabad. The journey which had taken us three days and nights
in the rowing-boat was now accomplished in as many hours. The road
was crowded with pilgrims on their way to the Mela. They travelled
in ekkas, clinging to them in half dozens, in tongas, motor buses, cars
and on bicycles. They also travelled on foot, men and women and
children plodding up the road with their faces wrapped in cloths to
avoid being asphyxiated by petrol fumes and choked with the dust that
rose from the dry verges of the road. There was a file of camels,
each with a man on its back seated on a wooden saddle. There was
even an elephant with a painted head, chained, all alone at the side
of the road. It was chewing grass and swishing its decorated trunk
up and down, curling it delicately so that it looked like the initial
letter on a page of illuminated manuscript but one that was constantly
changing its shape.

It was a beautiful day. The plain was a sea of sprouting wheat and
barley, dotted with groves of trees that were enchanting islands among
the lighter green of the crops. It was a day of spring rather than winter
in which everything seemed to be burgeoning, all except the man-made
objects, villages, tanks, and shrines – which were mostly crumbling
into dust. But as the sun sank behind the trees and the shadows leng-
thened, the fields assumed the same uniform greengage colour as the

river did when it flowed in the sunless places close to the high banks; except in one place where a single shaft of sunlight filtering through a gap in the trees illuminated a whitewashed tomb. Then it disappeared. Low in the west the sky became blood-red; higher it was purple; overhead it was deep blue; while low down close to the earth in the fields, the smoke from the village fires hung in swags and trailed away among the trees in woods which were no longer Arcadian but dark and mysterious-looking.

Because of the huge crowds, the bridge of boats at Jhusi on the left bank of the Ganges had been closed to motor cars, and by the time we reached the Curzon Bridge at the big bend of the river north of the city, it was almost dark and only the pools among the sandbanks upstream still shone in the last of the light.

The bridge itself was jammed with bullock-carts and tired pilgrims – men, women and children on their way to the Sangam, the confluence of the Ganges with the Jumna and a third invisible river, the Sarasvati. They were country people and what belongings they had they carried in sacks slung across their shoulders. It was a moving sight.

Eventually, we reached the Fort, and from the ramparts looked out over the sandbank which extended upstream for more than a mile from the confluence of the two rivers as far as the Izzot railway bridge.

It was more like the camp of an army on the eve of a great action than a holy place. The sandbank was hidden from view by a blanket of low-lying fog and smoke which was illuminated by the flickering light of the camp fires, and the glare of kerosene lanterns. The long lines of electric lights on long poles which marked the way to the bathing areas were the only lights actually to rise above the fog; while overhead the stars looked down, pale and remote.

It was eerie, for apart from a few hundred pilgrims who were seeing the night through huddled against the wall of the fort, there was not a human being in sight. Only a muted and continuous roar from the sandbank and the encampments announced the fact that a million people were settling down for the night. A sound that was punctuated by the beating of gongs and drums, the ringing of bells, the rumbling of trains on the railway bridges and the noise of the loud-speakers which blared out injunction to this vast multitude on how it should comport itself the next day, on the morning of Makara Sankranti, when the sun and moon would be of equal degree.

At five o'clock the following morning it was still dark. Down on the sandbank, the road which led from Akbar's great embankment on the north side of the fort to the landing-place was itself a tributary river of human beings all moving towards the Ganges. Down on the shores of the Jumna by the fort shoals of country boats propelled by sweeps were setting off, deep-loaded, for the Sangam. From the sandbank rose the same deep roaring sound we had heard the night before that was like the sound of a storm at sea.

At a quarter to six the sky beyond the Sangam was tinged with red and the wind-blown clouds were like the wings of a giant grey bird that had been dipped in blood. From the horn of sand where the rivers met, a further isthmus of boats extended far out into the Jumna and their masts and rigging, mooring poles and cordage were like a forest of trees and creepers against the sky.

Little bands of men and women who had travelled here together from their villages, some of them very old with skin like crumpled parchment, the women singing sadly but triumphantly, lurched bare-footed across the silt towards the pragwals, evil-looking men who performed their duties with an air of patient cynicism, in contrast with that of the pilgrims themselves who wore expressions of joy. They had all been shaven with varying degrees of severity in the barbers' quarter: women from the south and widows had had their head completely shaven; the men were left with their chhotis, the small tufts on the backs of their skulls, and those who had moustaches, but whose fathers were still alive, had been allowed to retain them; natives of Allahabad were allowed to keep their hair; Sikhs gave up a ritual lock or two. At one time the hair was buried on the shore of the river; now it was taken away and consigned to a deep part of the Ganges downstream. Like pilgrims everywhere they were not allowed much peace: shifty-looking men offered to guard their clothes while they were bathing; the dreadful loud-speakers exhorted them not to surrender their clothes to these same shifty-looking men and, at the same time, urged them to bathe and go away; boatmen importuned them; policemen and officious young men wearing armbands tried to move

them on, but they were in a state bordering on ecstasy, and were
oblivious to everything but the river which they had come so far to
see, bathe in and perhaps to die by this very morning; for some of
them were so decrepit that it seemed impossible that they could survive
the sudden shock of the immersion.

The women dressed in saris, the men in loin-cloths, they entered the
river, dunking themselves in it, drinking it, taking it in their cupped
hands and letting it run three times between their fingers with their
faces towards the still invisible sun. Shivering but happy and, if they
were fortunate enough to possess them, dressed in clean clothes, they
allowed the pragwals to rub their foreheads with ashes or sandalwood
and make the tilak mark. They offered flowers and milk to the river,
and those who had never been there before bought half-coconuts from
the pragwals and launched the shells filled with marigolds on the water,
which were afterwards appropriated by the pragwals to be sold again.
New or old pilgrims, these clients were his for ever, and so would
their descendants be and their names would be inscribed in one of his
books, according to their caste, as they had been for centuries.

The sun rose as a ball of fire, but was almost immediately enveloped
in cloud. A cool wind rose and the dust with it, enveloping the long,
dun-coloured columns which were moving towards the Sangam and
those whiter ones which were moving away from it. The camps of the
pragwals were labyrinths of thatched huts and tent-like constructions
in which saris and dhotis and loin-cloths hung on thickets of bamboo
poles drying in the wind and the smoke of dung fires. Over them, on
longer poles flew their banners, the rallying places of their clients who
squatted cheek by jowl below them in a dense mass, cooking, waiting
for their clothes to dry, or merely waiting. There were banners with
European soldiers on them in uniforms dating from the time of the
East India Company and there were banners decorated with gods. Some
poles had baskets and other homely objects lashed to the top of them
instead of flags. One had an umbrella.

Further north, towards the Banaras bridge, the encampment of the
sadhus was like a sea of saffron. There the Mahanta Krishna Mahatna
from the ashram at Paribragikachary, seated on cushions in a tent, was
discoursing to his followers, using a microphone. On the other side of
the river, on the sands at Jhusi a famous saint, the Beoraha Babu, who

is said to have walked across the Ganges on the water, was installed on a tower ten feet high. On the day after we had left Allahabad for Mirzapur, he had crossed the river by more conventional means to attend a meeting of pandits and sadhus at the foot of the living banyan tree inside the Fort; the one which is not accessible to the laity because it is in a military area.

The way from the Sangam to Akbar's embankment was a Via Dolorosa lined with beggars. To traverse it was to be transported into the Dark Ages. They were dressed in rags the colour of the silt on which they lay or crouched, and they were almost indistinguishable from it. The air was filled with the sound of their moanings. There were lepers and dwarfs and men, women and children so terribly mutilated – without limbs, eyes, faces, some with none of these adjuncts – that they bore scarcely any resemblance to humanity at all. Some lay contorted in little carts with broken wheels. Each had his or her begging bowl and a piece of sacking with a little rice spread on it, put there in much the same way as a cloakroom attendant at Claridge's leaves a few shillings in a plate to show that he is not averse to being tipped. The lepers were the most terrible of all, with fingers like black knots and with white crusts for eyes, or else a ghastly jelly where the eyes should have been. And to each of them the returning bathers, rich or poor, threw a few grains of rice and a few paise, confident that by so doing they were at least ensuring themselves merit in this world and perhaps even a little in the next.

'Why are you taking photographs of these people?' said a highly civilized Brahman. 'What will people think of India if you show pictures such as these?' He was genuinely angry.

He delicately sprinkled a handful of rice on the sacking of the beggar in front of him, looked at me with disdain, and went on his way.

There were mendicant sadhus, men lying on beds of thorns with a carefully concealed cushion to take their weight but still uncomfortable enough, and there were others with iron skewers through their tongues. These were the side-shows, together with the children six or seven years old, who had been skilfully made up as sadhus by their proprietors in little lean-to sheds which had been set up against the wall of the Fort for this purpose. They sat, cross-legged, plastered with mud and ashes, eyes downcast, garlanded with flowers, sadly ringing their little silver bells. This was a world with its strange constructions, barrels on the end of long poles, tented encampments and limbless creatures such as both Breughel and Hieronymus Bosch knew, and one that they would have understood.

But the ghats and the city above it, however many temples it contained, were nothing but a backdrop to the enactment of a ritual, incessantly performed, that was as natural and as necessary as the air they breathed and the water itself to the participants, but in which one could have no real part. However well-intentioned he might be, and however anxious to participate, for a European to bathe in the Ganges at Banaras was simply for him to have a bath. It was as if a Hindu, having attended a Mass out of curiosity, decided to take Communion; and although it undoubtedly had the capacity to engulf sin, the river did not here have the icy clarity that it had at Hardwar or the sheer volume that it had at the Sangam at Allahabad, or that rare beauty that it had on the lonely reaches of the river that had made it irresistible even to the uninitiated.

For initiation was difficult. There was no joining Hinduism in the sense that you could become a Roman Catholic with your name on a list somewhere, for there was nothing to join. No one ever suggested to another that he should become a Hindu.

Nor was it enough to read the books. So I had found for myself in the last cold winter of the war, inspired by a low diet and rash doses of Boehm and Eckhart, thinking myself on the way to becoming a mystic. It had been like trying to enter a theatre by the exit.

For us, the best time at Banaras was at dusk, in the labyrinthine alleys behind the ghats before the lights were lit. At this hour there were few people about and those who seemed unnaturally subdued. Even the small boys who make life hideous during the day with their ''ullos' and 'very well thank you's' had either departed to the land of nod or sat, drained of energy, at the doors of their houses.

Down these alleys, many of which ended in a heap of rubble where some buildings on the river front had collapsed, the darkness came while the sky overhead was still blue; but already the pigeons had ceased to wheel about the spire of the last of Aurangzeb's minarets and the kite-fliers had hauled down their kites. Soon the sky faded and the long, pink, streamers left over from the sunset stretched across it.

Now the walls began to exude a dampness and the smells of sewage as it trickled down between the houses to the river became more pronounced. Here, smelling these smells, it was not difficult to believe that this was part of Banaras, itself the city with a higher rate of infant and adult mortality than any other town or city in Uttar Pradesh, with the highest mortality of all; but it was worth being there if only for the anonymity conferred by the partial darkness.

The only commerce at this hour was small wayside stalls where old women bent over their scales weighing out infinitesimal quantities of herbs for equally old and shrivvelled customers. In the shops of the charcoal vendors the merchants and the men who carried the charcoal for them were as black as the pits in which they stood waiting for customers. These and the scarcely human figures of the women who still continued to plaster the walls with freshly kneaded cakes of dung were the only ones to be seen. Everyone else had withdrawn to eat the evening meal leaving the rooms on the ground floor unlit.

But what it lacked in people was more than made up by the cows. They were everywhere, and the ground underfoot was slippery with their excrement. They were in the forecourts of the temples. They were tethered in the yards of the houses. They were free, lurching up gradients, and floating down the alleys as if they were levitated; or they suddenly loomed up like great, ghostly ships running under a press of sail with the vapour coming from their nostrils in the chill evening air as if it was cannon smoke. They never hesitated. They simply sailed serenely on, and it was for us to get out of the way or be crushed against the walls. They were the chosen animals and they knew it.* They would never die a violent death, only more horribly, of old age, disease or malnutrition.

Now from the river came the sounds of the beating of gongs, the ringing of hand-bells struck with hammers and the rattling of a gourd-like instrument with some hard round object inside it. This was the committee of the Ganga Sava performing, as it did every night, at dusk, the Arti Puja offering the light of a five-branched candelabra to the river together with flour, milk and sweetmeats.

* It is quite common for Brahmans to leave their all for the endowment of homes for aged cows.

Further westward in the shopping lanes the lights were already lit:
in Kachauri Gali where they sold Mukhbilash, betel nut dipped in silver;
Esha Gol ka Bhusi – flaky crisp crimson stuff derived from the betel;
Pulfgllifhiria, tobacco dipped in silver; Kashria Supan, betel with saffron,
and Pan Khapa, all in round embossed tin boxes. They were lit in Vish-
wanath Lane, on the way to the temple where they sold religious objects:
tilak powder, lingams, conch shells, incense, lat-i-dana, the white sweets
used as offerings, Brahmanical cords, sandalwood and in shops selling
more profane articles – false hair, stuff for reddening the soles of the feet,
sweet-smelling oils, little packets of scented powders called chinasin-
door, small, jewelled beauty spots made of plastic, erotic scents and
scents so heavy they could only act as a tranquillizer, palankeens for wed-
dings, little lacquered figures of highland soldiers with blue and white
spotted bagpipes, gods, musicians and pop-eyed servants carrying plates
of fried eggs. The lights had come on too in Kunj Gali where the silk
shops were; in the Thatheri Bazaar where they sold hideous brass and
copper objects and in the Narial Bazaar they were beginning to glow
behind the curtains on the balconies of the brothels on the upper floors.

The peak time for bathing was between nine and one o'clock. By good
fortune we met Bag Nath and Hira Lal, our boatmen, who had taken
us down the river from Allahabad to Mirzapur. They insisted on taking
us out to the Sangam in their boat. They said it had taken them eight
days to tow it up from Mirzapur.

We bathed at the confluence where the long curving line of bathing
platforms and boats reached out across the Jumna and the Ganges ripped
across it.

It was one o'clock and the water was warm. Out in the stream
dolphins came to the surface, sighing like steam engines. This was the
meeting-place not only of the three rivers but of all humanity. All,
together with the lepers, submerging and coming up spluttering, for
this was the water that washed all sin away.

The Maharaja of Banaras went up the Jumna in his processional barge
with a heavy bodyguard of policemen in rowing boats. Long lines of
pilgrims were leaving now by boat or walking slowly up the bank of
the Jumna, under the walls of the Fort. The sun broke through the
clouds and the banners streamed against the sun.

## ARRIVAL AT CALCUTTA

The river was now more than three-quarters of a mile wide; and it looked big. The ebb was beginning now and it took us down close under the left bank, past decrepit nineteenth-century buildings in the district of Alambazar, some of which would have looked equally at home on the shores of Limehouse Reach or in old Portsmouth. The weed-covered steps that led down from them to the river were flanked by broken pillars, and up on the shore, in what had once been the riverside gardens, lay the skeletons of abandoned boats; while in the filthy water below the bank, among rotting piles with grass growing from their tops, an occasional solitary man or woman bathed, dressed in rags which might once have been white, but which were now the same uniform brown as the river itself.

We drifted down past these poor derelicts and past drab temples made of cement, and past inhuman-looking factories and rank neglected wastelands in which not even weeds flourished and past jetties and outfalls from which noxious effluents which were the colour of mulligatawny soup poured into the river.

The river was full of boats. Panswais far bigger than ours, and with far more energetic crews than our own, were being propelled upstream by six oarsmen, three on either side, who were plugging away standing up.

There were bigger boats called oolaks, with huge superstructures and balconies on their counters, which were havering about in the river with their single square sails empty of wind, slowly drifting down on the ebb which was beginning to run more strongly now. There were slabsided wooden lighters, loaded to the gunwales with sacks of sugar which were being guided rather than propelled by men wielding sweeps. There were huge rafts of bamboos which themselves constituted the cargo, floating down with raftsmen on board who were running from side to side, steering them with long poles. There were cargo flats built of steel, that were more than two hundred feet long, being hurried down river by tugs with yellow funnels. These great vessels with their corrugated iron roofs, each of which could carry seven hundred tons of cargo, were like floating dock sheds. Equally strange were the barges all going down on the ebb, piled thirty feet above the water with hay and straw which were like floating ricks. There were little fishing boats with ends that were so sharply upturned that only about a third of their total length appeared to rest on the water which was full of cabbage leaves, ashes, the heads of marigolds and little mud-coloured balls of jute, which had been thrown into it from the mills along the shore.

We came into the last big bend before the city. To the left there was a big power-station on the shore which dwarfed everything. Bamboo poles were planted in the river, and the ebb pulled at their tops which were pointing upstream. Here the wind came up, and the panswai went tearing away over towards the inside of the bend on the right bank.

The right bank was a weird, surrealistic place. Grass-grown jetties on the point of collapse projected into the stream; boats with broken backs lay half-submerged in the mud in forgotten creeks, on the shores of which engine houses stood roofless, open to the sky. What had been fine houses when they were built a hundred and fifty or more years ago were now either tenements, their façades obscured by lean-to sheds, or else completely abandoned and with pipal trees growing out of them and breaking them apart. There were endless boatyards where they were riveting the hulls of lighters which were supported above the foreshore on little piles of stones which were slipped in on the falling tide, and there were older yards where they were building wooden country boats, the ribs of which were golden in the sun. There were melancholy brickfields and places where the embankments were slipping slowly but surely into the river, and there were abandoned Victorian factories which had chimneys with cast-iron railings round the top of them, from which long green grass was sprouting; and then suddenly there was the great skeleton of the Howrah Bridge, rising out of the haze ahead.

Now the wind freshened still more and we raced down towards it, past the municipal burning ghats on the left bank in a river that seemed to be full of floating haystacks, all going down under sail towards the bridge which loomed three hundred feet above us, immense, silver and exciting, glittering in the sun. From it came the roar of traffic, the hooting of motor horns, the ringing of innumerable bicycle bells, outlandish cries and murmuring sounds like a swarm of bees, made by the thousands of people who thronged the footways, and from down-stream the sounds of the ships' sirens came booming up towards us. This was the East as Conrad saw it; the one which hooked many a young Englishman and made him an expatriate, fed-up and far from home.

We were through the bridge now and the captain was steering the boat in towards the left bank, happily anticipating an orgy of dispu-tation. At twelve-forty-five we grounded some way off shore in the mud by the Armenian Ghat. We had made it.

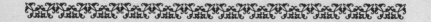

# Around the Mediterranean

## AN EVENING IN VENICE

IN THE WINTER of 1983, in the early stages of a journey round the shores of the Mediterranean, we arrived in Venice, en route to Montenegro, to find the city swathed in fog.

Long before we stepped ashore from the steamer on to Riva degli Schiavoni, the great expanse of marble quay off which Slavs from the Dalmatian coast used to moor their vessels in St Mark's Basin, darkness had added itself to the fog, creating the sort of conditions that even Jack the Ripper would have found a bit thick for his work down in nineteenth-century Whitechapel.

The fog dissipated what had seemed a romantic possibility when we left Chioggia but now seemed a crazy dream, that we might sweep into Venice from the Lido on the No. 11 steamer up the Canale di San Marco and see the domes and campanili of San Giorgio Maggiore and Santa Maria della Salute not as we had seen them once, coming in from the sea in the heat of the day, liquefying in the mirage, then reconstituting themselves again, something that would be impossible at this season, but sharply silhouetted, appearing larger than life, against the afterglow of what could equally well be a winter or summer sunset, with what would be equally black gondolas bobbing on the wine-coloured waters in the foreground. This was a spectacle we had enjoyed often, usually in summer, coming back after a long afternoon by the lifeless waters of the Lido with sand between our toes and stupefied with sun, our only preoccupation whether we would be able to extract enough hot water from the erratic hot water system in our equally decrepit hotel to allow us to share a shallow bath; and whether we could find another place to eat, in addition to the few we already knew, which was not infested with, although we hated to admit it, people like ourselves, fellow visitors to Venice who on any day in the high season, July and August, probably outnumber the inhabitants.

Never at the best of times a very substantial-looking city – even the largest buildings having something impermanent about them, due perhaps to the fact that they have not only risen from the water but, however imperceptibly to the human eye, are now in the process of sinking back into it – on this particular evening the fog had succeeded in doing what the mirage could only accomplish for a matter of moments – caused it, apart from its lights, to disappear from view almost completely.

Disembarking from the steamer, we turned left on Riva degli Schiavoni, passing the entrances to the narrow *calli* which lead off from it, Calle delle Rasse, where the Serbian material used for furnishing the interiors of the *felzi*, the now largely extinct cabins of the closed gondolas, used to be sold, and Calle Albanesi, the Street of the Albanians, down which some of our fellow passengers had already vanished. While walking along the Riva we just missed falling into what is, because it is spanned by the Bridge of Sighs, the best known and most photographed canal in Venice after the Grand Canal, the Rio Palazzo. This would have been a bore because besides contracting pneumonia (our luggage was already at the railway station), if we had inadvertently drunk any of it we would have had to rush off to the Ospedale Civile, San Giovanni e Paolo, in order to have pumped out of us a mixture the smallest ingredient of which was water. Then we crossed the Rio by the Ponte di Paglia, passing on our right hand the Palazzo delle Prigioni, from which the magistrates known as the *Signori di Notte al Criminale* used to look out at night for evil-doers, *malviventi*, arrest and try them, and if they were sufficiently low and common and criminal, sentence them to the *Pozzi*, otherwise the Wells, the cells at the lowest level of the *Prigioni*, which were reserved for the worst sort of common criminals.

On along the Molo, the furthest point pirates ever reached when attacking Venice, back in the ninth century when it was young, past the forest of piles where the gondolas were moored, now, in this weather, all covered with tarpaulins, as they would be in the Bacino Orseolo, the basin behind the Piazza San Marco where there is another big fleet of them moored. For no one on a day like this would have used a gondola, unless they were *sposi*, newly married, or were dead and being conveyed in a funeral gondola to Isola San Michele from one of the undertakers' establishments on the Fondamenta Nuove. In fact, today, scarcely anyone goes to the cemetery in one of the old funeral gondolas, which were picturesquely decorated with a pair of St Mark's lions in polished brass; now the undertakers' boats are almost all big, powered vessels.

Then we turned right into Piazzetta San Marco, with the Palazzo Ducale on one hand and the Mint and the Library designed by Jacopo Sansovino on the other, passing between the feet of the two immense grey and red granite columns that someone had brought here from Syria or Constantinople. Somewhere overhead, invisible in the fog, the grey column supported the bronze lion, really a chimera, a fire-breathing monster with the head of a lion, the body of a goat and the tail of a serpent, whether Etruscan, Persian or Chinese no one really knows, to which some inspired innovator has added wings.

All that was visible of this wonder of the world on this particular night in January were the enfilades of lights which hang in elegant glass globes under the arches of the long arcades of the *procuratie*, once the offices and residences of the Procurators of Venice, who were the most important dignitaries after the Doge, vanishing away into the fog towards the far western end of the Piazza where the wing known as the Ala Napoleonica, built to replace a church torn down by his orders, was completely invisible. Beneath the arcades there were some amorphous, will-o'-the-wispish smudges of light, which emanated from the windows of expensive shops and cafés. There were also some blurs of light from the elegant lamp standards in the Piazzetta di San Marco, where the fog was even thicker. All that could be seen of the Basilica were the outlines of a couple of bronze doors, one of them sixth-century Byzantine work: nothing at all of the great quadriga of bronze horses overhead in front of the magnificent west window, copies of those looted from the Hippodrome at Constantinople by Doge Dandolo after he had taken the city, plunging ever onwards, stripped of their bridles by the Venetians as a symbol of liberty, on their endless journey from their first known setting-off place, the Island of Chios, through what were now the ruins of the world in which they had been created.

Now the giants on top of the Torre dell'Orologio began banging away with their hammers on the big bell, as they had done ever since they were cast by a man named Ambrosio dalle Anchore in 1494, some 489 years ago, the year Columbus discovered Jamaica, a slice of the action the Venetians would like to have been in on, the year Savonarola restored popular government in Florence, something they themselves were already badly in need of. They made things to last in those days. No question of replacing the unit if something went wrong.

It was five o'clock. Soon, if it was not raining, or snowing, or there was no *acqua alta* to turn it into a paddling pool, and there was none of this damn fog, the better-off inhabitants, those who wanted to be thought better-off and those who really were badly-off but looked almost as well-dressed as the rest, which is what you aim at if you are a Venetian, having changed out of their working clothes would begin that ritual of the Christian Mediterranean lands, something that you will not see in a devout, Muslim one, the *passeggiata*, the evening prom- enade, in Piazza San Marco and in the Piazzetta, in pairs and groups, young and old, the old usually in pairs, the young ones often giving up promenading after a bit and congregating on the shallow steps that lead up from the Piazza into the arcades, the ones that in summer have long drapes hanging in them to keep off the sun, which gives them a dim, pleasantly mysterious air. So the Venetians add themselves to the visitors who swarm in the Piazza at every season of the year, costing one another's clothes, casting beady, impassive eyes on the often unsuit- able clothes of the visitors, as their predecessors must have done on various stray Lombards and other barbarians down on a visit, and on the uncouth Slavs and Albanians who came ashore at the Riva degli Schiavoni. Those on whom they had not looked so impassively had been the Austrians who filled the Piazza in the years between 1815 and 1866, the period when, apart from a few months of brave but abortive revolution in the winter of 1848–49, the Venetian States were under the domination of Austria, to whom they had originally been sold by Napoleon in 1797. (He got them back again in 1805, only to lose them when Austria received them yet again at the Congress of Vienna, a couple of months before Waterloo.) In those years the Austrian flag flew in the Piazza in place of what had been that of the Republic of St Mark, an Austrian band played, which it is said no true Venetians

opened their ears to, let alone applauded, and one of the two fashionable
cafés that still face one another across its width, the one which was
frequented by Austrians, was left to them.

Meanwhile other, less elegant but equally ritualistic *passeggiate* would
be taking place in the principal *calli*, *campi* and *salizzadi*, in other parts
of the city, and there the younger ones would probably flock to some
monument and drape themselves around the base of it. There would
also be crowds in the Merceria dell'Orologio, *merceria* being a haber-
dashery, which is still, as it always was, filled with rich stuffs which
the Veneziani love, a narrow street which leads from the clock tower
into Merceria di San Giuliano and from that into Merceria di San Salva-
tore, once the shortest route from San Marco to the other most important centre of the city, the Rialto. This was the way the Procurators
and other important officials used to follow on their way in procession
to enter the Basilica, and the one followed by persons on their way
from the Rialto to be publicly flogged.

Then, quite suddenly, after an hour or so, except at weekends or
on days of festa, old and young suddenly disappear indoors, many of
them having to get up what is in winter horribly early in order to
get to work on the terra firma, leaving the Piazza and other places of
*passeggio* to visitors and to those making a living by catering to
their needs.

Tonight the *passeggiata* was definitely off. The pigeons had long since
given up and gone to bed – that is if they had ever bothered to get up
in the first place, and the only other people on view were a few dark
figures with mufflers wrapped round their mouths, hurrying presumably homewards, some of them coughing as they went. The only
people, besides ourselves, who were not on the move were a lunatic
who was sitting at the feet of the Campanile gabbling away happily to
himself, and a pretty young girl, dressed in a smart, bright red skiing
outfit, to which even the Venetians could not have taken exception,
and those après-ski boots with the hair on the outside, that make the
occupants look as if they have forgotten to shave their legs. She was
leaning against a pile of the duckboards the municipality puts down in
various parts of the city when an *acqua alta* is expected, listening in on
her earphones and reading *Fodor's Guide* with the aid of a pocket torch.

'Hi!' she said, removing her earphones and switching off, at the same time displaying a mouthful of pearly white teeth that had not been near a capper's. 'Would you mind repeating that? I didn't get it.'

'We said, "Good evening, it's a rotten night."'

'Yes, it certainly is a lousy night. This is my first time in Venice. What an introductory offer! My sister and I came down this afternoon from Cortina. The son of the guy who runs our hotel there gave us a lift but once we got out of the mountains we couldn't see a thing, not even Treviso. It was like being out in the boondocks. It's brilliant in Cortina. My sister's back where we're staying, not feeling so good. I guess we should have checked out on the weather. We've got to go back tomorrow. Maybe it'll be better tomorrow. I haven't even seen a gondola yet.'

'There are some over there,' I said, 'moored by the Molo. But you have to watch your step. We nearly fell in.'

'I'll check on the gondolas on the way back to the hotel,' she said. 'I was just boning up on the Piazza San Marco, about it being beautiful at all times of day and night and all seasons of the year, one of the only great squares which retains a feeling of animation when there are very few people in it. Personally, I don't think this Fodor person was ever here in a fog. He says bring plenty of colour films. What a laugh! Personally, I think it's kinda spooky, what with that poor old guy over there hollering away to himself and that bell going on all the time out on the water. Why, it wouldn't surprise me if we saw some old Doge.'


## IN AND OUT OF A PYRAMID

Although not technically speaking on the Mediterranean, the Pyramids are not objects to which travellers around its shores are likely to give a miss: and we were no exceptions.

As no one at the El Nil Hotel, one of the less expensive caravanserais, seemed to have any idea what time rosy-fingered dawn occurs over Cairo in mid-January, we settled for a 4.45 a.m. departure to get us to the Pyramids in time to witness it.

At 4.15 a.m., rather like a *corps-de-ballet* all taking off on the same foot, everything began to happen at once. The alarm clock went off. The telephone waking system jangled into action, operated by the night porter who a few seconds later – we were five floors up – was thundering on the door with what sounded like an obsidian sledgehammer, announcing, 'Your limousine, Mister!' I opened it a couple of inches to tell him that we had got his message and would he kindly desist, and a chambermaid the shape of a scarab beetle slipped in through this chink and began dusting my hat. She was followed by three humble but dogged-looking men, the sort I imagined who had been forced to build the Pyramids. They began shutting our bags, apparently under the impression that we had already had enough of Cairo and were on our way to the exit, although we had not checked in until midnight, having come straight from a party that was probably still going on. In the face of all this, still dressed in pyjamas, I felt my reason going.

'*Ma fish bakshish.*' ('There is no baksheesh.') 'Try again Monday,' I said, the last bit in English, when we were finally ready to go.

'*Mas es-Salama!*' 'Go with safety,' they said, hoping that I would be preserved that long, raising some sickly grins.

Take plenty of baksheesh, ladies and gentlemen, when visiting Egypt under your own steam, unprotected by couriers. Wonderful how it softens the hardest Muslim or Coptic heart, better than any nutcrackers. And do not begrudge it; most people, even those quite far up the social scale, are poorer than it is possible for most of us to imagine.

Then in the limousine, an immense, black, air-conditioned Mercedes, we howled up the road to the Pyramids, the six-mile-long, dead straight Shari el-Ahram, built by the Khedive Ismail for the visit of the Empress Eugénie of France on the occasion of the opening of the Suez Canal in 1869. Then, having traversed it at more than a mile a minute, we climbed on to the escarpment on which the Pyramids would have long since been descried if it hadn't still been pitch black night with a sandstorm in progress.

After a bit we stopped and the driver, a distinguished-looking Egyptian of fifty-odd on whom constant intercourse with the limousine-using classes had conferred the manners of a Firbankean cardinal, assisted us out of the vehicle by the elbows as if we were antiques.

'Good place, Sir,' he said.

'Good place for what?' Apart from a small segment of flying sand,

In Venice in winter you can often
hear more than you can see of it: the
melancholy crying of gulls, the tolling
of a bell on a buoy moored out in
one of the channels and, occasionally,
angry cries as helmsmen set on
collision courses record near misses.

Giza: encampment of the Nagamas below the Great Pyramid. They specialize in giving visitors camel rides and driving them round the bend with their attentions. Some people, myself included, believe that the Nagamas commissioned the building of the Pyramids as a tourist attraction. While resting from their labours they feed their camels bright green foliage.

*Above:* Cairo.

*Right:* Inhabitants of one of the labyrinthine cities of the dead now occupied by the very poor.

*Left:* The trouble with Irish roads is that they begin at a cross miles from anywhere and end up at a similar one – neither of them furnished with signposts.

*Opposite below and below:* Two views of the great annual horse fair at Spancil Hill, County Clare.

Wanda – done in, in Ireland

illuminated by the headlights, one could see nothing. The only thing it seemed adapted for was a witches' coven.

'Good place for seeing Pyramids,' he said, gently, as if humouring a couple of loonies, which I suppose, thinking about it in retrospect, was what we were. 'From up there,' pointing into the murk. 'Up there, where there are weruins, broken buildings in the desert, Sir.'

'Is it safe?' I asked. 'I mean for my wife and I to be here alone? It's horribly dark.'

'Safe, Sir, safe? What is safe?'

'I mean are there any bad people?'

'No bad peoples, all good peoples here,' he said, raising his hands in an expansive gesture, as if embracing the teeming inhabitants of the Valley and all those scattered over the three million-square-mile expanse of the Sahara Desert, then dropping them and entering his vehicle.

'Here, I say,' I said, genuinely alarmed at the thought of being left alone in such a spot. 'What time's dawn, actually?'

'Dawn, Sir, actually? About dawn, Sir, actually, I do not know. Will that be all, Sir? Thank *you*, Sir, Madam!' receiving from me a generous helping of closely folded baksheesh which a lifetime of experience told him was an ample sufficiency without actually counting it. And he drove away.

It was now 5.15 a.m. and bloody cold with the wind that was raising the sand around us coming off the snowbound High Atlas in Morocco, 2500 miles to the west, with nothing in between to slow it down as it droned over the debased 'weruins' up to which we climbed. Underfoot they felt like what they were (I had forgotten to bring a torch), a bulldozed brick barrack block with sheaves of those metal rods that are used to keep reinforced concrete together protruding from them, and lots of broken glass, all of which made it impossible to walk or even run about in order to keep warm. We tried running on the spot but it was exhausting. Then we tried slapping one another, but I did it too hard and we had a row.

Then, around 6.15 a.m., the terrible wind suddenly ceased, as if whoever was in charge had switched it off at the main, the sand fell back to earth where it belonged, the sky over the Gulf of Suez and Sinai turned an improbable shade of mauve, overhead the morning star shone down brilliantly out of a sky that had suddenly become deep indigo, and the Pyramids of Giza – two huge ones, of King Cheops and King Chephren, a lesser one of King Mykerinos and three little ones, one behind the other – appeared to rise up out of the ground with the rapidity of mushrooms in a slow-motion film, the only Wonders of the Seven Wonders of the ancient world – first designated by Antipater of Sidon in the second century BC, six of which were on the shores of the Mediterranean (the other, which was not, was the Hanging Gardens of Babylon) – to survive more or less intact.

And now, across the mist-filled Valley of the Nile, the sun came roaring up from behind a black rampart of cloud that was resting on top of the escarpment of the Mukattam Hills, turning what is a seven-hundred-foot limestone escarpment into what looked like a colossal mountain range. It shone palely at first on the southern faces of the three big Pyramids, but diagonally so that the countless thousands or millions of stones that composed them stood out in such a way that each individual one was distinct from its immediate neighbour and one had the crazy feeling that with enough patience one could have counted them.

As the sun rose it shone down into the thick white mist that filled the valley and illuminated the tops of what must have been some immensely tall palm trees which rose up through it, producing an unearthly effect, as it would be, I imagined, to look across the Styx.

It also illuminated the hideous 'weruins' in which we were imbrangled, and for a few moments it filled the whole of this vast landscape, in which, apart from ourselves, there was not a living thing to be seen, with a vinous, purply light. Then everything turned suddenly golden. It was like the springtime of the world and we set off downhill into the eye of this golden orb for what must be, for no one has so far come up with a scheme to make you pay for looking at them, the greatest free show on earth.

Then, just as the Pyramids had seemed to rise out of the earth, so when we were at last among them, did a picturesque, elderly, shifty-looking Beduin, mounted on a camel and with a donkey in tow, close in to the Pyramid of Chephren. Perhaps he had spent the night in one of the innumerable, lesser tombs with which the plateau is riddled.

'Good morning, King Solomon,' he said, dismounting from the camel which made a noise like a punctured airbed as it sank down, 'I kiss your hand,' seizing it and doing so before I could stop him. 'Good morning, Queen of Sheba, I kiss your hand also.'

'Oh no you jolly well don't!' said the newly-elevated Queen, dexterously avoiding this attention. 'You kiss your own.'

To tell the truth, he was a distinctly smelly old Beduin. If he had come out of a IVth Dynasty rock tomb then he needed a re-embalming service. He was a Nagama, one of a highly sophisticated tribe of Beduin who for uncountable centuries (they may have commissioned the Pyramids as a tourist attraction) have descended like swarms of gad-flies on visitors in order to suck them dry of life-giving baksheesh, in return offering their victims camel, horse and donkey rides and, until recently, when some kill-joy forbade the practice, assisting them up the outside of the Great Pyramid, at the same time contriving to manoeuvre female ones wearing skirts into positions of peculiar indelicacy, not all of them fortuitous.

Now he offered us a selection of these various services, including the opportunity to take his photograph in one of the stylized poses the Nagamas permit themselves in this traffic with the infidel. To all of which, not wishing to hurt his feelings but enjoying being called 'King Solomon' as much as I enjoy being addressed as 'Squire' by London taximen, I replied, 'Later, later!'

'Laters, laters! See you laters, alligators! In a whiles, crocodiles!' said the Son of the Desert, getting the message finally that we were a no-show, fishing a transistor designed to look like a military transmitter out of his saddle bag, plugging in to Radio Cairo and departing in a blast of harem music round the south-west corner of the Pyramid of Chephren, which was now the colour of Kerrygold butter but with added colouring, with his donkey in tow.

Close in under the cold, sunless north face of the Great Pyramid, looking up its fifty-one degree slope to a summit eighty-five feet higher than the cross on top of St Paul's, I had the impression that a petrified seventh wave to overtop all seventh waves was about to fall on us and rub us out. Outside the original entrance and another forced entry made by the Caliph al-Mamun in AD 820, which made it look as if it had been gnawed by giant mice, there were two notices: NO SMOKING

IN THE PYRAMID and NO CLIMBING THE PYRAMID. Across the way from these holes in the Pyramid two young Japanese, a man and a pretty girl, and an elderly American couple were hovering indecisively outside an office advertising trips to the interior at £2 ($2.80) a head. '*O-nayo-gozaimasu!*' the Japanese said, bowing as if welcoming us to a tea ceremony, baring what looked like a couple of upper and lower sets of silicon chips.

'They don't open till ten,' said the American gentleman whose name, he told us, was Henry Haythorn. 'Can you beat it? Rosie and I got up specially to be here before the coaches. I guess now we'd better go on back down to the Mena House, grab breakfast and come back up again.'

Guarding the entrance to the still-locked interior was a Tourist Policeman, member of an admirable force specially recruited to protect visitors to Egypt from being defrauded and other forms of molestation.

'Gom on,' said this resourceful representative of law and order. 'No need of a ticket. You go now. Many peoples later. Give me one half pound each. Gom on!'

Inside, the Pyramid was surprisingly hot. The smell was not what we had steeled ourselves to support, what someone had described as being like the inside of a public telephone box. Instead it was the stench of the deodorants with which mad humanity now sprays its nooks and crannies in order to suppress more natural, feral odours. The going was hard. Anything that isn't horizontal in the Pyramid has a gradient of twenty-five degrees, one in two, and I was carrying a suitcase which contained cameras, quantities of baksheesh, passports and some great tomes about pyramids, everything I felt we might need in a pyramid and which I was reluctant to entrust to a policeman, even a Tourist Policeman, as I had no key with which to lock it.

'The Great Pyramid of Gizah,' Davidson* wrote, 'is a building well and truly laid, perfect in its orientation, and built within five points symbolising the five points of the fulness of the stature of Christ . . . four define the corners of the base square – symbolising the foundation of Apostles and Prophets – the fifth point the Apex of the Pyramid

---

* David Davidson was the author of an enormous book *The Great Pyramid: Its Divine Message* (London, 1932).

. . . the Headstone and Chief Corner Stone, Jesus himself as the Head of the Body; the Stone rejected by the Builders.'

Because we had entered the Pyramid by al-Mamun's forced entrance we had failed to travel down the Descending Passage as far as the First Ascending Passage, a stretch which for Davidson symbolized 'The Period of Initiation into the Elements of the Mysteries of the Universe in a Spiritually Degenerate Age, from the time of the Pyramid's construction to the time of the Exodus of Israel', which he dated 2625 to 1486 BC. By doing so we had avoided one of the worst fates in Davidson's Pyramid Game, which was getting into the dead-end of the Descending Passage. This passage began below the First Ascending Passage and, once into it, any member of the human race descended irrevocably towards Ignorance and Evil. We had missed it because al-Mamun's forced entrance had carried us across the Entrance Passage on what was the equivalent of a spiritual fly-over.

However, by missing the way down to Eternal Damnation, we had also missed the entrance to the First Ascending Passage which begins at the date of the Exodus, 1486 BC, ends at the Crucifixion and is symbolized by the granite plug which blocks its lower end, 'sealing up all the Treasures of Light, Wisdom and Understanding'. It was also the 'Hall of Truth in Darkness' up which 'Nation Israel progressed under the Yoke of the Law towards the True Light, the coming of which was to lighten the Darkness of the World'.

There was no doubt about the fate of those who rejected the Messiah. It was awful. Borne swiftly along the horizontal passage leading off from the top of the Hall of Truth in Darkness, symbolizing 'The Epoch of Spiritual Rebirth', they found themselves in the Queen's Chamber, otherwise the 'Chamber of Jewish Destiny' and, the way Davidson interpreted it, a spiritual dead-end.

But by now we were no longer engaged in what had been beginning to resemble a game of snakes and ladders, with rules invented by Davidson, played out on an evolutionary, spiritual plane. Instead we were plodding on foot what seemed interminably upwards in al-Mamun's most awesome discovery, the Great Gallery, which leads into the heart of the Pyramid. Nearly thirty feet high, a hundred and sixty feet long, its walls of polished granite seven feet apart at their widest point but diminishing in width towards the ceiling, and so finely jointed that it is impossible to insinuate a hair between them, it is a place of nightmare.

It was also Davidson's 'Hall of Truth', a direct route, symbolizing the Christian Dispensation, up which we were climbing at the rate of one pyramid-inch a year, with no chance of taking a wrong turning, from the Crucifixion (7 April AD 30 according to the Old Style, Julian Calendar), to the first day of the Great War (4–5 August 1914, according to the Gregorian, new one). It was rather like being on a moving staircase in a chic department store which normally takes you to the restaurant on the roof without stop-offs but has ceased to function so that you have to foot it.

At the top, having hauled ourselves over a monolith known as the Great Step, which symbolizes 'The Great Epoch of Science for the Consummation of the Age', we passed, bent double, through 'The First Passage of Tribulation' which led from 4 August 1914 to 11 November 1918. From there, after the Armistice, we successfully negotiated 'The Chamber of the Triple Veil' which would have been a continuous period of woe and tribulation, lasting until 1936, if Divine Intervention had not shortened it so that it ended 29 May 1928.

With the goal almost in sight we passed through 'The Passage of Final Tribulation', which extended from 1928 to 1936 – a period (was it a coincidence?) that almost entirely covered my schooldays – after which came the end of all toil and pain and the end of human chronology in 'The Chamber of the Mystery of the Open Tomb', better known as 'The King's Chamber' to non-pyramidologists.

It was a tense moment, the one before entering it. In theory it should have disappeared on the night of 15–16 September 1936, and everything else with it, but it was still there, an astonishing construction at the heart of an edifice in which the epithet loses force from sheer over-use.

In it is what archaeologists believe to be the empty, lidless tomb chest of King Cheops, cut from granite so hard that saws nine feet long with jewelled teeth and drills tipped with diamonds or corundum had to be used to cut it and hollow it out; what some pyramidologists believe to be a symbol of the Resurrection in a chamber in which 'The Cleansing of the Nations in the Presence of the Master of Death and the Grave' should have taken place back in 1936, a happening I would have dearly liked to witness from a safe distance, and judging by the smell inside it something of which they still stood in need. Others believe that it embodies a standard of cubic measure left for posterity to do what it will with.

And above this chamber, which is entirely sheathed in polished granite, unvisitable, are five more chambers, one above the other, with floors and ceilings each composed of forty-three granite monoliths and two enormous limestone ones at the very top, each of the granite ones – many of them badly cracked by an earthquake thought to have taken place soon after the presumed burial of the King – weighing between forty and seventy tons. Here, 300 feet or so below the apex of the Pyramid, 200 feet from the nearest open air (the King's Chamber is connected with the outside by two long ducts), and with the ever-present possibility that another earth tremor might bring down something like 4000 tons of assorted limestone and granite monoliths on our heads, I felt as if I was already buried alive.

There was a sudden flash, brighter than a thousand suns as it bounced off the polished walls, caused by the Japanese gentleman letting off a fully thyristorized, dedicated AF 200-type flash on top of a Pentax fitted with a lens that seemed more suitable for photographing what lay on the floor at our feet than the actual chamber. Perhaps this was what he was photographing, this unsuitable human offering on the floor.

'Holy hat!' said a fine hard voice that I recognized as that of Rosie, the Girl from the Middle West. 'Who in hell laid that? Don't say it was the cop. They got a sign outside, "No Smoking". What they want's one saying, "No Crapping".'

## VIEW FROM A HILL – FEZ

Of all the Muslim cities on the Mediterranean littoral none is more intricate and virtually unknowable by foreigners than Fez. It is not the *muezzins*, the regular summoners to prayer, who are the first to sound reveille in Fès el-Bali, Old Fez, which they do with such notable effect at the first intimation of light in the east. Long before there is any suggestion that the *fejer*, the dawn, is on the way, back in the middle watches of the night, the Companions of the Sick, ten devout Muslims chosen, like the *muezzins*, for their voices and provided for by a bequest made long ago by one who was himself sick and required moral sustenance in the night, begin their weird and hauntingly beautiful chanting, changing over throughout the night at half-hourly intervals. Failing this, half an hour before the dawn, there is the *ábad*, the thrice-repeated cry of praise to God which begins, 'the Perfection of God, existing for ever and ever'.

Eventually, after what seems an age and the *ábad* has been repeated for the second time, first light seeps into the world away to the east over the northern outliers of the Middle Atlas, and the *muezzins* go into action from the minarets, the only really tall edifices in a city in which there appear to be no buildings of European inspiration at all (apart perhaps from some now long-disused foreign consulates), announcing that 'Night has Departed . . . Day Approaches with Light and Brightness . . . Prayer is Better than Sleep . . . Arise And to God Be Praise!' The whole cry is repeated in its entirety four times, once to each cardinal point of the compass, in parts twice.

And now the Old City is revealed behind its crenellated, turreted walls. It is a city set in a valley, an amphitheatre or an open shell, tilted so that its western end is higher than its eastern and its northern end higher than its southern, with a river and other streams, most of them invisible until you actually stand on their banks or fall into them. All of these streams run down from the plateau up at the western end on which New Fez, Fès el-Jedid, which is not new at all, was founded in 1276.

The walls of Old Fez, thirty or forty feet high, twelve or thirteen feet thick at the base, are made of *tabia*, clay mixed with chalk and cement which sets rock-hard, and their angles are reinforced with masonry. They were built by Christian slaves for their masters, the Almohads, in the twelfth century. Many more centuries were to pass before there was any pressing need to import Negroes as slaves, to supplement what seems to have been an unending supply of Christian captives taken by Barbary corsairs or in battle – who, when they breathed their last, usually from over-work, were often added to the mixture to give it more body.

A completely Muslim city, one of the most revered in the Muslim world. We are looking at it from out beyond the northern walls up on the hill called el Kolla among the tombs of the nomad, Berber Merinid sultans and others.

In a few minutes the sun comes racing up behind the tall, modern houses perched on an escarpment above the lower, eastern end of the amphitheatre in which the city stands and floods it with brilliant light, at first honey-coloured, then golden, transforming houses that a moment before were drab rectangles of a shade that someone, rather unkindly, compared to unwashed bed-sheets, into golden ingots. It illuminates the green-tiled roofs of the mosques, the *médersa*, the Islamic colleges, and the tall, square minarets that are so different from the tall, slender, circular minarets of Cairo and Istanbul, some of which have golden finials and are embellished with ceramic tiles. And it shines on the leaves of those trees that have managed to force their way up into the open air from the courtyards of the houses, like grass forcing its way through concrete.

And as the city is drenched with light that is more and more golden as the moments pass, it comes to life. The air fills with the haze of innumerable charcoal fires and with what sounds like the buzzing of innumerable bees, the noise made by some 250,000 human beings telling one another that night has departed, prayer is better than sleep, wishing one another good morning across the deep, cobbled ditches between the buildings that serve as streets, or else having the first row of the day in Berber or Arabic.

The night is over and two sharply-dressed youths have already spotted us from the ring road and are even now weaving their way up towards us among the tombs and other debris of past civilizations on a motorcycle. They turn out to be identical, juvenile twins with identical, embryonic moustaches and identically dressed. In Britain they would be thinking vaguely about not taking O-level examinations at some still distant date. In the United States they would still be in the tenth grade. Here, they seem as old as the surrounding hills and are planning retirement at our expense and other unfortunates like us.

They are from Modern Fez. They live, we later discover, in what was known when it was built as 'The New Indigenous Town', the brain-child of the French town planner Ecochard, which is sited, with the fine contempt for the potential inhabitants which characterizes town planners everywhere, on a bare and arid hillside, the sort of site traditionally reserved for the poor everywhere. It preserves little or nothing of traditional Muslim town planning which might make life in it more comprehensible to the 60,000 inhabitants who find themselves hoiked into the twentieth century in this dreary place.

'Hallo, Sir! I will be your guide, Sir!' says the one who is riding pillion. 'You cannot visit Fez alone, Sir! Bad mens, Sir, in Fez!' And so on, similar tosh. Fez may be confusing but it is not dangerous, unless you play the fool at some shrine or mosque, or openly eat ham sandwiches in its streets. In fact we are speaking to two of the most dangerous people we are likely to meet.

'Thank you. We have already had a guide. With him we have seen everything we wish to see with a guide.' It is true. We have already spent an entire day with a highly cultivated guide, arranged for us by the Tourist Office, the only sort worth having. Now we want to retrace some of the routes we travelled together, but alone.

We both want to do this, but in our hearts we know that it is going to be very difficult, if not impossible. By climbing up here in the early hours we had hoped to escape, at least temporarily, the hordes of self-styled, self-appointed guides and touts, most of whom know less than the most ignorant visitor armed with the most primitive guide book can learn about Fez in twenty minutes. They infest every hotel and every place of interest, waiting for their prey to emerge, and their maddening and, if thwarted, threatening attentions make life such a misery that for many visitors travelling by themselves, as opposed to travelling with a group, the memories of innumerable encounters with these pests become the most enduring of all their memories of Morocco.

Eventually we escape, but only at a run, swerving among the tombs of lesser men than Merinid sultans to the ring road which encircles the Old and New Cities where, by a miracle, we manage to board a bus in which the passengers are so crushed together that if they adopted the same positions in the open air they would be arrested.

It lands us in the Place du Commerce, outside the royal palace in Fès el-Jedid, to the south of which lies the Mellah, our next refuge, the one-time ghetto of the Jews and there we find the twins waiting for us astride their motorcycle, and the whole boring business begins again.

'You do not like Moroccan peoples,' says the pillion-riding twin, a cunning ploy at this stage of the torture, when the victim, now nearly insane, may quite easily hoist the white flag, fall on his knees and blubber, '*Please, please,* be my guide.'

'I *do* like Moroccans,' I shout. 'We *do* like Moroccans.' By this time a small crowd has collected and is looking at me as if I had committed some misdemeanour. There is not a policeman in sight. 'We're just fed up with *you*! NOW FOR CHRIST'S SAKE GO AWAY!'

And to escape them we set off together at a shambling trot which eventually leads us into the Mellah.

'FUCK YOUR MOTHERS!' shouts the boy on the pillion, before dismounting and setting off in leisurely pursuit.

'AND FUCK YOUR FATHERS ALSO!' shouts his brother at the helm, the one who up to now had preserved a sombre silence, doing a kick-start and revving up preparatory to heading us off in case we make a swerve in some other direction. All of which seems to prove that in Fez, among the motorcycle-owning classes at least, there has been a marked decline in the use of religious imagery, if not in the actual practice of the religion. A few years ago they would have called us Christian dogs and hoped that our parents' bones might rot in their graves.

In the Grande Rue, we stop to buy a very large tray of beaten aluminium with a folding stand which took our fancy during our guided tour. A Fasi craftsman's answer to the problems of the air-age, previously it would have been unthinkable to make such an object in anything but solid copper or brass and therefore untransportable. It would, nevertheless, give Air Maroc a few headaches. I only hope they won't fold it in half to get it into the machine. While we are negotiating this purchase, a twin arrives and, in a decidedly threatening manner, demands commission on the sale, in which he has taken no part, from the shopkeeper. One would have expected the shopkeeper, who is twice his size and age, to give him a thick ear and send him packing, something I have been longing to do for some time myself, being something like four times his age and three times his size. Instead, the shopkeeper shows every sign of being cowed and frightened. Is there a protection racket? We leave them to it.

The Grande Rue leads into a big open space, a *mechouar*, enclosed by high, crenellated walls, at the far end of which is a gate, the Bab es-Seba. Above this gate, the Infante Ferdinand of Portugal was exposed, pickled, naked and upside down in his entirety for four days or years, no one seems quite sure which, six years after he had been taken prisoner while on an unsuccessful expedition against Tangier in 1437: after which he was exhibited, stuffed as well as pickled, in an open coffin, for another twenty-nine days, or years. It was here, also, that the Franciscan, Andrea of Spoleto, far from home, was burned to death in 1523. Here, too, a Merinid sultan is said to have had himself walled up above the gate after his death. The Bab es-Seba is not a particularly cheerful spot, but then very little of either Old Fez, New Fez or Modern Fez can be said to be exactly jolly.

The Bab es-Seba leads into the Old Mechouar, another walled court-yard, with, so far as can be made out with the aid of an old map, the Oued Fès, the principal river of Fez, flowing secretly beneath it.

Like the square at Marrakech, the Old Mechouar has always been a gathering place for story-tellers, snake-charmers, who carry coils of snakes wound round their necks, jugglers and such like, but now in decreasing numbers. A gate in the wall to the right leads into the Bou Jeloud gardens, which are a kind of no-man's land between New Fez and Old Fez. Here we acquire several more 'guides', but Wanda manages to get rid of them by speaking only Slovene. Puzzled, angered and, finally, half-convinced and unable to understand her, they go off in search of easier prey with much fucking of our mothers.

In these gardens the Oued Fès emerges to form a series of pools among groves of bamboo, weeping willows, olives and cypresses, all of which flourish here. From them a waterwheel, said to have been brought here by the Genoese, scoops up water and distributes it into conduits lower down, which take it down through the gardens of the palaces in what was the Belgravia of Old Fez. Here the rich and culti-vated used to live, families who kept their own bands of musicians, and here the consulates, around which the always very small foreign colony would congregate in the hope of not being slaughtered, used to be found.

In the Bou Jeloud Gardens, looking down on the abundant waters of the Oued Fès before it continues through the amphitheatre in which the old city stands, one begins to understand why the two cities came to be built where they were. Enormous quantities of water were needed for drinking purposes, for watering pleasure gardens, for fountains, for all the other more mundane domestic uses and for the ritual ablutions of countless thousands of Muslims.

The way into Fès el-Bali, the Old City, is through the Bab Bou Jeloud. A fine gate with an arch in the form of a keyhole and embellished with brilliant blue and green tiles, it looks old but isn't. It was only built in 1919, but like almost everything in Morocco made or built by craftsmen using traditional methods and materials, it is an instant and total success.

Once inside the Bab Bou Jeloud you are in the Souk of Talaa (Talaa being one of the eighteen wards into which the city is divided), and as if by the waving of a wand, back in the Middle Ages. In it a street is an alley about 9 ft wide, in which five people might with difficulty walk abreast, off which lead innumerable alleys, no wider than trenches, in which it is often impossible for two people to pass one another without one of them turning sideways. For long stretches of their courses, these various ways are roofed with rushes, through which the sunlight, if it reaches into them at all, filters down on the crowds moving purposefully and apparently endlessly below, casting on them a tremulous light, as if they were underwater. It falls on men wearing a fine variety of clothing: skull caps decorated with geometrical designs, felt caps called *shashia*, like sugar loaves, with silk tassels hanging from them, turbans, hooded *jellabs* and *selhams*,* and on their feet yellow *babouches* with their backs turned down exposing heels as hard as rawhide.

It falls equally fitfully on men in rags lugging bunches of live chickens in either hand as if they were bunches of bananas, or pushing wheelbarrows, the only wheeled vehicles to be seen; on porters bent double under the weight of huge sacks and packing cases; on donkeys loaded with charcoal, brasswork, brushwood, maize, newly-fired pottery,

---

* The *selham* is the Moroccan version of the burnous. It is made from a rectangle of fine woollen material, white or dark blue, with a hood made from the trimmings cut from the fronts, which are not joined together as they are in the *jellab*. The *selham* is a much more aristocratic garment than the *jellab* and is, or was, the only one permitted to be worn in the presence of king or sultan. It is sometimes worn over the *k'sa*.

mounds of pallid, slimy goatskins on the way to the dyeing vats down
at the bottom of the hill, or else on the way back from them to some
drying ground on the outskirts of the city, now a brilliant red, dyed
with what may still be, if a dye of the highest quality is required, the
juice of a berry. And it dapples the boys balancing boards on their
heads, loaded with round loaves which they have collected unbaked
from the housewives and are taking to the ovens for them, and on the
bearded merchants perched on corn-fed mules, dressed in a sort of
fringed, cream-coloured toga, six yards long and nearly two yards
wide, made of woollen gauze, which they wear with one end lapped
over the head, a garment, called the *k'sa*, which gives them – for they
are already stern-looking – a really awesome air.

The noise is incredible. All of them, riders, porters and boys with
boards on their heads and anyone else in a hurry, are shouting at the
tops of their voices, '*Balèèèk! Balèèèk!*' 'Make way! Make way!', and if
you don't they or their animals simply shove you out of it.

Here, men with more time to spare, having prudently made way,
greet one another by pressing their fingertips together, then to their
lips, then to their hearts, crying 'God be praised!' meanwhile gazing
into one another's eyes. From then on the air is full of cries of 'Peace
be unto you.' 'And to you be peace.' 'How art thou?' 'Thy house?'(an
enquiry which contrives to include the women without actually naming
them as such). 'Thy relatives?' To which the reply is, 'All well, thank
God.' Or, if it isn't, 'God knows; everything is in the hands of God.'

There are many women. Those squatting in the rare open spaces
selling bread and vegetables are often fairly negligent about the veil,
or do not wear it at all. Those who are better-off, who are buying
rather than selling, are dressed in the *häik*, the equivalent of the *k'sa*,
a long, white, fine rectangular woollen wrapper. They also wear the
*litham* – as do some of the men but for a different reason – which is a
white veil bound round the face, hiding what to the Muslim is the
sacredness of the nose, ears, nostrils and the mouth, but not the huge
almond eyes with the edges of the lids blackened with antimony, which
are left uncovered like huge, old-fashioned car headlamps, to dazzle
and disturb the beholder.

Most of these people are Arabs and Berbers, people of the Atlas,
the indigenous inhabitants of the Maghreb, otherwise Morocco, or a

mixture of both. Some Berbers are light skinned, so pallid that romantic theories are advanced about their antecedents: that they are descendants of Vandals, some 80,000 of whom crossed the strait of Gibraltar to North Africa from Spain in 429, taking Carthage from the Romans, and thus depriving them of their principal granary, as a prelude to their attack and sacking of Rome itself; or that they are descendants of the tribes expelled from Palestine by Joshua; or that they were of the race of Shem, Amalekites descended from Esau; or kinsmen of the Agrigesh (Greeks), or are from the Baltic, or are descendants of Celts.

Other Berbers are as black as Negroes from Central Africa. Some have blue eyes and rosy cheeks, which may be due to the familiarity of their women with Christian mercenaries and slaves.

There are many Negroes. Men and women dressed as Moorish Muslims, descendants of the slaves, who, when the supply of Christians began to flag and long before that, made the awful hundred-and-fifty-day journey across the Sahara with the slave traders to Morocco, as well as to Algeria and Tunis, from Timbuktu and Bornu in the western Sudan, with their children slung on either side of mules, their price a block of salt large enough for one of them to stand on, six or seven inches thick.

And there are ourselves. To tell the truth, now that we have succeeded in casting off our shadows, we feel a little lonely, going down into the souks of Fès el-Bali. Few of these Fasi even deign to notice us, however outrageous we must appear in their eyes, both in our behaviour and in our dress. If they do look at us at all, it is incuriously. Then they put us out of mind. They do not want us in their holy city, or anyone else like us, unbelievers from the far side of the Mediterranean.

I wish we could speak with them, these Fasi, perhaps become friendly with one of them, that is as much of a friend as a Nasrany (Christian) or any other sort of unbeliever can ever be with followers of the Prophet. They, the most reserved of all Moroccans, are known for their intelligence, their skill in business, their particular intonation – which is made fun of by other Moroccans who intone less well – the niceness of their natures, their argumentativeness, their avoidance of sunlight which might darken their skins, their alleged lack of courage, their appreciation of the pleasures of conversation and of, what some say is the best of all, their food. Facets of their characters that casual visitors, such as ourselves, can never know or experience, pursued as they are by westernized Fasi (themselves the living embodiments of the change they fear so much), and locked in the equivalent of a prison by ignorance of all but the most basic fragments of their language and divided from them by impassable gulfs of belief and antecedence.

Here, at this upper end of Old Fez, in the Souk of Talaa, you can buy painted hard-boiled eggs, *seksou* or *couscous*, which if dried in the sun will keep for years, *smeen*, green-streaked rancid butter to eat with it, best when it has been buried in an earthenware pot for a year – by which time it smells a bit like gorgonzola – chick-pea paste, the best mint from Meknès to flavour the sweet tea the Moroccans love, and other flavourings: red rose, marjoram, basil, verbena, *toumia* (which tastes of peppermint) and orange blossom.

Here, the butchers display their products, some of them ghastly to look on: flayed sheep's heads, still with their horns *in situ*, suspended from cords so that the owner of the stall can attract attention by setting them swinging under the light of the paraffin pressure lanterns (this part of the souk is always very dark); miles of entrails, cloven feet chopped off short, with the hair still on them, tongues and eyes and testicles. Who eats eyes voluntarily? Are they bought to be offered to a non-believer at a feast as a *pièce de résistance*, to test his courage?

Up here, there are minute restaurants in which, if you are not too squeamish, you eat well for next to nothing. We shall return to one of them later on, after midday, to eat *harirah*, meat soup with egg and coriander, or *kodban*, meat on skewers, or *seksou* and the stew made specially to go with it, among the ingredients of which are ginger, nutmeg, coriander, turmeric, saffron, fresh marjoram, onions, bread, beans and raisins or, if we are not really hungry, *seksou* with fruit, such as quinces, or whatever is in season.

Grander restaurants are hidden away in fine old houses in the labyrinths further down the hill. They serve such dishes as *bastilla*, cakes of puff pastry stuffed with minced pigeon, sprinkled with sugar and cinnamon, which is not as sickly as it sounds; and *tajine*, dishes of chicken, pigeon or mutton, either cooked whole or stewed, and dressed with olives, beans, almonds, apples, artichokes, carrots, or whatever else is appropriate and in season.

To dine in one of these beautiful dim lofty silent places populated by grave, equally quiet, picturesquely clad serving men, one needs a companion while the ritual unfolds itself: while the cone-shaped, lidded dishes are lined up, and while, squatting in what is excruciating discomfort on the cushions, one washes one's hands over an elegantly embellished copper pan. Alone, one would feel like an unloved sultan, without even his food taster.

The Talaa Kebira, the street in which the Bou Inanya College stands, continues to descend into the Old City, past mosques in various stages of dilapidation, blacksmiths' booths, a *guelsa*, which is a sort of halting place on the way to the Shrine of Idriss II, with lamps burning before it, some tea houses, and down through *souks* with endless rows of shops on either side of it, shops that are nothing more than cupboards with doors that can be locked at night, each more or less a carbon copy of its neighbour and, in a *souk* selling the same commodities, displaying almost identical goods.

In them the shopkeepers sit – telling the beads of their rosaries, the *tasbeeh*, which can be of amber, fruit stones or simply plastic, ninety-five of them, with five more at the end to record repetitions – hour after hour, year after year, dreaming of money and the *houris* who will be at their disposition when at last they are wrapt away to Paradise, scarcely moving except to stretch out a languid hand to reach some item of stock in which a passerby has betrayed some interest. Shops into which the customer hauls himself up, sometimes with the help of a dangling rope, to settle down, slipperless, for – if the object is of sufficient interest to warrant it – a long period of bargaining which usually ends with the shopkeeper feigning despair or exasperation and saying to him, 'Take it and begone!' Shops in which the proprietors take siestas in the long, torrid, insufferable summer afternoons.

This street also has some *fondouks* in it. *Fondouks* were partly caravanserais and partly, some still are, warehouses in which the goods and raw materials for the craftsmen were stored before being auctioned and distributed throughout the various *souks*. At one time there were said to have been 477 *fondouks* in Fez. They are the equivalent of the *han* in Asia. They are built round a central courtyard in which the caravan animals were tethered, with storerooms on the ground floors and with accommodation on the upper floors for the caravaneers where they awaited the auctioning of the merchandise and recuperated from the rigours of the journeys across the deserts. Some of these upper rooms in the poorer sorts of *fondouk* were barely large enough to allow the occupants to recline at full length. The guests provided their own bedding but the landlord supplied each of them with a large brass plate, a teapot, teacups and a receptacle in which to boil water. On either side of the entrance gate to the larger sort of *fondouk* there was usually a coffee stall where what was generally regarded as the best coffee in Fez was to be found.

Then the henna *souk*, where the Moristan, the mad-house built by the Merinids, stands, in the indescribably filthy cells of which, well into the twentieth century, the occupants were kept chained to the walls with iron collars round their necks.

Down here is the glazed white pottery *souk*, the *souk* of the carpenters, a *souk* selling salt and fish from the Sebou, the *souk* of the eggs, a *souk* which sells yarn in the morning and corn in the evening, and the *souk* in which, until the beginning of this century, the slaves were sold, having previously been fattened up, taught some vestigial Arabic, enough of the religion and ceremonial practices of Islam to enable them to be deemed to have embraced it, and having been given one of the particular names reserved for them, such as, for men, Provided for, Fortunate; and for women Ruby and Dear.

And beyond these are the *souks* of the tailors, the *souk* of rugs and fabrics, the *souk* selling *häiks, selhams, jellabs* and other clothing, a *souk* where antiques are sold, and the *souk* of the coppersmiths.

And there is the Kisaria, otherwise the Market Place, which is not a market place at all, but the final labyrinth within a labyrinth, a network of covered *souks*, with gates which are locked at night, each with its own nightwatchman, as in the Great Covered Bazaar in Istanbul, and, like the Great Bazaar, burned down innumerable times, always to rise once more, phoenix-like, from its ashes.

In Old Fez, the craftsmen are members of guilds according to the particular craft they are engaged in. At the beginning of the century there were 126 of them. Such guilds bear scarcely any resemblance to the trade unions of the western world. Their members think of themselves primarily as belonging to the *Ummah*, the community of believers which, in theory, although it is difficult to know to what extent in actual practice a Fasi craftsman today would subscribe to this, transcends nationality, creed, and even ties of race and blood, a community held together by belief in the Oneness of God. One of the best ways of giving this practical expression was by becoming proficient in a craft, as a member of a guild working first as a *mubtadi*, an apprentice, then for long years as a *sani*, an artisan under a *mu'allim*, a master craftsman. The master of such a guild, who had wide powers – he could order the most draconic punishments for those who behaved dishonestly, for example – was the *shaykh*, the descendant of a line of *shaykhs* going back to two companions of the Prophet, Ali ben Abi Talib and Salman al-Farisi, and beyond them to Shem, the son of Adam.

Here in Fez, looking at the works performed by these craftsmen in mosques and *médersa* and secular buildings, one begins to understand that there is no division between religion and secular activity in traditional Islam and that what they were working for, collectively, was the Glory of God: in plaster and cedarwood and stone, in ceramics, firing the amazing, lustrous tiles, forming the bowls and vases decorated with the dark blue and jade green arabesques in the potteries out by the Ftouh Gate in the Andalus quarter on the right bank of the river, working in brass, binding the books in the soft red goat leather which required twenty different operations to produce it, 13 carried out by the master, his artisans and apprentices, the remaining 7 by other specialists, embroidering the single coloured silks.

Behind the *souks*, many of them reached by the narrowest of alleys are what appear at a distance to be the great honeycombs of houses in which the Fasi live, those apparently interlocking cubes we had seen this morning from the hill, none of them, despite a superficial uniformity, ever quite repeats the form of another; a lack of symmetry which is an inherent part of the Muslim ethos, and one which manifests itself in every sort of art and artefact, from the asymmetry in the design and even the shape of a Berber rug, to the near perfection of a keyhole arch in a mosque courtyard.

These dwellings, large or small, inhabited by rich and poor were designed and built, not for the requirements of a husband, wife and children, childless couples, the aged whose families have left home, or

even for individuals but as centres of family life to house the entire
extant hierarchy of a family comprehending several generations. There
is no word for 'home' in the Muslim vocabulary and in Morocco the
nearest approach to it is *wakr*, which is almost exclusively used to
describe the lair of a wild beast.

A typical Fasi house is an irregular quadrilateral, built of mud bricks
and clay, the same material that was used to build so much else in Fez
from walls to mosques. If there are any windows opening outwards
onto the street they are high up and covered with wood or iron gratings.
The only embellishment on these outer walls will probably be the hand
of Fatimah, the Prophet's daughter, delineated in hen's blood, to ward
off evil.

In such a house the courtyard is surrounded with a sort of cloister
in which columns, which may be partly tiled, partly decorated with
plasterwork, support richly encrusted arches. In the centre there is
usually a fountain with a tile or marble surround into which water
splashes soothingly. In the courtyard there may also be orange trees,
vines and figs. On the upper floors long, lofty rooms, some of them
bedrooms, surround the well of the courtyard and look down on it.

The roof, surrounded by walls and trellises, is the retreat of the
women of the house, from which they can look out over the city and
down into it without themselves being seen. Like all Moroccans the
Fasi use the rooms on the upper floors of their houses in winter, the
lower ones in summer. Then during the hot nights the inner court
collects the cooler air which descends into it; by day the stifling heated
air flows across the mouth of it, leaving the lower floors and the courtyard cool.

Such a house, although it appears to be inextricably locked together
with its neighbours, is not. There are no communal stairs. Each
windowless, walled dwelling that goes to make up the mass is completely cut off from its neighbour, without any possibility of being
overlooked, except perhaps from the roof. Each one is essentially a
sanctuary, demonstrating as well as anything material can the essential
duality of Islam. The huddle of houses displays the unity of all within
Islam, the walled sanctuary, the place where the head of the family is
its *imam* and in which his person, and those of his family, are intensely
private, inviolable, *harām*, forbidden to others, as inviolable as the

Zawiya, the shrine of Moulay Idriss II. Some say that he was the founder of Old Fez in 809, others that it was founded by his father. Together with the tomb of his son, the mausoleum of Idriss I is the most venerated shrine in Morocco.

The alleys surrounding the Zawiya are packed with Fasi and pilgrims from the furthest parts of Morocco, all of whom come to obtain a *baraka*, the Saint's blessing. They are also crowded with beggars who crouch against its outer walls, demanding alms 'For God and my Lord Idriss!'

Such beggars, men and women, are said in Islam to 'Stand at God's door', and what they receive is described as being 'God's due'. For those who appear reluctant to give them this due, a familiar prayer is 'May God give thee something to give!' To which the hard-of-heart or the penniless may reply, but rarely do, so close to the shrine, 'God open the way for us and thee to prosperity!'

# A NIGHT IN MONTENEGRO

The main road to Cetinje by way of the Lovčen Pass was a wild one even by Montenegrin standards; lined with ruined forts, it climbed through plantations of oak and pine ravaged by fires that had only recently swept the mountainside. It was loosely metalled, full of pot-holes, had twenty-four major hairpin bends on it and was only one vehicle wide, with lay-bys. Its outside edge frequently overhung preci-pices and at some places gaps in the masonry, as they did in so many places on the Adriatic Highway, showed where vehicles had been driven clean through the protecting walls taking the occupants on what had been, presumably, a spectacular exit to eternity.

Our ascent of it was made more difficult by a large caravan of pictur-esquely-clad gypsies who were descending it from the Pass in horse-drawn carts, on foot and with numbers of animals running loose along with them; but finally, having emerged from a tunnel that had been driven through one of the outlying spurs of the massif, we reached the Pass, which was literally white with sheep. Here the sky was

threatening and a few drops of icy rain fell. Already old women in
long, rusty black skirts and white-moustached men wearing little
round black pill-box hats and waistcoats and what looked like baggy
jodhpur breeches of heavy, brown homespun were urging the flocks
and the cattle that had been grazing around the head of the Pass
down to the little village of Njeguši in anticipation of the coming
storm.

Just below this pass there was an inn, a *gostiona*, which is the Montenegrin way of spelling *gostilna*, where we stopped for a drink.

Inside it four men, one of them the proprietor who was in his shirt-
sleeves, were drinking the Albanian brandy called XTRA. All were
drunk and beginning to be acrimonious. It was not a place to linger.
The three customers had their vehicles parked outside, one of which
was a large petrol tanker, and when we got up to go one of them, who
turned out to be the driver of the tanker, easily identifiable by his
overalls, got up, too, clutched one of the lapels of my coat in order to
keep himself in an upright position and, swaying backwards and forwards on his feet like some Cornish rocking-stone, announced that he
was about to drive his tanker down to Kotor by the road we had just
climbed to the Lovčen Pass. How he was proposing to do this and
remain alive was a mystery.

By the time we emerged from the *gostiona* the storm was directly
overhead and for an instant a single, blinding flash of lightning turned
the grey limestone of the mountain a dazzling white. It was followed
by a single, deafening roll of thunder which reverberated among the
rocks. Then an apocalyptical wind blew, bending the trees as if they
were reeds. Then the heavens opened.

Thanking our lucky stars that tonight we would sleep in a Grand
Hotel instead of in the back of a van unconverted for this purpose,
which was what we had now been doing on and off for months, we
set off downhill through the downpour into what, insofar as we could
see anything at all, resembled a crater filled with twisted rocks, narrowly missing a head-on collision with a bus that was groaning up
through the hairpin bends on its way to Njeguši, loaded with what we
later discovered was part of the day shift of the 'Obod' factory in
Cetinje which made refrigerators and other electrical appliances, the
'Košuta' footwear factory and the 'Galenika' factory for processing

pharmaceutical preparations, all of whom would have been a serious loss to the economy.

By the time we reached the city it was completely dark and the rain that had been clouting down had given place to a monotonous drizzle; so dark that in a dimly-lit boulevard opposite what had once been the building occupied by the Italian diplomatic mission I ran over and killed a black cat which darted across the road in front of us. However, even this melancholy incident failed to dampen our spirits completely. For we were looking forward to staying the night at the hotel, which was not just any old hotel but the Grand Hotel of Vuko Vuketič, as it used to be known, otherwise known as the Lokanda, one of the last hotels of its kind in the Balkans: the Balkans strictly speaking being the mountains in Bulgaria that extend across the country from the Yugoslav border to the Black Sea: but in the sense in which I interpret it, the one in which it is commonly used, of the Balkan Peninsula, the lands between the Adriatic and the Black Sea.

I had last stayed in it in the 1960s. I remembered it as a rather splendid cream- and yellow-coloured building with a sort of semi-circular foyer that was a bit like a Victorian greenhouse. Originally built in 1864, it was the first hotel to be constructed in Cetinje and to it were sent the official and honoured guests of what was then the Montenegrin capital, which even in its heyday never had more than 5000 inhabitants. (Now it had more than 10,000 inhabitants and had several large factories producing, as well as electrical appliances, shoes, pharmaceutical products and white bauxite.) At one time the hotel housed the United States diplomatic mission. Reconstructed in 1900, and enlarged in 1929, it had two restaurants and forty bedrooms. In its remarkable foyer and in other public rooms, all rather dingy when I was last there, tall old men in national costumes with huge white moustaches, some, almost unbelievably, still with Lugers and Mausers and other weapons stuck in their cummerbunds, sat sipping away at their *rakijas*, their Albanian XTRA brandies and various other strong drinks for hours on end while remembering old blood feuds, an activity which in Montenegro had been raised to an art form. In fact one visitor, the author of the excellent *Companion Guide to Jugoslavia*, J. A. Cuddon, records one of these Montenegrin mountaineers taking out his pistol and shooting a mad dog in one of the dining rooms.

The hotel stood in what had been a windswept square when I was last there, for although it was already spring down on the Adriatic, 2100 or so feet below, up here at Cetinje, which is invariably snowed up for five months of the year from October until the end of February, there was still snow on the ground.

Now, on this really foul, wet night, we looked forward to the hot baths which could usually be had in it, sometimes to the accompaniment of alarming clanking noises from the plumbing system; to the big drinks, the scalding hot lamb soup we planned on ordering, and the great gobbets of Montenegrin pork, all brought to the table by ancient servitors; and after that to retiring to bed in one of the large and shabby but clean bedrooms. All things I remembered about the hotel with pleasure from my previous visit and of which I had spoken enthusiastically and perhaps too frequently to my fellow traveller. I could even remember the way to it, through little streets lined with lime and black locust trees, the latter a form of acacia.

By the time we reached the square in the centre of the town in which the hotel stood a thick mist had descended on it and as it was ill-lit I got down and set off on foot to look for it, leaving Wanda in the vehicle.

There, at the southern end of the square in which I remembered it as standing, I was confronted with what looked like an enormous pancake but on closer inspection turned out to be a mound of yellowish rubble. There was no sign of the hotel.

'Excuse me,' I said to a passerby who had halted, curious at my interest in a heap of rubble, speaking in Italian, which sometimes serves in these parts of the world. 'Do you happen to speak Italian?'

'Yes,' he said.

'Can you please tell me the way to the Grand Hotel?'

'Grand Hotel,' he said. 'That is the Grand Hotel,' pointing at the mound of bricks and plaster.

'But what happened?' I asked.

'It was the earthquake,' he said. 'The great earthquake of 1979. It destroyed not only the Grand Hotel. It also damaged and destroyed a large part of the city.'

'Is there another hotel?' I asked him, remembering that back in the sixties although the Grand Hotel had been the only one of any consequence in Cetinje, there had been some talk of another hotel, although whether it was built or about to be built I could no longer recall.

'No,' he said, 'there is no other hotel. The Grand Hotel was the only one. Tourists are no longer allowed to stay in the town. In fact there is no longer even a Tourist Office.'

*       *       *

In spite of the drizzle and the fog it was the hour of the *passeggiata* in the main street, which although many of its buildings had been badly damaged was either being rebuilt or had already been built in their original, old-fashioned form.

Young, tall, dark and incredibly handsome men, moustache-less and pistol-less, and equally beautiful girls wearing jeans and as upright as if they had been brought up to carry pots and heavy weights on their heads, as they probably had, walked up and down in little bands past the lighted shop fronts of the pleasant, pale-coloured buildings I remembered, talking animatedly, smoking cigarettes like chimneys and eyeing one another. Apart from the two of us there was not a tourist in sight and the Tourist Office, as my informant had already told me, was closed, with a notice in the window to that effect.

We dined well on the sort of huge pieces of pork we would have been offered at the Grand Hotel if only it had remained standing, quantities of bread – there were no vegetables of any kind on offer – a delicious pastry stuffed with figs, a sort of baklava, but softer than the Greek variety, and drank copiously of a robust red wine of the region called Vranač Plavka in an effort to banish the thought of another night in the open, in a restaurant which resembled a brick-lined *bier-keller*, except that it was on the ground floor. The waiters, who were all well over six feet tall, wore white shirts and black trousers and black waistcoats. Male guests drank oceans of beer straight out of the bottles, spurning glasses; and old men of the sort I remembered with moustaches like racing bicycle handlebars kissed one another before settling down, as I had remembered them doing, to speak nostalgically, according to Wanda who could understand some of what they said, of what had been until quite recently an almost unbelievably violent past.

'He who revenges himself is blessed,' was one of the dicta of family

life in a country where male children used to have loaded firearms
placed in their hands before they could even stand on their two feet,
let alone fire them, in order to prepare them to be good Montenegrins,
worthy members of the only Balkan State that was never subdued by
the Turks. For Montenegro, until the Second World War, was a man's
country in which a woman's lot was to perform menial tasks such as
agriculture, beget as many male children as possible to make up for
the constant death roll among the men, and attend the funerals of their
lords and masters when they failed to survive a *ceta*, one of the predatory
raids they spent so much of their time either planning or taking part
in. The results of such expeditions were subsequently recorded for
posterity by *guslari*, minstrels, many of them blind, who used to accompany their recitals of these bloody doings on the *guslar*, a one-stringed
instrument rather like a lute, made of wood, or clay, or copper, sometimes even of stone. Some of the ballads, which the *guslari* knew by
heart, were anything up to seventy thousand words long and are still
recited today in some parts of what is the smallest Yugoslavian republic.
Now these feudal practices were ostensibly no more in Cetinje.

After dinner, having ascertained that there was no official camp site
in Cetinje and therefore no camping, which put us in a rather difficult
position, we drove hurriedly away and hid the van and ourselves with
it behind one of the walls of what had been the royal park, outside the
Crnojević Monastery, otherwise the Monastery of the Virgin, so
named after Ivan Crnojević who built it in 1484. This original monastery, which he surrounded with a moat and heavily fortified, was razed
to the ground by the Turks in 1692, again in 1712, and again in 1785.
Above it on a hill, when I had last been in Cetinje, there had been a
round tower called the Tablja which the Montenegrins used to decorate
with the skulls of Turks, emulating by so doing the Turks who built
the Celé Kula, the Tower of Skulls, at Niš in Serbia which they decorated with a thousand Serbian skulls, a few of which are still in position.
Whether the Tablja was still standing or whether it had fallen a victim
to the earthquake it was impossible to say because it was dark, and the
following day, with the fog still persisting, we forgot to ask.

What with earthquakes, the Turks who had set fire to it and
destroyed it three times, and the Austrians, Italians and Germans, who
had each consigned it twice to the flames, it was a wonder that there

was anything left of Cetinje at all. One of its proudest possessions, now in the Treasury of the Monastery, is the skull of the Vizier Mahmut-Pasha Busatlija of Shkodër in Albania, one of Montenegro's greatest enemies and the last Turkish leader to fight his way into Cetinje and destroy it and the Monastery, in 1785, who was killed in a great battle with Petar I Njegoš in 1796.

We also saw the residence of Petar II Petrović Njegoš who reigned from 1830 to 1851 and was six feet eight inches in his socks, ex-monk, poet, traveller, crack shot, player of the *guslar* and a thorn in the sides of the Austrians and Turks. His palace was called the Biljarda because it was to it that the Prince had a full-size, slate-bedded billiard table from England manhandled three thousand feet up what was then a mule track from Kotor to the Lovčen Pass, then over the Krivačko Ždrelo Pass and then 2000 feet down through a chaos of limestone to the Palace where it was installed without the slate being broken.

There, behind the wall, we spent, as we anticipated we would, an awful night, which not even the good red wine of Vranač Plavka we had drunk alleviated. Soon after we arrived some policemen drove up in a car to the Monastery, obviously in search of us, and we only narrowly escaped discovery.

Meanwhile the rain, which had become torrential again, drummed on the tinny roof of the van making sleep impossible. Finally, in the early hours of the morning, when the rain had finally ceased and we had at last succeeded in dropping off, we were besieged by a pack of savage dogs, one of a number of such packs that infested the park and which had already made the night hideous with their barking and fighting. Why they chose to surround our van was a mystery. Perhaps they could smell a salami that we had hanging up in it.

At the Art Gallery of the Socialist Republic of Montenegro, which is housed in the former Government House, the Vladin Dom, the largest building in Montenegro, we were kindly received by the Director, a cultivated man who was very upset about the siting of the 'Obod' electrical appliance factory, which had been plonked down in a prominent position in the town and had done nothing to improve its appearance. He himself, as director of the gallery, had suffered an almost worse aesthetic misfortune in the form of an enormous inheritance of paintings known as the Milica Sarić-Vukmanović Bequest which, although it did contain a number of good paintings, including works by foreign artists, was largely made up of post-war kitsch of a particularly awful sort which he had not only been forced to accept but put on permanent display, completely swamping what was otherwise an interesting and representative collection of Montenegrin art from the seventeenth century to the present.

Then, having admired the outsides of various buildings, some of which had once housed the Russian, Austro-Hungarian, Turkish, French, English and Italian diplomatic missions, some of them wonderfully eccentric buildings, and having failed to find the Girls' Institute, one of the first girls' schools in the Balkans, founded in 1869 by the Empress Maria Alexandrovna of Russia, with which Montenegro had a close relationship before the First World War, we left Cetinje with genuine regret, and took the road to Albania.

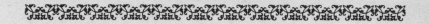

# On and Off the
# Trans-Siberian Railway

## NEW YEAR'S NIGHT ON THE RED ARROW

Leningrad is a city of canals, a northern Venice of such beauty that there is no absurdity in the comparison, and as the taxi raced down the Nevski Prospekt, here nearly 120 feet wide, over what looked like pure ice to the station where I was to catch the night express to Moscow, it seemed, with the huge flakes of snow drifting down into it out of the darkness of the northern night, yet another enchanted, frozen waterway, brilliantly lit.

It was New Year's Eve 1964. At 11.30 p.m., having entrusted a two-kilo tin of the finest procurable caviar to the engine driver who stuck it on the front of his steam locomotive in order to keep it cool, I boarded the *Krasnaya Strela* (the *Red Arrow*), and after disposing of my baggage took a seat in the restaurant car.

The *Krasnaya Strela* is one of the Soviet Union's most famous trains. It covers the 410 almost dead straight and completely bumpless miles to Moscow in eight hours and thirty minutes, arriving at the Leningrad Station on Komsomolskaya Square at 8.25 the following morning, on the dot. The line has a sentimental place in the hearts of Russian railwaymen as it was the first major line to be built entirely within the frontiers of Russia; it took 50,000 serfs working from sunrise to sunset – and who were flogged for the privilege of doing so – eight years to complete. Thousands of them died.

Almost everything about the *Krasnaya Strela* was good. It was warm, even too warm, and the dark blue brass-buttoned greatcoats and fur hats worn by the conductresses who sometimes smiled, sometimes scowled, sometimes were inscrutable – Russian officials of either sex are as unpredictable as fruit machines – were of the finest quality. And it was not only the conductresses who were fitted out in a sumptuous manner: the appointments of the two-berth 'soft-class' compartments, which is how the Russians describe their first-class *wagons-lits*, were redolent of another age – the headboards fitted with linen covers embellished with drawn-thread work, the dark green curtains, the pleated silk shades on the massive cast-iron table lights, the glittering water decanters, the long druggets in the corridors (instantly soiled by the snow-covered hooves of the passengers as soon as they boarded the train), the dazzling white curtains and bed linen, the multiplicity of mirrors – all were satisfactory to the most exacting bourgeois taste and therefore not only to me but to the sort of Russians who were my fellow travellers in 'soft class', many of whom had the air of commuters. It was not surprising that at one period of the war this rolling stock had been used by Hitler and other top members of the Nazi Party, or so someone told me later that night.

In fact, the only remotely criticizable thing about the *Krasnaya Strela*, apart from the thought that I might be occupying a berth once used by Himmler, which was rather off-putting, was the menu in the restaurant car, of which I had been offered an English translation covered with gravy stains, in which all the more agreeable items and most of the less agreeable ones were unavailable. 'Beluga Belly Flesh', 'Goose', 'Roasted Duck wit Garnisch' and 'Plum Cake "Stolichny"' were all out of stock. All that was currently on offer was some luke-warm noodle soup, great gobbets of some unidentifiable meat which looked as if it had been hacked to pieces by a maniac with an axe, and what were literally smashed potatoes.

It was therefore little wonder that I and my fellow diners, all of whom were Russians and therefore endowed with the native facility of making the best of what would have been disastrous for anyone else, had recourse to the bottles with which the restaurant car was well supplied, and on which they had already made a start before I arrived.

The only other passenger at my table was a large man as tall as an early Romanov with glossy black hair, wearing an expensive, hand-built black suit, a black knit tie and a white shirt with a Madison Avenue-type button-down collar with a fashionable swerve to it. He was in his early forties and looked a formidable customer. Anywhere west of the Iron Curtain I would have put him down as the man in charge of the J. and B. Rare or the Smirnoff Account. Here, I identified him as a member of the *apparat*, and a trusty one who had spent a lot of time abroad.

He was uncommunicative – just a very curt nod – but hospitable. He had just filled a glass with Stolichnaya from a bottle and now he did the same for me, which emptied it. We clinked the big glasses and turned them bottoms up in the Russian fashion. I ordered another bottle. Into the Valley of Death.

It was now a quarter to twelve.

'Where are you going?' he said suddenly. He spoke English with a fine voice as deep as he was.

'To Moscow.'

'Of course,' he said impatiently, making me feel like a small boy of about seven, 'but after Moscow?'

'To London.'

And that was the end of that conversation. At 11.50 the *Krasnaya Strela* left for Moscow.

In the course of the next ten minutes of what was becoming a New Year's Eve carouse we emptied the second, smaller bottle. I must say it is a boring way of drinking, this ritual. Then, having ordered a bottle of Ukrainian pepper vodka a minute or two before midnight by the restaurant clock, he leant forward across the table and said, portentously, 'Do you know Nakhodka?'

It was like the beginning of that boring joke that begins, 'Do you know Omsk?', which I had heard so many times in my years as a commercial traveller, but instead of waiting for a couple of hundred *versts* to pass as do the protagonist and the blundering reciters of this chestnut half as old as time, he carried straight on.

'You should go to Nakhodka,' he said, 'by the Trans-Siberian Train. From it you will see Siberia and the great progress our peoples have made in developing the country. It is the longest railway in the world and it was built by Russians.'

By now, somewhere in the outer suburbs of Leningrad, it was 1 January 1965, and any further conversation of a coherent sort in the restaurant car was rendered impossible by great gusts of singing, the drinking of further enormous toasts and an outbreak of bear-hugging among the entire company. It was half past one before I finally got to bed, having sung 'Auld Lang Syne' three times by popular request to great applause and having drunk to peace in our time in beer so often that it should last at least two thousand years, leaving the rest of them still hard at it. Nevertheless, overcome as I was, the man in the black suit had planted the seed of an idea in my fuddled brain.

At 8.26 a.m. I was decanted on to the platform of the Leningrad Station in a city still shrouded in gelid night and one that I have never really grown to like however hard I have tried. There I repossessed myself of my two-kilo can of *beluga malossol* which was thickly coated with hard snow – it had been a risky business sticking it on the front of the engine as caviar begins to disintegrate around 20°F, but less risky than having it simmering itself into a Russian version of *bouillabaisse* inside the *Krasnaya Strela* where the temperature was up in the 70°s and 80°s.

Then I queued for a taxi to take me to the National Hotel, where I planned to leave my treasured possession in a cool caviar chamber for the next week or so before taking the Ost-West Express to Liverpool Street by way of Brest, Warsaw, Berlin, Rotterdam and the Hook. It was a long queue with few taxis at the end of it, and while I was shuffling forward in it I suddenly recalled through a haze of distilled potato juice the words of my brief acquaintance whom I was to see no more.

'You should go to Nakhodka [wherever that was] by the Trans-Siberian Train. It is the longest railway in the world and it was built by Russians.'

In my hand luggage I had a copy of *Cook's Continental Timetable* and in a few moments I was deep in the USSR section of that heady work, studying the timetable headed MOSKVA–IRKUTSK–KHABAROVSK–NAKHODKA. TRANS-SIBERIAN RAILWAY.

The whole thing appeared even more simple than my perennial optimism about travel would have allowed me to believe. The train, which was called the *Rossiya* (the *Russia*), was due to leave for Vladivostok in approximately one-and-a-half hours' time from the Yaroslavl Station, which was so close that I could see it from where I was standing. There was no need for a taxi and I already had a porter.

By reading the small print I discovered that, being a foreigner and therefore not allowed to enter Vladivostok, which was a naval base, I would have to change trains at Khabarovsk on the Amur River, 5331 miles from Moscow and would arrive at Nakhodka on the Sea of Japan on the morning of the ninth day from Moscow. From Nakhodka I could take either a Russian steamer to Yokohama in about 52 hours or one to Hong Kong in 174.

I was terribly tempted. If I did decide to go I would have made the entire journey from the Nevsky Prospekt across Asia, a street of which Sacheverell Sitwell wrote (in *Valse des Fleurs*):

> Down at the far end, which tails off as the crow flies, towards Moscow, the buildings, the people, and even the colour of the sky are already Asiatic, in the extent to which the word means wars and plagues and barbarian invasions. The first suburbs of another and an endless world, all plains and distance.

This is what, in spite of feeling rather ill, my heart yearned for at this moment – those vast nomadic steppes which in their southern parts extend for more than 4000 miles without interruption from the Danube to the Great Wall of China. For I am one who believes that a golden opportunity once rejected is seldom put on offer again.

With me I had everything I needed: a Russian visa which was valid for another ten days and which, as a transit passenger on the railway, I would have little difficulty in extending if the need arose. Even if I failed to get an exit permit at Nakhodka for Yokohama or Hong Kong, neither of which was the exit point named on it, I could always fly back from Khabarovsk to Moscow and get my exit visas there for Poland and East Germany. For once I even had plenty of money on my person. There was time, too, to buy food for the journey, which seemed a good idea as 'Roasted Duck wit Garnisch' would presumably, more often than not, be 'off'. Anyway, with a couple of kilos of caviar I would not lack for friends *en route*, and if I did I could always stick it on the front of an engine.

It would be a quiet time, something in parentheses in a life that was sometimes almost too full of movement, and yet I would be moving, cocooned in the white sheets and with the heavy water decanter to hand (I would steer clear of burly men in black suits and button-down collars who gave me 200-gramme slugs of Ukrainian Pepper Vodka and bear-hugs at midnight into the bargain), and I would re-read Tolstoy's *Resurrection*, something of which currently I was badly in need.

But this moment of euphoria soon passed. I was also a newspaperman with a piece to transmit to London, and there were others to be written in Moscow in the next few days. How I wished I had a brace or two of carrier pigeons which I could release at intervals beyond the Urals. 'National Hotel,' I said, sadly, when my turn came to board a taxi. More than twelve years were to pass before I finally caught the *Rossiya* from the Yaroslavl Station and made the journey of the Trans-Siberian Railway.

## THE BIG RED TRAIN RIDE

For eleven years I roared around the world, but during that time the opportunity to travel on the Trans-Siberian Railway never arose, although I often thought of writing a book about it. Railways, like rivers, are difficult subjects for writers because they go on and on. They are less difficult for writers of fiction who can populate their trains with corpses, villains, beautiful people and *wagons-lits* attendants with seven o'clock shadows. If they get bored they can blow them up or derail them. A non-fiction writer is lucky if anyone pulls the communication cord.

When the opportunity finally arose I discovered that there were three possibilities open to me. One was simply to apply for a transit visa for the USSR, buy a ticket from Intourist in London and make the journey from Moscow to Nakhodka without getting off the train at all, except to inspire fresh air on the station platforms along the route. An alternative would be to make the journey, stopping over for a day or two at Novosibirsk, Irkutsk and Khabarovsk, these being the only cities along the route open to foreign visitors in 1977. The third way, and the most complicated and expensive, was to make the journey under the aegis of the Russians themselves and let The Novosti Agency provide one of their representatives to accompany me. The Agency is regarded by

Western intelligence services as an arm of the KGB. The theoretical advantage of this was that it might be possible to stop off at places that were not on the normal Intourist agenda and see things denied to ordinary foreign tourists, and this was the course that I eventually decided upon. It required a Finnish publisher to pay a large sum of money to Novosti, which they eventually did.

Which was why, in the depths of Arctic January 1977, I found myself keeping a tryst with a senior representative of The Agency in a sauna bath in the West, not much more than a biscuit's toss from the Iron Curtain.

Mr Oblomov (for that is what I shall call him to spare his blushes), whom I was now regarding through a haze of steam in this subterranean hothouse, was a splendidly endowed fellow in every way, both physically and mentally. Dressed in a Western bespoke suit he had been impressive; now, wearing nothing but a piece of towelling and flagellating himself with a bunch of birch twigs, he looked like a pentathlon gold medallist, and when we plunged into the spacious pool after the torture was over he swam like one.

Later, when I had swum two lengths of the bath under water to show him that, although I was not in the same class as he, I also kept fit, we sat swathed in towels, drinking beer and mapping out a programme for him to present to his superiors.

Two days and three bottles of whisky later – there were others in on this act – I left for London. It had been a thoroughly successful meeting so far as I was concerned. Mr Oblomov had a list of Siberian Wonders as long as your arm, which if I was able to see only a few of them would have turned me into a Siberian Marco Polo. It included visits to active volcanoes, to the coldest place in Siberia where the temperature descends to −90°F, to the descendants of the Golds, aboriginals, who until comparatively recently had worn suits of fish skin, to railway construction sites in the remotest wilderness, to gold and diamond mines, ginseng root-collectors and bring-them-back-alive Siberian tiger-hunters. 'I shall also,' said Mr Oblomov, 'recommend that at least part of your journey should take place while there is still snow on the ground. A visit to Siberia without seeing it under snow is like . . .'

'A rose without a thorn?' I suggested.

'I was going to say,' he said, mischievously, 'like a writer without a head.'

The day after I got back to London I received a message to say that I would not be able to make the journey through Siberia with snow on the ground. No reason was given. I suppose they think it makes the place look untidy.

'Your other proposals,' the message said, 'are being considered.'

They were still being considered when I caught the train.

There were four of us travelling to Siberia together: Otto, a German photographer on a mission of his own, who was Jewish and with whom we were travelling as it was cheaper to share an interpreter; Mischa, a member of the Agency, who had spent some time in India and who was almost certainly godless; me, as British as a Bath bun and a lapsed member of the Church of England (although still crazy about old churches, preferably with singing going on inside); and lastly Wanda, my wife, a Slovene and a Roman Catholic, who dislikes Mass in the vernacular and whose observations during our long journey together in the two-berth 'soft-class' compartment on the *Rossiya* were interesting to record. Put all these unlikely ingredients in the same compartment, stir in a bottle and a half of vodka, leave to simmer for a couple of hours, light the blue touch paper and stand clear!

Besides being singularly ill-assorted, we were also exceptionally heavily laden, apart from Mischa who was apparently set on going a quarter of the way round the world and back with two shirts and a mohair pullover. It was not altogether our fault. We had been warned to 'dress as you would for an English spring', which is a damn sight more difficult than being told that you are going to the Sahara in summer, or the Arctic in winter; besides which, we were loaded with the tools of our trade.

I had a barely portable library of Siberiana and all sorts of other works which included a timetable for the entire route in Cyrillic. I also had two 1:5,000,000 maps which took in European Russia, Siberia and most of the rest of the USSR.

These maps were contained in a four-foot-long cardboard tube which drove everyone mad who had the custody of it for more than two minutes, including myself. I also had, among others, an underwater camera (because it was also dustproof), six Eagle H pencils, a rubber, a pencil sharpener, three pens and a Challenge duplicate book. All of which worked extremely well throughout. Otto had a large, highly professional metal box, which although made of aluminium was as heavy as lead, full of cameras, and a tripod which also drove everyone mad who had anything to do with it.

On the way to the Yaroslavl Station, the boarding point in Moscow for the Trans-Siberian train, we made a detour to the National Hotel in Manezhnaya, now 'Jubilee of the Revolution', Square where Lenin, who had as keen an eye for the bourgeois comforts of the bed and the board as any of his successors, put up for a spell in March 1918. As we drove to it we passed through Dzerzhinsky Square, so named after the Pole, Felix Dzerzhinsky, whose statue has brooded over it since 1958. Dzerzhinsky was head of the Secret Police from its formation in December 1917, when it was called the CHEKA (Extraordinary Commission for Combating Counter-Revolution and Sabotage), until his death in 1926 from natural causes, something rare in his profession, by which time it had become the OGPU (the State Political Administration). Now, in 1977, its direct lineal descendant the KGB was, almost unbelievably, preparing to celebrate the first sixty Glorious Years of the existence of the Secret Police by giving parties.

At the top end of this square, which is the size of a modest airfield, an immense wedge-shaped reddish building rises on a desirable island site. The pre-revolutionary headquarters of an insurance company, it has been added to and rebuilt many times, the last time in 1946. The back of these premises faces on to a dark and draughty street which for years was shunned by Muscovites like the Black Death, and by almost everyone else in the USSR who happened to be in its vicinity – and still is by those who cannot rid themselves of the habit.

'What's that building?' I asked Mischa. It was intended as a joke. I knew what it was, or what it had been, as well as he did, and so did everyone else in Moscow, where it was as well known as Wormwood Scrubs and the Bloody Tower to Londoners, or the Tombs to the inhabitants of New York – so infamous that some years previously my son, while still a schoolboy of the smaller sort, had tempted providence by photographing it with a rather noisy camera. 'It's some kind of office block,' Mischa said airily. I was damned if I was going to take this from anyone, let alone a 'fellow journalist', even if he was a card-carrying member of the you-know-what. '*You* know what it is, don't you?' I said to the taxi driver, a cheerful fellow who spoke some English. 'Yes,' he said, 'I know what it is.' 'Well, what is it?' 'It's the Lubyanka,' he said.* And he roared with laughter, exposing a perfect row of stainless steel teeth in the upper storey.

The station, at which we arrived one-and-a-half hours before the train left, is an astonishing building, even in Moscow, where this epithet, especially when applied to architecture, can become seriously over-used. From the outside it looks like the work of a horde of gnomes of the class of 1900, although actually built in 1907 by F. O. Schechtel.

The inside is very different. Entering the waiting room, I had expected to find the customers perched on toadstools. Instead I found myself on an Eisenstein set for a twentieth-century sequel to *Ivan the Terrible* – medieval-looking chandeliers powered by electricity, a complete absence of natural light, squat black marble columns with granite capitals, and filled to the brim with all the extras waiting for the stars to appear and the cameras to roll, hundreds of what could have been Tartars, Komis, Udmurts, Mordvins, Nanays, Chuvashs, Buryats, Koreans, Latvians, Germans, Kazakhs, Bashkirs, Maris, Evenks, Tofas, Ukrainians and possibly some genuine Russians – just some of the people who inhabit the regions through which the Trans-Siberian Railway passes on its way to the Soviet Far East.

I say 'could have been' because even an ethnologist might have found himself stumped, unless he had an identikit with him. None of them, apart from a few Uzbeks in little round hats, whom even I could identify, having once visited their country, wore anything remotely resembling a national costume, so well had the rationalists done their work. The men were dressed in Western-type suits that looked as if they had been cut with a chopper – the Soviet tailoring industry shares the same master-cutter with the Turks – although some of the younger ones were wearing plastic jackets. Most of the adult males had on the sort of cloth caps worn by British working men before the war. The

* One of the three prisons in or near Moscow which housed political prisoners, and since December 1917 the headquarters of the Secret Police.

women wore headscarves and velour topcoats which made them look as if they had been dumped in the waiting room in sacks.

The Uzbeks were at the wrong station, anyway, although they probably didn't know it and if they did, being Uzbeks (and therefore by nature nomads), probably didn't care. They should have been next door, at the Kazan Station (architect A. W. Shchusev, who was also responsible for Lenin's Tomb), waiting for Train No. 24 – 'soft' and 'hard' class, with dining car – to whirl them to their capital Tashkent, 2094 miles away, beyond the Aral Sea. They had plenty of time to find out that it wasn't the Kazan Station – their train didn't leave until 11.20 p.m., and it was now 8.30 a.m.

As in every other railway waiting room in every other communist country I had ever visited, this one was the exclusive preserve of the *lumpen proletariat*, the hoi-polloi. There was not a single traveller to be seen in it of what one might call the administrative or managerial class. I knew, from previous experience, that if any such chose to travel by train they would arrive at the station by taxi or office car, as we had, not as the occupants of the waiting room appeared to have done, on foot and a couple of days early; and they would arrive just before the advertised time of departure. Then their neat luggage would be wheeled up the platform in front of them by porters to whom they would give tips, just as their counterparts in East and West Berlin, Paris, Prague, Warsaw, Rome, Bucharest or Peking would do; everything here is just as it was under the last of the tsars, and just as it still is at Waterloo, King's Cross, Victoria, Euston, Paddington and Liverpool Street under Elizabeth II in my own country – that is, if anyone can find a porter to tip at any of these six last-named termini.

It was a bit different in the waiting room. Here, the submerged classes, most of whom displayed a stoic attitude which under the circumstances was most surprising, were laid out for inspection, in some cases quite literally. The majority of them were sitting or sprawling on the varnished wooden settees with which, just as in every other waiting room in a main station anywhere, this one was inadequately provided: sleeping, sawing away at huge, dark loaves as if they were cellos, talking, quarrelling, belching, smoking cigarettes, laughing, crying, taking milk from the breast, extracting gobbets of meat from horribly greasy parcels, engaging in dreadful spasms of coughing, or just sitting, surrounded by black bags made from American cloth, cheap suitcases and cardboard boxes, all bulging at the seams and held together with bits of string. Those who could not find a seat – and I never saw one unoccupied for an instant unless it was piled high with bags or coats which indicated that it was already somebody's property – either stood, supporting themselves with unfurled, unopened umbrellas, or squatted among their possessions with which they had walled themselves in like settlers preparing to resist an attack by Red Indians. Some simply lay on the floor. Of these, the most determined to find peace and quiet had flaked out in a little enclave that led off the ticket hall one floor up, built in 1964; vast, airy, full of natural light, the complete opposite of this lugubrious place, but almost empty because there was nothing to sit on except the floor.

Meanwhile, down on the ground floor others queued to buy lumps of boiled chicken and equally pallid sausages, Scotch eggs and delicious-looking macaroons, washing these delicacies down with Russian coke, squash or coffee – no beer, vodka or even tea available at the station, apparently, except possibly in the restaurant on the upper floor, outside which a queue had formed. A good thing, too, judging by the Bacchanalian scenes enacted outside in the vicinity of Komsomolskaya (Young Communists') Square, even at this unseemly hour, by what I hoped were non-fellow-travellers.

Over all hung the smell of Russians *en masse*; no worse than the smell of an *en masse* of English or Italians, or inhabitants of the Côte d'Ivoire, or any other nationality; but just different. A smell that one traveller compared, I think inaccurately, to that of a laundry basket on the weekly collection morning; inaccurate not because it is impolite – it is impossible to describe smells of people *en masse* politely – but because the smell to my mind is more pungent, and I think comes in part from eating the strong, black bread. I wondered what we smell like to them.

In these surroundings it was not surprising that Otto, a somewhat conspicuous figure in Russia, although he could never understand why (his jeans – the going black market rate for which was in the region of £100 – his Nikons and Leicaflexes were under continual offer from the locals) contrived to get himself arrested twice in the space of an hour: the first time by the Railway Police for photographing an elderly lady on one of the platforms in the rain (which, apart from one miraculous day, had been falling more or less incessantly ever since our arrival in the country); the second time, which was far more serious, by the Military Police, for taking pictures of some conscripts from the borders of Outer Mongolia, who were on their way to be turned into soldiers elsewhere in the Soviet Union.

The clothing of the conscripts was exiguous. Mischa explained that they were wearing their oldest clothes because, on their arrival at their training depot, their clothes would be burned, as was the Red Army custom. One had a paper hat on made from a sheet of *Pravda*. It seemed a shame to burn that. They looked cold, tired, hungry, fed up, and far from home. I felt sorry for them and I felt alarm for Otto, but I also sympathized with the lieutenant in charge of the draft who had called on the Military Police to take Otto away to their home-from-home in the station. He was as grumpy as an Irish Guards officer would have been at Paddington Station, lumbered with a similar collection of recruits straight from the back blocks of Connemara and Mayo and on his way with them to the Training Depot at Pirbright, if he found them being photographed by a Russian.

It was fortunate that I saw Otto being marched off as Mischa was elsewhere; otherwise we would have started looking under trains for him or calling up hospitals. As it was, Mischa had to produce the small, oblong red pass entombed in plastic, the one I never managed to get a really close-up look at in the weeks to come, which sometimes worked in difficult situations. This time it did work; but only after much serious telephoning.

## THE FLOWERY STEPPE OF ISHIM

At around 0.55 on 29 May, the third day of our progression across Europe and Asia (God knows what it was locally – the time-zone map was vague about demarcations), the *Rossiya* pulled into Ishim on the Ishim River. It was pitch dark and there were no signs in sight. I only knew it was Ishim because some fellow, presumably employed to do so (usually it is done over a loudspeaker which no one can understand,

even Russians), was walking past outside chanting 'Ishim . . . Ishim!'
reminding me of the man who plods past the Simplon Express, 288
miles from Paris at its first stop in Switzerland, groaning 'Vallorbe . . .
Vallorbe'. At the same time a colleague, who also meant well, was
tapping the axles.

Of Ishim I knew nothing, and at 12.55 a.m. cared less. It was not
until I returned to England that I discovered that this was a place
where Friedrich Heinrich Alexander, Baron von Humboldt, the famous
scientific explorer, was taken for a secret agent and very nearly shot.

At about half past one I woke again, this time to experience a new,
more gentle motion. Dawn had just broken (about four-thirty local
time), and as if to show respect for it the *Rossiya* had stopped behaving
like an overloaded plane trying to take off. Instead, it was drifting
through a world only a fraction of which seemed to be made up of
landscape, an enormous, endless prairie covered with rich, fine, gently
waving grass, interspersed with fields of black earth in which crops
were already sprouting, groves of silver birch and here and there, where
there was a stream or marshy place, a few aspens and willows. And
there were flowers, too, thousands of them: anemones, buttercups,
kingcups, forget-me-nots, dandelions. The rest, about 90 per cent, was
sky, still streaked with high cirrus, as it had been over Tyumen the
previous evening but now, in these brief minutes before the sun would
transfigure it, the colour of the lees of wine.

We were in the Steppe of Ishim, just a small part of the vast plain
which, under various names, stretches out from the foot of the Urals
across the Irtysh, the Ob and the Yenisei over 35 degrees of longitude
and about 20 degrees of latitude before breaking at the foot of the
Siberian upland in the Krasnoyarsky Kray almost 1200 miles to the
east. We were in Siberia, and it was large. There was no doubt about
that. Just as I had imagined it. You could put the whole of the United
States into it and all of Europe except Russia and still have several
hundred thousand square miles to spare. And apparently it was empty,
this bit of Siberia between the Urals and the Yenisei and the Altai
Mountains to the south, although statistics show that more than 13
million people live in it.

The *Rossiya* stole on to the south-east with her living cargo, most of whom were asleep, as if she was under sail, a ship moving through a Sargasso Sea of grass, so quietly that, as in a sailing ship, I could hear the creaking of tackle and her rivets working: a ship in which, ever since it had been towed by a diesel, the cabins had been covered with a fine layer of metallic dust which smudged like grated carbon when it was touched. The only other passenger on view was a boy with a Ronald Colman moustache, coming off shift after another night of lipstick with his conductress.

And now, from the general direction of the Pacific on which it had been shining for a good five hours, the sun came shooting up over an horizon that looked as if it had been ruled with one of my H pencils, into a sky that turned first an improbable shade of puce then a fiery red, as if someone was stoking a furnace. Soon it was a great, bloody sphere, sometimes over the *Rossiya*'s port bow, then, as the line wove its way among some sunken, half-dry watercourses, over the port quarter. Then for a while it was invisible while we ran past a halted freight train that must have been more than half a mile long, made up of sealed vans and flat cars loaded with secret-looking objects covered with tarpaulins, and hauled by four giant diesel locomotives. After that we halted at a little station for a rare, non-scheduled stop. As if by magic Lilya appeared from her little boudoir, looking remarkably spruce, and let down the steps to the line. We were on the frontiers of the second and third time-zones and it was either 3.30 or 4.30 a.m. local time.

There was not a soul in sight, not even a male or female station-master. Except for a disembodied voice coming from a crackly loud-speaker stuck up on an iron pole, addressing a world that was still asleep, the place might have been deserted. Then that too ceased. The silence was uncanny.

Beyond the station there was a village of low log houses with iron roofs, now shining in the light of a sun that looked as if it was on a collision course with the earth with about five minutes to go. The only living things on view were half a dozen magpies which were using a telephone wire as a trampoline. Ahead, the track, two parallel but apparently converging lines (something about which I had learned in the chapter on perspective in the *Wonder Book of Why and What* when I was small), stretched away into Siberia. A light, warm breeze was blowing up from the south, bringing with it the smell of earth, grass, a whiff of wood smoke and a feeling that it emanated from vast, nomadic spaces.

'Good place,' said Lilya, giving me one of her golden smiles that to me, any day, were worth about double whatever was the current price of a fine ounce of the product, and were more bracing than a whole bottle of Wincarnis tonic wine. 'No pipple.'

It was Sunday morning.

# AMURKABEL

'Listen, Mischa,' I said at breakfast, which we consumed together with the local rep from The Agency, after arriving at Khabarovsk, 5331 miles from Moscow, 'I know we've only got one day in Khabarovsk now, but on the way back from Nakhodka we've got another day or two here if we want them. Before we came to Russia I sent your people a list of things I would really like to see. For instance, I would like to go to some village in the *taiga*, and see how the people live.'

'Unfortunately it is impossible to visit a village in the *taiga*, because of the insect that causes encephalitis.'

'The *clesh*?'

'Yes. None of you have been inoculated against it.'

'Well, why can't we visit that man who captures Siberian tigers alive? Ivan Bogachev, I think his name is?'

'Ivan Bogachev is dead and, besides, the reserve is near the Ussuri River and you are not allowed to go without special permission.'

'But I asked for special permission.'

'It has not come through.'

'Well, what about visiting the men who look for *ginseng* roots, or the ones who go after the deer for their horns, the *panti*. I asked for permission to see them, too.'

'The permissions for these have also not come through,' Mischa said, rather wearily, as if he was answering a lot of unanswerable questions posed by a child, which in effect was what he was doing.

'Well, at least, can we see the Arboretum?'

'Yes, you can see the Arboretum this afternoon,' said Mischa, 'but this morning we are going to Amurkabel.'

'What's Amurkabel?' Otto asked, emerging from what appeared to be a trance.

'Amurkabel is the largest wire-making plant in the Far East. It employs 2500 workers.'

'Listen, Mischa,' I said. 'You and Wanda and Otto can all go to the wire-making factory if you want to. Personally, I've seen so much wire in so many wire factories in my life that if it was all put into a heap it would cover more ground than the Matto Grosso.'

'If you do not go to Amurkabel,' Mischa said – by now he was becoming very angry – 'you will cause grave offence and I will be forced to report to Moscow that you are a trouble-maker. You are a writer, and you are supposed to be writing a book about Siberia and the Trans-Siberian Railway. I do not care whether you write it or not, but you must go to Amurkabel.'

We all went to Amurkabel.

Amurkabel was housed in a largish factory on the outskirts of the city. Next to it there were some blocks of flats that housed the workers. When we arrived the technical information bureau chief, a Mr Beresnev, and a number of faceless satellites were waiting for us.

'The cars of the workers,' said Mr Beresnev proudly, pointing to fourteen vehicles parked outside, as we swept through doors held open by professional door-openers into the administration building.

'But there are 2500 workers. Do only fourteen have cars?'

'Only half the workers are on shift,' said Mr Beresnev, completely unperturbed. 'This is the day shift.'

'But the day shift's 1250 people!'

'They don't need their cars because they live next door,' said Mr Beresnev, and I began to wonder if I was going round the bend.

After enduring the *mineralniye vody* treatment for an hour or so in the boardroom we were taken on a tour of the plant, shown the various machines that reeled up cable core coming from a continuous-process vulcanizer, coated the wire with enamel, and braided it with fibre glass, as well as machines for drawing the wire out from whatever stuff it was made from, and so on. Amazingly, none of them was working, and apart from one or two men and women who were either repairing machines or walking around stroking them with oily cloths, there were no workers.

'Where is everyone?' Otto said, loaded down with equipment and fed up with all this. 'How am I supposed to take photographs of a factory with no workers in it?'

'This is the dinner break,' said Mr Beresnev. 'All the workers are in the canteen.'

'Well, then, let's go to the canteen.'

When we reached the canteen, it was populated by about forty or fifty men and women, many of them elderly, some of them wearing white coats – none of them wearing the sort of dungarees that the machine-minders had on. It was obvious from their garb that, whoever they were, they all hailed from the clean-hands departments, and that this was *their* canteen. There was not a single grease mark of the sort that the grimy beings we had seen could not have failed to leave on the surface of the spotless tables; and, anyway, the canteen was much too small to accommodate even a third part of the day shift. Wherever the workers ate it was not here.

'Well, where are the workers?' Otto said.

'Unfortunately,' said Mr Beresnev, 'they have just gone back on shift. But now,' he went on, indicating a table at which other managerial persons were hovering, waiting for us to join them, covered with a spotless cloth and with a whole battery of wine and other glasses at each place setting, 'it is time for us to eat.'

'Tell me,' Mr Beresnev asked, leaning across the table towards me, in the course of what was proving to be a copious and excellent luncheon. 'Do you believe in God?'

It was an unusual question to be asked by the technical information bureau chief of a wire factory, even though it was 5300 miles east of Moscow.

'Mr Beresnev,' I said, 'I don't know what your feelings are about this matter, but one thing I am certain about is that, if there is no such thing as God, you wouldn't be showing me round your wire factory.'

Later that afternoon a small, highly intelligent woman, who had an excellent command of English, took us round the Arboretum of the Far East Forestry Research Institute. It was a charming, old-fashioned place, founded in 1935 on the site of a tree nursery, set up about 100 years ago to supply Khabarovsk with saplings. Now hemmed in by buildings, it was almost miraculously preserved, together with its 1300 sorts of trees and shrubs indigenous to the Soviet Far East.

While we were ambling about it, Mischa showed signs of impatience, as he always did whenever we visited anything faintly old or of pre-revolutionary date; but at last he succeeded in getting us back into the waiting cars. There was a further delay while our guide went off to get for me the last copy the Arboretum possessed, other than its file copy, of a descriptive pamphlet to it written in English.

'Vod is dis life,' she said, ignoring Mischa and his colleagues, as she presented it to me, 'if full of care, ve haf no time to stand and stare.'

## NIGHT TRAIN TO THE GREAT OCEAN

That evening at 6.25 p.m. local time (11.25 a.m. Moscow time) we boarded the *Vostok*, the night train to Nakhodka. By this time the *Rossiya* had already been six hours in Vladivostok, and in another four hours fifty minutes would be starting on the return journey to Moscow.

The *Vostok* was made up of a half-dozen green passenger cars, drawn by an electric engine, and from the outside looked no different to any normal Russian passenger train. On the inside it was fantastic, a train-that-never-was, something that might have been designed by Beaton for Garbo, using for money the three-year box office take from *My Fair Lady*: the perfect train, kept forever behind the wall in Plato's Cave, of which only distorted shadows are seen in the outer world, all shining mahogany, brass and scintillating glass.

Each of the two-berth compartments was loaded with mahogany, some of it gilded. The mahogany armchair was covered in red plush (and so was the brass door chain) and the coved roof was also banded with mahogany. The finely chased door furniture was solid brass, and the screws in the brass door hinges had been aligned by some artisan so that each of the cuts in the heads of the screws was parallel with the ones below it and next to it. The mahogany table had a brass rim round it; there were brass rails around the luggage compartment overhead to

stop the cabin trunks crashing between one's ears, the ashtrays were
solid brass, and the cut-glass ceiling light had a brass finial on it.

On the floor there was a thick red and green Turkey carpet. On the
beds snow-white pillows had been arranged in a manner that suggested
that this work had been performed by a parlourmaid who had majored
in household management around 1903. The sheets were freshly ironed
and so were the white voile curtains which were also supported on a
brass rail.

In the bathroom, with which the compartment was connected by
way of a mahogany door, there was a full-length looking glass, a
stainless steel washbasin as big as a font, furnished with nickel-plated
taps (the sort that stay on once you have turned them on), and the
stainless steel lavatory basin had a polished mahogany seat. The shower
head was attached to a flexible tube. The towels were thick and sumptuous and the heavy water carafe held two litres. Illumination in the
bathroom was provided by a frosted glass window which gave on to
the corridor. On the outside this window was embellished with an
art-nouveau motif, also in solid brass, and in the corridor this motif
was echoed in the decoration of the ceiling lights. The corridor, in
which golden curtains oscillated with the movement of the train
(which, admittedly was far more bumpy than that of the *Rossiya*), was
provided with a number of tip-up seats, also upholstered in red plush,
for those who had grown weary while on the way to and from the
restaurant car, and the carpet was the same as those in the compartments.

And everything worked. If this was not enough, our particular car
was equipped with the most beautiful conductress I had seen on the
Russian or any other railway system. She was reputed to be of Czech
origin. Perhaps the whole thing came from Czechoslovakia, for it was
newly built, and she with it. If it was built in Russia, where had the
Russians found the artisans to build it? From the same source that
produced the men and women who refurbished the Summer Palace at
Tsarskoye Selo?

The train trundled out of Khabarovsk past allotment plots, soldiers
laying track in a siding; over level crossings with long queues of lorries,
their drivers fuming; through marshalling yards in which disembodied,
gravelly voices were giving instructions through loudspeakers mounted

*Preceding page:* Occupant of a fine wooden house – one of many such scheduled for demolition at that time (1976), in the city of Irkutsk: five time zones, and 3244 miles by the Trans-Siberian railway, east of Moscow.

*Opposite top and bottom:* Seller and buyer on a station platform somewhere east of the Urals.

*Above:* Pilgrim in the austerely beautiful cathedral of the Troitska in Zagorsk; the air resonant with the constant chanting of the plea '*Gospodi pomilui!*' ('Lord have mercy upon us!').

*Above: I Castagni* — for twenty-five years our home in Italy.

*Opposite top:* A formidable brace of conductresses on the *Rossiya* (Russia) which for Soviet citizens used to take seven twenty-four-hour days (170 hours and 5 minutes) to cover the 5810 miles from Moscow to Vladivostock. For foreigners, who had to go to Nakhodka, the journey took almost eight twenty-four-hour days, 192 hours and 35 minutes, which included a stopover from day seven to day eight at Khabarovsk on the Amur River. From Nakhodka you can take a ferry to Japan.

*Opposite bottom:* Would-be passenger.

*Left:* Woman of Sassalbo, a lonely village below the main ridge of the Apennines – a picture taken twenty years ago.

*Opposite:* Signor Giuseppe and Signora Fernanda, who lived next door to us at *I Castagni*.

*Below:* Dinner for our neighbours.

*Overleaf:* Attilio.

on poles; past long trains of red, yellow and black tank waggons being shoved up inclines by bright green diesels, the *Vostok* mooing, the factory chimneys belching black and yellow smoke; running past stagnant ponds and fatigued-looking trees, out into the country where the ponds were clearer, red in the now-setting sun: out between the two hills, now with mist rising around them, that we had seen from the one-time site of Muravyev-Amursky's statue that morning. On to Vyazemskiy, a very-close-to-the-Chinese-frontier town which was immediately to the west across the always invisible Ussuri. There the train halted for five minutes, long enough for Wanda to borrow a bike from the station-mistress and go for a ride on it.

It was a brilliant evening. To the east the country was open and rolling. The fields along the line of the railway were full of strawberries in flower, currants and raspberries and sweetcorn.

All through the twilight the *Vostok* rolled along the frontier with long views, across expanses of open plain, of hills and mountains that were in China. To the right of the line in one section there was a continuous wire fence with a splayed top. It was about seven feet high and showed signs of being electrified. Beyond it there was a wide strip of freshly raked earth. At kilometre mark 8672 the fence turned away westwards towards the heights above the Ussuri on the Russian side, where the watch towers were silhouetted against an apple green sky that had small, black bands of cloud floating in it.

Then we had dinner. If the restaurant car was anything to go by, there was not a single Russian passenger on this train. In fact, the *Vostok* was not a train run for the benefit of Russians. It was the boat train for the Russian ferry service from Nakhodka to Yokohama and Hong Kong, and the passengers, all of whom were from capitalist countries, were bearers of valuable foreign currency. The Japanese on board were nothing like the little men in black suits who work for Mitsubishi and get married by numbers, but up-to-date people who regarded a suit as something you got buried in. The Americans were mostly one-time love children from Haight-Ashbury, now grown up and thinking about their mortgages: the men had moustaches and suits from the Cable Car Clothiers, and their girls were in easy-to-pack cotton jersey; and from what one could hear, all of them had made the great leap forward into the Psychobabble era while living in Marin.

But it was fun in the restaurant car with the lovely big drinks coming. No shortages on this train, of anything, and the pretty waitresses smiled and stopped to chat, after bringing to you items that were always 'off' on the *Rossiya*. But in spite of it all I still thought nostalgically of the *Rossiya*, simply because we had spent so much time together.

'And now,' Mischa said, 'we are going to a conference with the Mayor of Nakhodka.'

We were sitting in the lounge of a hotel on the outskirts of the town. From its windows there was a view that included Partizanskaya Creek, the sugar loaf hill which was called the 'Sister', and some spoil barges. It was as cold and grey as ever. With us was a 'journalist' who never left us and never opened his mouth in our presence, except to put food in it: if he was a journalist, which seemed highly unlikely, he must have worked for a paper catering for the deaf and dumb. There was also a rather nice girl from Intourist.

'Listen Mischa,' I said. 'As we were coming into Nakhodka on the *Vostok* you asked me if I wanted to meet the Mayor and I said I didn't. Remember?'

'I don't want to meet the Mayor, either,' said Otto.

'There isn't any point in my meeting the Mayor,' Wanda said. 'I don't want to photograph him and I don't want to interview him.'

'What we really do want to see is the fishing port, and we also want to go on board one of the big fishing ships,' I said. 'And before that we want to see the ferry leave for Yokohama.'

'It is all arranged, the meeting with the Mayor. He is already waiting for us. It was arranged from Khabarovsk. Besides, there is no fishing port at Nakhodka,' Mischa said. By this time he was becoming angry.

'Well if there's no fishing port, how do you account for Nakhodka being the base for your ocean-going fishing fleet in the Far East?'

'That is so,' said the girl from Intourist, proud of her native place. 'There is a fishing port. It is the biggest.'

'You're playing us a dirty trick, Mischa,' I said, really very angry myself by this time. 'Just because you want to get some copy out of the Mayor of Nakhodka there's no earthly reason why we have to go too. You go. We want to see the ferry leave for Yokohama.'

'Watch what you're saying, Newby, or it will be the worse for you,' he shouted, and went off in a fury, taking the journalist and the Intourist girl with him, no doubt to give her a rocket for letting him down over the fishing fleet.

After a few minutes he came back, with the journalist but without her, having cooled down a bit by this time.

'The fishing port is being reconstructed, and you cannot visit it,' he said. 'I have cancelled your visit to the Mayor, and will go and see him myself. He was extremely displeased. This gentleman and the Intourist guide will accompany you to the ferry terminus.'

We stood on the quay outside the ferry terminal building, which resembled a huge, old wooden hunting lodge in Red Indian country, watching the other passengers from the *Vostok* going up the gangplank of the good ship *Baikal* past a frontier guard who stood at the foot of it. The Japanese were so heavily laden with loot from Europe that some of them failed to get up the gangplank with it and had to make two journeys. Soon the ship's side was manned by dozens of our newly found, and equally soon to be lost, friends, all waving.

They continued to wave for the next thirty minutes until twelve noon, when the *Baikal* cast off and the tugs began to take her out, until she was far from the quay, and we had no alternative but to wave back at them all this time, without stopping, as the three of us were the only people seeing them off.

'Lucky bastards,' Otto said. 'Providing they don't run into a typhoon in a couple of days they'll be sniffing cherry blossom.'

'In June, in Yokohama?' I said. 'You must be joking.'

Late the following afternoon I stood with Wanda on some high ground above the port area beside an enormous hoarding with a poster stuck on it which showed a female worker making WHAM! POW! with her clenched fist and shouting 'Peace to the People!' There was a bitter wind from the north-east, the sea was choppy and the temperature was around 41°F. Looking down on the fishing port, which in spite of what Mischa said seemed to be flourishing, its fish-canning and can-making factories, its miles of quay, its shipbuilding yards, its 300-ton floating crane, one of two in the USSR (the other is in the Black Sea) which had been towed round the Cape of Good Hope, and its big dry dock which had been brought 15,000 miles from Klaipedia in Lithuania by the same route, it was difficult to believe that at the end of the war there had been nothing here but a few shacks. Now Nakhodka was a city of 120,000 people and the biggest commercial port in the Soviet Far East; and when Vostochnyy, the Eastern Port, really gets going, around 1990, it will have five times the annual turnover of Nakhodka, which is now 9 million tons a year, 75 per cent of which is foreign trade cargo. We had been to Vostochnyy, by boat across the bay, and had damn nearly frozen to death there. It was almost completely automated and utterly eerie, out there in the wilderness, with huge yards for exporting lumber which was moved about by Hitachi travelling gantries each of which could lift 16 tons; and it was also a stop-off for containers from the United States and Japan which from here were sent by the Trans-Continental Route to Europe. It was being built with Japanese capital, and somewhere there on the shores of Vrangel Bay the 10,000 men and women who were building it were living in huts, although we saw no more than half a dozen all the time we were there.

Over both these ports and the Tchadaudja Oil Harbour (over the hill from Nakhodka) and also over the city itself, an air of super-secrecy and security brooded. The whole place was crawling with frontier guards. When foreign sailors wanted to go ashore for the evening they were met at the gangplank by buses which took them straight to the International Seamen's Club and, when the evening was over, straight back to the ship. In winter the only thing that doesn't freeze at Nakhodka is the sea, which is why it was built there.

'I've had enough of Nakhodka,' Wanda said. Her teeth were chattering. 'It's a hell of a place. What's more I've had enough of Siberia, and we've all had enough of Mischa, and I'm fed up with your damn maps. I want to go home.'

So we did.

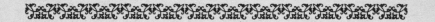

# A Long Bike Ride in Ireland

## BICYCLES

IN NOVEMBER 1985, more or less on the spur of the moment, we decided to go back to Ireland and travel through as much of it as we could, in the space of three months or so, starting in the south. The north could wait. If things improved there, so much the better. We were not going to travel in the guise of sociologists, journalists or contemporary historians. We were not going there, we hoped, to be shot at. We remembered it as it had been twenty years previously, when it had been idiosyncratic and fun. In short, we were going there to enjoy ourselves, an unfashionable aspiration in the 1980s.

We decided to begin our journey at the end of November. The reason we chose to begin it in this dead season was simply that at home in Dorset in the not-so-dead seasons we are engaged in extensive gardening operations, including in them a large kitchen garden in which we grow all our own vegetables.

We decided, Wanda with some reluctance, to travel by bicycle.

The heart of rural Dorset is not the easiest place to find out about the latest developments in the world of bicycles, but by good fortune our local newsagent in Wareham had a copy of a magazine called *The Bicycle Buyer's Bible, 1985/6* on its shelves. By this time the question of what sort of bikes we were going to take with us if we were going to get moving before Christmas was becoming extremely urgent. *The Bible* gave detailed specifications of about three hundred machines with prices ranging from £105 to £1147, and £1418 for a tandem.

The machines that interested me most were the mountain bicycles, otherwise ATBs, All Terrain Bicycles. Everything about a mountain bike is big, except for the frame, which is usually smaller than that of normal lightweight touring bicycles. They are built of over-size tubing and have big pedals, ideal for someone like me with huge feet; wheels with big knobbly tyres which can be inflated with four times as much air as an ordinary high-pressure tyre; very wide flat handlebars, like motor-cycle handlebars, fitted with thumb-operated gear change levers; and motorcycle-type brake levers connected to cantilever brakes of the sort originally designed for tandems, which have enormous stopping power.

Most of them are fitted with 15- or 18-speed derailleur gears made up by fitting a five- or six-sprocket freewheel block on the rear hub and three chainwheels of different sizes on the main axle in the bottom bracket where the cranks are situated; a sophistication so conspicuously unnecess-ary that it would have had Thorstein Veblen ecstatically adding another chapter to his great work, *The Theory of the Leisure Class*, had he lived to see it. This equipment produces gears ranging from 20″ or even lower (which can be a godsend when climbing mountains) or 90″ or even higher for racing downhill, or with a following wind on the flat.* Not all these gears are practicable or even usable, however, for technical reasons.

These mountain bikes looked very ugly, very old-fashioned and very American, which was not surprising as they were the lineal descendants of the fat-tyred newspaper delivery bikes first produced by a man called Ignaz Schwinn in the United States in 1933. To me they looked even older. They made me think of Mack Sennett and Fatty Arbuckle and Jackie Coogan. If I got round to buying one I knew that I would have to wear a big flat peaked cap like Coogan's. Eighteen gears apart – perhaps she would settle for fifteen – and providing we could find one with an open rather than a man's diamond frame model, this seemed exactly the sort of bike, in the absence of the beloved conventional Italian Bianchi bicycle that Wanda had owned during the war, that she now needed to carry her the length and breadth of Ireland and even up and down a holy mountain or two.

---

* The gear ratio (as a single figure) in inches is calculated by dividing the number of teeth on the chainwheel by the number of teeth on the rear sprocket and multiplying the result by the wheel diameter, in the case of most mountain bikes, 26″.

'"To buy a mountain bike now",' I read, '"is to win yourself a place in the first of the few rather than the last of the many."'

It was a wet Sunday evening in Dorset. We were in bed surrounded by the avalanche of catalogues and lists I had brought down on us by clipping out the coupons in *The Bicycle Buyer's Bible*. One dealer, in what seemed to me an excess of optimism, had also sent order forms which read:

PLEASE SEND . . . MOUNTAIN BICYCLE(S), MODEL(S)
. . . FRAME SIZE(S) . . . COLOUR(S) . . . PLEASE GIVE
ALTERNATE COLOUR(S). I ENCLOSE A CHEQUE/
BANKER'S ORDER, VALUE . . .

'I don't want to be one of the first of the few,' Wanda said.

'Shall I go on?' I said. 'There's worse to follow.'

'Okay, go on.'

'"From prototype to production model they have been around for less than a decade. In that short time they have been blasted across the Sahara, up Kilimanjaro, down the Rockies and along the Great Wall of China."'

'Isn't it true that the Great Wall of China's got so many holes in it that you can't even walk along it, let alone cycle along it?'

'Yes, I know,' I said, 'but there is a picture here of two men sitting on their bikes on the top of Kilimanjaro. And anyway, just listen to this: "With each off-the-wall off-the-road adventure, with each unlikely test-to-destruction, the off-road-state-of-knowledge has rolled the off-road-state-of-the-art further forward."'

'Read it again,' she said. 'More slowly. It sounds like bloddy non-sense to me.'

'There's no need to be foul-mouthed,' I said.

'It was you who taught me,' she replied.

I read it again. It still sounded like bloody nonsense and it came as no surprise when I later discovered that some of the early practitioners of this off-the-road-state-of-the-art mountain bike business hailed from Marin, that deceptively normal-looking county out beyond the Golden Gate Bridge on the way up to the big redwoods, which gives shelter to more well-heeled loonies to the square mile within its confines, all of them into everything from free association in Zen to biodegradable chain cleaning fluid, than any other comparable suburban area in the entire United States.

'Read on,' Wanda said.

'"You don't have to be some gung-ho lunatic to get your kicks",' I read on. '"Take a mountain bike along the next time the family or a group of friends head off for a picnic in the woods. There'll be plenty of places to put the bike through its paces and it sure beats playing Frisbee after lunch [interval while I explained the nature of this, I thought outmoded, pastime to Wanda]. Or take the bike on a trip to the seaside – rock-hopping along the beach is a blast."'

'That's enough,' she said in the Balkan version of her voice. 'I can just see you on your mountain bike, a gong-ho (what is gong-ho?), Frisbee-playing, rock-hopping lunatic.'

'I say,' I said, some time later when the lights were out, 'I hope all this isn't going to make you lose your enthusiasm.'

'Enthusiasm for what?'

'For these bikes, and Ireland and everything,' I said, lamely.

'Not for these bikes, I haven't,' she said. 'I've never had any. Nor for Ireland in winter. If I come it will only be to make sure you don't get into trobble.'

'What sort of trouble?'

'In Ireland all sorts of trobble,' she said, darkly.

# A STAY IN BALLYVAUGHAN
## or
# ROUND THE BURREN

The whitewashed cottage we were to stay in at Ballyvaughan (looking at it no one would have guessed that it was built with breeze blocks), at which Wanda had already arrived in the car of a local man called Tom, with her bike strapped precariously on top, had a thatched roof and a green front door with a top and bottom part that could be opened separately so that if you opened the bottom and kept the top closed, or vice versa, you looked from the outside as if you had been sawn in half.

The ceiling of the principal living room went right up to the roof and was lined with pine. The floor was of big, olive-coloured grit flagstones from the Cliffs of Moher, and there was an open fireplace with a merry fire burning in it, fuelled by blocks of compressed peat. There was a large table which would have been ideal if I had actually been going to write a book instead of thinking about doing so, which I could do better in bed, and traditional chairs with corded backs and seats. To be authentic they should have been upholstered with plaited straw, but straw had apparently played hell with the guests' nylons.

The rugs on the floor, all made locally in County Cork, were of plaited cotton which produced a patchwork effect, and there were oil lamps on the walls with metal reflectors behind the glass shades, but wired for electricity. A wooden staircase led to a room above with two beds in it, the equivalent of a medieval solar. Leading off the living room was a very well-fitted kitchen, and there were two more bedrooms on the ground floor: altogether, counting a sofa bed and a secret bed that emerged from a cupboard, there were eight, a lot of beds for the two of us. The rooms, primarily intended for the visiting Americans, could be made fantastically hot: they had under-floor heating, convectors, a portable fan heater upstairs, infra-red heating in the bathroom, plus the open fire. Gary, Tom's son, was bowled over by all this. He was even more pleased with it than we were. 'Never,' he said, 'in all my born days' had he seen anything like it.

'When I get married,' he confided, 'I'm going to bring my wife here for our honeymoon.'

'How old did you say you are?'

'Eight.'

'Tell me,' I said, 'is there any girl you really like?'

'There's one in First Grade. I like her.'

'How old is she?'

'About six.'

'But would you marry her?'

'I would not.'

'Why wouldn't you?'

'Because she's an O'Hanrahan. You can't marry an O'Hanrahan in the parts we come from.'

Later, after he had eaten three apples, a banana and a large plate of salted nuts and drunk three large bottles of Coke, left as a welcoming present by the proprietors (together with a bottle of gin for us), Wanda asked him if he spoke Gaelic.

'No way!' he said firmly.

'But I thought they taught you Gaelic in school.'

'No, they only teach us Irish,' he said.

After this we went to a pub where he ate all the nuts on sale there and drank three large orange juices.

*        *        *

The next morning was cold and brilliant with an east wind, and with what looked like a vaporous wig of mist on the mountains above. While we were eating rashers and eggs we received a visit from an elderly man wearing a long black overcoat and cap to match who offered to sell me a walking stick he had made – one of the last things I really needed, travelling on a bicycle. 'I'll bring you a pail of mussels this evening, if you like,' he said, negotiations having fallen flat on the blackthorn. The whole coast was one vast mussel bed where it wasn't knee-deep in oysters, but as the tide was going to be in for most of the morning and it was also very cold, it seemed sensible to let him gather them for us.

Our destination that day was Lisdoonvarna: '"Ireland's Premier Spa,"' I read to Wanda in excerpts from Murray's *Guide* (1912) over breakfast. '"Known since the middle of the 18th century . . . situated at a height of about 600 feet above the sea . . . its climate excellent . . . the rainfall never rests long upon the limestone surface. The air, heated by contact with the bare sun-scorched rock of the surrounding district, is tempered by the moisture-laden breezes from the Atlantic three or four miles distant, and is singularly bracing and refreshing owing to the elevation."' It also spoke of spring water conveyed to the Spa House in glass-lined pipes, thus ensuring its absolute purity. More modern authorities spoke of a rock which discharged both sulphurous and chalybeate (iron) waters, rich in iodine and with radioactive properties, within a few inches of one another, the former to the accompaniment of disgusting smells.

The town was equally famous as a centre of match-making. Farmers in search of a wife were in the habit of coming to stay in the hotels in Lisdoonvarna in September after the harvest; there they found unmarried girls intent on finding themselves a husband. The arrangements were conducted by professional match-makers, in much the same way as sales of cattle and horses are still concluded by professional go-betweens at Irish fairs. This marriage market is still said to thrive, although to a lesser extent than previously. Professional match-makers, masseurs and masseuses, sauna baths, sun lounges, springs, bath and pump houses, cafés, dances and pitch-and-putt competitions, all taking place on a bed of warm limestone – it all sounded a bit like Firbank's *Valmouth*. With the addition of a black masseuse it could have been.

We set off in the sunshine in the general direction of Lisdoonvarna, this being the nearest thing attainable in this part of the world to going from A to B by the shortest route. All was well at first. The road ran through meadowy country interspersed with hazel thickets, 'fairly level but with a strong upward tendency' as the Cyclists' Touring Club *Irish Road Book* of 1899 rather charmingly put it, en route passing close to the Ailwee Cave, closed for two million years until its discovery in 1976, and now closed again because it was winter.

At this point the 'strong upward tendency' began in earnest – a succession of steep hairpin bends up Corkscrew Hill. At the same moment the sun vanished and we found ourselves in what seemed another world, enveloped in dense, freezing cloud which whirled across our path borne on the wings of the east wind and reduced visibility to not more than twenty yards. In spite of all this, once she had stopped changing up instead of down, and falling off when her Wild Cat subsequently ground to a halt, Wanda very nearly succeeded in winding her way to the top, and only had to get off and push the last fifty yards or so.

From the top, if it really was the top, there was nothing to be seen of the famous view over the Burren to Galway extolled by every guide book. Indeed it was difficult to imagine that on every side now, enveloped in what resembled cold gruel, were a host of natural wonders, some of them so extraordinary as to be positive freaks of nature: what are known – how uncouth the terms used by geologists sometimes sound – as clints, grykes, glacial erratics, and potholes and turloughs (what Wanda knew in her own country as *doline* and *polje*).* Here, the last glaciation took place only about fifteen thousand years ago, making this one of the most recently created landscapes in the whole of Europe. What we were riding over now was hollow; beneath us rivers ran, quite literally, through caverns measureless to man down to a sunless sea.

About the only thing currently visible on the High Burren and able to continue growing there throughout the winter was grass. The limestone retains the heat of the summer sun, turning it into a species of giant storage heater and making the hilltops and the higher valleys much warmer than the low-lying country below. For this reason the cattle are left high up to forage for themselves from November to late April and are then taken down to the lowlands for the summer months, the reverse of what happens in most other places. Herds of wild goats perform an invaluable function in keeping down the hazel scrub which rampages in summer.

At this moment, as if wanting to prove to us that they really were living up there, a herd of Burren cattle came sweeping round a corner towards us in close formation, steaming and smoking and completely filling the road, and looking to me very much as the Sixth Iniskilling Dragoons must have done to the French infantry when they were being charged by them on the afternoon of Waterloo. We did what the French would probably have done had it been available: took refuge in the entrance to the Corkscrew Hill National School, built in 1885 and now abandoned, while they thundered past it and on down the hill, apparently unaccompanied, in the direction of Ballyvaughan. Where did they think they were going? To the seaside for a dip?

For the next seven miles the only living soul we met with was a young Australian girl, sopping wet, padding gamely through the muck

---

* *Clints* are the blocks of limestone paving. *Grykes* are the open crevices in the clints. *Glacial erratics* are rounded blocks of limestone, some of them very large, deposited in the wake of an ice-cap. *Turloughs* are grassy hollows, sometimes created by the collapse of the roof of an underground cavern and often filled with water from below (*doline* being the smaller ones and *polje* the larger ones, the biggest of which is the Carran Depression in the eastern Burren).

in her training shoes with a big, rectangular pack on her back the size of a large suitcase. She was a bit pissed off, she said, having been given a lift from Ballyvaughan post office by this old guy who said he was bound for Lisdoonvarna, but then changed his mind and dumped her at a fork in the road, with a six mile hike to go. Unfortunately, there was nothing we could do to help her. 'You should have brought a tandem,' Wanda said to me. 'Then you could have given people lifts.'

Lisdoonvarna, when we reached it after a gratifying downhill run, came as a bit of a shock after all the build-up it had been given by the various guide books I had consulted. In fact I wondered if some of the authors could have been there at all. Admittedly, no resort looks its best in the depths of winter – that is, unless it is a winter resort – and Lisdoonvarna, with the east wind hurrying clouds of freezing vapour through its streets, was no exception. I tried to imagine excited farmers with straw in their hair, accompanied by their match-makers, pursuing unmarried ladies through its streets and down the corridors of the Spa Hotel, which had broken windows and looked as if it would never open again, but failed.

Now, in December, it seemed a decrepit and terribly melancholy place, like the film set of a shanty town. Its hotels, souvenir and fast-food shops had closed down in October and would not re-open until March, some of the hotels not until June. But would what the Irish call the crack – what others call the action – start even then? Rough-looking youths stood on the pavement outside a betting shop, one of the few places open at this hour. The wind struck deep into the marrow of one's bones; in spite of being dressed in almost everything we possessed we were frozen, and took refuge in a pub, the Roadside Tavern, run by two nice ladies, the walls of which were covered with picture postcards. They stoked up the fire for us and we gradually thawed out in front of it while we ate ham and soda bread and I drank the health of the priest at Crusheen in Guinness, while Wanda drank port.

Too fed up with Lisdoonvarna to seek out the various sources of its waters, smelly or otherwise, and the various pleasure domes in which customers were given the treatment, we quitted Ireland's premier spa, and set off westwards up yet another cloud-bound road. Suddenly, as suddenly as we had left it at the foot of Corkscrew Hill, we emerged into dazzling sunshine on the western escarpment of the Burren. Below us it dropped away to a rocky coast on which, in spite of the wind being offshore, heavy seas were breaking, throwing up clouds of glittering spray. Just to look at the shimmering sea after the miseries that had gone before gave us a new lease of life – and we roared down towards it via a series of marvellous bends with the Aztec Super brake blocks on our Shimano Deore XT cantilever brakes screaming (a malfunction) on the Rigida 25/32 rims (for the benefit of those who like a bit of technical detail from time to time), past the ivy-clad tower of Ballynalackan Castle, a fifteenth-century seaside house of the O'Briens perched on a steep-sided rock high above the road, with a magical-looking wood at the foot of it, and on down to the limestone shore.

We were at Poulsallagh, nothing more than a name on the map. Somewhere out to sea to the west, hidden from view in their own mantle of cloud, were the Aran Islands. To the right dense yellow vapour flooded out over the Burren escarpment as if in some First World War gas attack, over a wilderness of stone, interspersed with walled fields and extravagantly painted cottages, their windows ablaze in the light of the declining sun, while high above, squadrons of clouds like pink Zeppelins were moving out over the Atlantic. Here, the haystacks were mound-shaped and covered with nets against the wind, or shaped like upturned boats, hidden behind the drystone walls. To the left, between the road and the sea, were endless expanses of limestone on which the glacial erratics rested, like huge marbles, rolled down from the screes above. Here and there a walled field gave shelter to giant sheep solidly munching the green grass. At Fanore, six miles north of Poulsallagh, we spoke with the first human being we had set eyes on since leaving Lisdoonvarna. He was a small man of about fifty, who was working in a plot beside the road. He had a large head, abundant flaxen hair with a touch of red in it, of the kind that always looks as if it has just been combed, a high forehead and very clear blue eyes like T. E. Lawrence. And he had a voice of indescribable sadness, like the wind keening about a house. After exchanging remarks about the grandness of the day I asked him about the absence of people.

'Ah,' he said, 'there are more than meet the eye; but most of them are old, and are by their fires, out of the wind. You can see the smoke of them.'

'But what about the school? It's quite new. There must be some children,' Wanda said.

'There are children,' he said, 'but when those children leave the school, their parents will leave Fanore, and the school will be closed. They are the last ones.'

'But what will happen to their houses? Surely they won't be allowed to fall into ruin?'

'The old ones will be allowed to fall into ruin. The newer ones will be holiday houses. Many of them are already.'

'And what will you yourself do when the old people are dead, and the children and the younger people have all gone away?'

'I will give an eye to the holiday houses,' he said.

By the time we got back to Ballyvaughan, having covered a modest thirty-six miles, the wind had dropped completely and in the afterglow the still waters of the bay had a vinous tinge about them. Thirty thousand feet or so overhead jets bound for the New World drew dead straight orange crayon lines across a sky still blue and filled with sunshine. There was a tremendous silence, broken only by the whistling of the oystercatchers and the gulls foraging in the shallows. The inhabitants of Ballyvaughan were eating their evening meals and watching telly. If we hadn't seen them going about their business we might have thought they were dead. Looking at what they presumably subsisted on lining the shelves of the supermarkets, it was surprising that they weren't. Did they really eat prepacked mashed potato and tins of meat and fish that could easily have doubled as pet food with a change of labels, on which the additives listed by law read like the formula for something nasty?

Famished, we took the edge off our appetites with scones and raspberry jam – the mussels had arrived and stood outside the door in a sack, a huge quantity for £2, enough for two copious meals. Then we went to O'Lochlan's pub and sat in its glittering interior, a bit like an Aladdin's Cave with newspapers on sale. Mr O'Lochlan, it transpired, was a member of one of the historically most powerful septs in this part of the Burren. They had owned the great hazel thickets which still grow at the foot of the Cappanawalla mountain, and the great stone fort of Cahermore up among the limestone pavements, and the Ballylaban Ringfort, down near sea level, which contained a single homestead and which, with its earth walls crowned with trees and its moat filled with water, is as romantic as the limestone forts are austere.*

By the time we got to Ennistymon and had been deposited at the top of its main street by a large Gothic Protestant church with an octagonal tower and a handless clock face, it was eleven o'clock and the first shops up at this end of the town were beginning to show tentative signs of opening, like early daffs. We put up at Mrs Mary MacMahon's B and B which was situated in Church Street above a pub of the same name, of which her husband was the proprietor.

We were given a room next door to the TV Room on one of the upper floors. The TV Room was unlike any other TV Room I had ever seen. It was full of religious images executed in plaster-of-Paris, all balanced on a rather precarious-looking what-not, and on a facing wall was a large oleograph of Jesus with his heart exposed and flames coming out of it, surrounded by a circle of thorns with a cross on top. There was a lot of blood about. Religion was everywhere. Even the lavatory had the Virgin and Child of Kiev balanced on top of a spare roll of paper on top of the cistern, which made use of the arrangements extremely hazardous. In fact as soon as I set eyes on it I began to rehearse how I would break the bad news to Mrs MacMahon, who was religious and nice with it, that her picture of the Virgin and Child of Kiev had just fallen down the hole, and please where could I find the nearest religious picture repository for a replacement.

Fifteen years previously Ennistymon, which at the last count had 1013 inhabitants, had forty-eight pubs. According to Mr MacMahon, when they were last counted, a few days previously, there were twenty-one – out of a total in Southern Ireland of 10,000 (in 1985 there were 11,000) and numbers were closing every day. The town is also famous for some of the best shop fronts in Ireland. On the left-hand side going down Church Street was C. O'Lochlen, Draper and Outfitter, with what was probably Mr O'Lochlen transferring some of his stock on

* According to Bord Failte's *Ireland Guide*, 1982, there are between 30,000 and 40,000 of these ringforts in Ireland North and South. No one can be sure who lived in most of them, or when: the hundred or more sites excavated in Ireland show evidence of occupation as early as the Bronze Age and as late as the Middle Ages, the most populous period being the early Christian one.

to the pavement outside, having come to the risky conclusion that it wouldn't rain today. Down from him was Keane's, Saddler and Harnessmaker; a butcher who described himself as a victualler; Nagles, a pub that was also, conveniently, an undertaker's; and on down the road, in a little square, Killybegs Fresh Fish Stall was doing a brisk trade.

On the right hand was C. Hayes, with a perfect austere pub façade, bottles of Paddy in the window and a dim interior full of drink, which never opened during our stay and now probably never would; the premises of Twoney Walsh, Outfitter and Draper, in which Wanda bought a two-yard skirt length of expensive-looking tweed for £9. Next to that, more or less in the same line of business, was T. J. Mahoney, who emerged from his premises to present her with a card on which was printed '*Very Special Value – T. J. Mahoney*'. The drapers in Ennistymon carried stocks that would have made department store buyers curl up and die from apprehension. One of them, in a town with a thousand inhabitants, stocked five sixty-yard lengths of identical material all in the same colour. Others had enormous stocks of shoes and clothing in outmoded styles and would, I felt, if asked, produce a pair of 1950s winkle-pickers at the drop of a hat.

And so on, past more pubs, open and shut, for sale and haunted, than I had physique to visit and record, among them E. Burke, with another beautiful façade. Then Considine and Sons, a pub now a gift shop;* Hyne's, mysterious dark façade, closed, use unknown; Vaughan's, black-shuttered and said by an old man with a bike to be haunted, also use unknown; Nagle's Bar, 'Traditional Musicians Welcome', closed and for sale; McGrotty's Medical Hall, open; O'Leary's Undertakers with the smallest possible window filled with artificial flowers. Here at the far end of Church Street, perched on a hill, were the remains of a church and a cemetery.

---

* A pub in Ireland can sell anything. In Kinvarra, where King Guaire Aidhneach had his Easter Banquet spirited away by angels, there was a dark, cavernous pub that had its windows dressed with cans of weedkiller.

## TO THE FAIR AT SPANCIL HILL

The next day, Monday, was the day of the Fair at Spancil Hill which
we had first heard about from Mr O'Hagerty while drinking at his
establishment at the Crusheen crossroads in County Clare the previous
December. As it turned out, it was extremely difficult to find out
anything more. Although almost every Irish man, woman and child
knows at least some words of the immortal song 'Spancil Hill' – The
cock crew in the morning, he crew both loud and shrill / And I woke
in California, many miles from Spancil Hill – far fewer have any idea
of where Spancil Hill actually is; the most precise directions we heard
were 'somewhere up or down Limerick way, or thereabouts'. It doesn't
appear on the half-inch Ordnance Survey map of the appropriate area;
that otherwise trustworthy compendium of fairs and cattle marts, *The
Genuine Irish Old Moore's Almanack, 1986*, has not a word about it, and
all the other guides I had read were silent on the subject.

Eventually one of Bord Failte's spies in County Clare came up with
the information that it was held at a 'crass' somewhere between Ennis
and Tulla, and that 'if the parties concerned were still in Galway city
they'd best get a move on as the fair had been going all night, and the
latest news was that there had already been a bit of fighting, but not
with sticks, so far'. We managed by a whisker to catch the Expressway
Service to Ennis, 43 miles away. During this journey, while Wanda
snoozed, recharging her batteries for whatever horrors lay ahead, I
took the opportunity to bone up on The Divorce Question, as dealt
with in a couple of reject newspapers I had found on board that had
been used for packaging sandwiches. I soon got bogged down in the
letter pages, most of whose correspondents were respectfully suggesting to their opponents that they should read the Gospel according
to Mark, chapter 10, verse 10; while their opponents retaliated with
Matthew 19, verse 9, in which Our Lord appeared to give a conflicting
judgment on the subject to the wretched Pharisees. Various Irish ecclesi-
astics also used these columns to tell the laity that they should do what
they had been told to do, and not to push their luck. All of which soon
put me in a coma, too.

The bus deposited us at Ennis railway station which, like so many
Irish railway stations and most Indian ones, was sited more for the

convenience of the builders of railways than for the inhabitants of the
towns the names of which they so misleadingly appropriated. And if
you don't believe me, try doing a four-minute mile from Ennis to
Ennis station, or for that matter from Ballinasloe station to Ballinasloe
*centre ville*. From here we telephoned for a taxi, which arrived like
lightning, driven by a female who thought she knew everything,
including the whereabouts of the Fair at Spancil Hill but, as became
painfully clear, didn't. When we found ourselves well on the way to
Magh Adhair, the Inauguration place of the Kings of Thomond on the
banks of the Hell River, a site we had 'done' back in December, I
shouted 'Whoa' and asked her to reconsider her position vis-à-vis our
proposed destination.

'It's not much of a thing at all, I'm told,' she said airily, when she
finally deposited us at a 'crass' which, if not the right one, was somewhere pretty near it, if the vans, horse boxes, lorries, cars, jeeps and
trailers, all parked with fine abandon, were anything to go by. To
which I would have replied if I had had my Irish curse book handy,
'*Ualach se' chapall de chrè na h-ùir ort!*' or 'Six horse-loads of graveyard
clay on top of you!', for being such a pain-in-the-neck. At the same
time I handed her the £5 Irish she asked for, which seemed little enough
considering the miles we'd travelled together, albeit many of them in
the wrong direction. The only soul in sight to ask the way of was a
middle-aged, horsey-looking individual with a pair of very bright
brown eyes and a beaky nose, who was wearing the remains of what
must once have been a gabardine raincoat with huge, padded shoulders
which made him look a bit like an over-size, moulted bird of prey.

'It's way down from the other crass, way up there past Duggan's
place,' he said, pointing with a switch he had just cut in a hedgerow.

This in answer to my absurd English, 'I say, excuse me, could you
possibly tell me the way to Spancil Hill, the Fair I mean,' which,
judging from the facial contortions he had to indulge in to stop himself
literally falling about with mirth, must have sounded as extraordinary
to him as his 'crass, way up dere' did to me. One of the few major
pleasures of travelling is that of hearing what others do to one's own
native tongue, a pleasure equalled by the amusement they get from
listening to your version of theirs.

We had a drink at Duggan's, which was full of smoke, debris, and human beings in various stages of decay. I asked one of the barmen if it had been quiet, remembering to keep a low profile and not to call him 'old fruit' and he said, yes, it had been pretty quiet, on account of their having closed at 2 a.m. and only opened again when the customers could see their hands in front of their faces without the aid of lights.

Just up the road an official sign read 'Cross of Spancil Hill', and here the air began to be full of the sort of murmuring noises flocks of starlings make when talking to one another, in this case emanating from the punters at the fair.

There's no hill at the Cross of Spancil Hill, just a farm building and nearby, according to the map, the remains of a castle invisible from the road. From it a lane leads off to a hamlet marked on the map as Fair Green, the principal ingredients of which consist of Brohan's pub, an outbuilding or two and Kelly's which, on this grand morning, was serving cooked breakfasts and, from 11.30 on, dinners as well. After this momentary flirtation with city lights it leads out into what the Germans, who, with Americans, still make up the largest number of visitors to Ireland, call the *Ewigkeit* – in this case the eternity of rural Ireland.

The actual scene of the action was the lane outside the pub, and a field on the other side of it edged with trees, and entered through newly whitewashed gateposts which acted as a navigational aid for those leaving the pub with a skinful. The ground around it was now a sea of glutinous mud. Beyond this more fields extended away gently upwards to something you might conceivably describe as a hill if you'd never seen a real one. It was a beautiful day. In a sky of indigo blue a warm wind was ushering towering masses of cumulus in across the Atlantic from the New World, as if it was moving day.

The lane itself was more or less choked with fish and chip vans, burger stalls, stalls at which quoits could be pitched and tossed, tables with roulette wheels ready to roll, tinkers finding-the-lady or playing heads-or-tails surrounded by little circles of men and boys, the players, all looking skywards when the coin went up as if expecting the Second Coming. And there were junk sellers, and little tinker boys with bleached hair, riding sixteen-hand hunters bareback up and down it, showing them off to the customers, and there was all sorts of music.

And further down the lane, beyond Brohan's and Kelly's, there were some barrel-shaped tinkers' carts, most of them now occupied by very self-conscious *Stonehengevolk* masquerading as tinkers, with their ladies ostentatiously suckling their offspring on the steps, some of whom looked big enough to be clamouring for second helpings of muesli. Any real tinkers living on this hard hat site would have been in sumptuous motorized caravans, their interiors ablaze with polished brass. Meanwhile, out in the field, there were any amount of stallions, geldings, mares and their foals, Connemara ponies, donkeys and mules, all waiting to change hands, either tethered, or hobbled, or being made to show their paces or display their teeth or their hocks. There were even a few goats. And there were any number of two-wheeled flat carts pulled by donkeys, and pony carts, all running around loaded with the fancy. And there were people selling tea, and sausages and saddlery, and other tack.

And there was every sort of horse-fancying man, woman and child for miles around, and further. If no mishaps had befallen them there would be Josie Kerrin from Ballyla, and Thomas Conroy and Thomas Ford from Tubber, and Paddy Lynch from Newmarket-on-Fergus, and all the Cashes, and Harold Lusk from up north, and Patrick O'Connor from Kanturk, and Michael O'Looney from Ennis, and Mick Moloney and Michael McKenna from Ogonneloe, and Mick Sheehan from Kilbane, and Michael Scanlan from Carranboy and John Ryan from Boher, and Frank Casey from Ennis and a power of others. And somewhere out there, though we never found him, must have been our old friend Mr O'Hagerty from Crusheen.

And the air was full of neighings and whinneyings and breakings of wind and the ghastly noises donkeys make when they think themselves unloved, and such remarks as:

'Sure, and hasn't he got a fine chest on him, like the Great Wall of China!'

'Looks a bit narrow to me. Put a bit of weight on him and he'll knock his legs about something terrible.'

'He's not narrow at all! Look at his great chest, will you! Like a barrel of porter!'

'Looks a bit shallow to me. Shouldn't wonder if he wasn't short-winded.' At the same time pinching the animal's wind-pipe and when that failed to provoke a reaction, pinching it again – 'See what I mean, short-winded.'

'And what a nice eye he's got!'

'Looks like a pig's eye to me.'

Occasionally, but you had to wait a long time to see it happen, like waiting for the cameras to roll on location, a sale would be made and the third party presiding over the deal would make sure buyer and seller both spat on their hands before the handshake that clinched it. Meanwhile, across the lane, in Brohan's, which was a bit like a parish hall in urgent need of restoration, the clientèle were ten and fifteen deep at the bar, all intent on ordering enough of the nourishment in one go to make it unnecessary to put in another requisition until evening. What Brohan's did for customers for the other 363 days and nights of the year when there was no fair was unclear. They probably made enough to see them through to the following one. When it closed, at 4 a.m. on Tuesday morning, the Fair would be finally over.

Altogether it was a great day, more lively than ever, the experts said, with moderate prices ranging from £1700 for a chestnut likely to make a hunter, to £3000 in the heavy hunter class, and equivalents in the pony, donkey and mule departments. Hours later, back on our bus to Galway, we passed a solitary figure leading a horse he had bought, or failed to sell, a good seven miles from Spancil Hill.

'Any questions?' said Wanda, as one or other of us always does when confronted with a not very exciting water source. Now, thirty-five miles from Sligo, from where we had set off that morning, at the feet of the boulder-strewn Cuilcagh Mountains, on the border of the Republic with Ulster, we found ourselves in a muddy field, looking down into a hole in the ground surrounded by trees and bushes, into which water was bubbling up from somewhere below. To get to it we had had to break through a cordon of cattle, determined to defend to the last their right to foul it up.

What we were looking into here, 256 feet above sea level, and 224 miles from its mouth at Loop Head, was Shannon Pot, the source of the Shannon, which ends up by draining one-fifth of the entire area of Ireland.

The only guidebook I had with me was what was left of Murray's

*Guide*, 1912. Opening it at the appropriate page to read to Wanda, I immediately wished I hadn't. '. . . The traditional source,' wrote John Cooke, quoting a maddening but no doubt perfectly correct pedant named Hull,

> 'is a tributary stream which takes its rise in a limestone caul-
> dron ("the Shannon Pot") from which the water rises in a
> copious fountain. The real source is, however, not at this
> spot, but at a little lough, situated about a mile from the
> Shannon Pot . . . The waters from the little lough flow in a
> subterranean channel till they issue forth at the so-called
> "Source of the Shannon". Mr W. S. Wilkinson has proved
> by experiments the truth of this, having thrown hay or straw
> into the little lough, which on disappearing, has come up in
> the waters of the Shannon Pot.'

'Do you mean to say,' said Wanda, after digesting this information with much the same relish as one would a fishbone, 'that after five and a half hours' cycling here from Sligo and another half hour going up and down and round and round looking for it, this isn't the source of the Shannon?'

'Well,' I said, 'not strictly speaking. That is, if Cooke, Hull and Wilkinson are anything to go by.'

'In that case,' she said, 'Cooke, Hull, Wilkinson, and you, too, should bloddy well be shot.'

# At the Foot of the Apuan Alps

SIGNORA ANGIOLINA was hovering in her vegetable patch outside her house, awaiting our arrival. As she told us, she had just finished feeding her rabbits which lived in a large wooden hutch at the back of the house.

The house looked bigger than it really was as she had rented a large room on the ground floor to a communist social club which was, at the moment, like the communist cell at the seventeenth bend, more or less moribund, but not completely so, and subsequently it started up with evenings of very un-communist pop which would have made Lenin turn in his grave.

Signora Angiolina's husband had died a couple of years previously and because of this she was in deep mourning, which meant that she was dressed in black from head to foot: black headscarf, black cardigan, black skirt, reaching below the knee, black woollen stockings – normally she wouldn't have worn any at all before the cold weather set in – and black felt slippers.

The only item that wasn't black was her apron which was dark navy with small white spots on it, which helped to cheer her outfit up a bit.

Later she told Wanda that she was fed up with being in mourning – the navy apron was probably a first sign of rebellion against it – and she was looking forward to leaving it off and quite soon she did so, which raised her spirits no end.

Signora Angiolina was in her sixties when we first met her, and was very slim. She had nice, bright-blue eyes and she cried easily. She had greyish-brown hair drawn back tightly from her forehead in a bun, now hidden by her headscarf. And she had a really lovely smile.

It was a tragic face but a beautiful one, a beauty, one felt, that would endure and in fact it did, until the day she died. Even seeing her briefly for the first time it was obvious that at some time in her life something awful had befallen her but we had to wait until we were on more intimate terms with her in order to discover what it was.

Like most *contadini* she was wary of people such as ourselves who came from cities and were foreigners but, in spite of this, she did bestow on us this lovely smile.

However, when Wanda asked her if she would take us to see the house and unlock the doors for us so that we could see the inside, which was the purpose of our visit, she suddenly looked serious, shrugged her shoulders in a way that was almost imperceptible, and said '*Ma!*'.

This seemed like bad news. In my experience almost all the Italian *contadini* I had ever met who used this expression had done so in a negative sense, one that usually boded ill.

When, for instance, while on the run in Italy during the war, I had asked the *contadini* for whom I was working in exchange for food and a roof over my head, if I had any chance of remaining free when the snow fell in the Apennines, something I had been thinking about for some time, there was no doubt as to what they meant when they said '*Ma!*'. They meant 'No!' And they were right. But Signora Angiolina's '*Ma!*' was of a different sort. One she used in the sense of '*Chissa?*' ('Who knows?')

But this was not her only interpretation of '*Ma!*'. If you asked Signora Angiolina, '*Che sarà successo?*' ('What can have happened?'), a question that we would be asking all and sundry in this part of rural Italy for the next twenty years or more, one which could cover any sort of calamity – a blow-back in a septic tank, the sudden disappearance of the roof, or the cessation of the water supply – her first reaction would be to say '*Ma!*', implying that she didn't know.

What she meant by '*Ma!*' in this particular instance, as Wanda subsequently explained to me, being more practised in the understanding of such things, was that she was not the actual owner of the keys, and was therefore expressing trepidation at the thought of having to be responsible for opening doors to rooms to which she may not have had access previously, unless someone had died in one of them, in which case she might have entered it for the wake.

Worst of all, for her, was the idea of opening them up for a couple of unknown persons who might quite easily turn out to be robbers.

But in spite of all this, the implication was that she would do it. It was all rather confusing.

Her other favourite expression, one which she used when confronted with a *fait accompli* which had on the whole turned out well, as, for example, if I had cut down, as I subsequently did, one of two trees, and it turned out to be the right one I had felled, not the wrong one, was '*Hai fatto bene!*' ('You have done well!'), uttered in resounding tones.

I loved it when Signora Angiolina gave me one of her '*Hai fatto bene!*' broadsides. It always gave me the feeling that I had just received an accolade from the Queen for saving her corgis from being run over, or that I had just been kissed on both cheeks by General de Gaulle after having been decorated with the Croix de Guerre avec Palmes for doing something frightfully brave and important – 'Well done, Eric!'

In fact if Signora Angiolina called me anything it was what everyone else called me in this part of the world, that is if they called me anything, which was 'Hayrick' without the 'H', 'Eyrick', or failing that 'Enrico'.

So now, having delivered her '*Ma!*', Signora Angiolina went off to get the keys from some hiding place, five of them altogether, all very old, three of them large and very beautiful works of art.

Then, having armed herself with a small reaping hook and giving it a preliminary sharpening on a special sort of sharpening tool embedded in a large log, she set off down the track, leading the way, to the place where Signor Vescovo had written that there was a curve to the right off the main track. From this point it then made a very steep, slippery descent to a little bridge which, at that point, spanned a stream.

'The track goes down through a chestnut wood,' he had written, 'which is why the houses and the locality are known as *I Castagni*.'

The bridge which spanned the stream was nothing but a couple of cement drain pipes covered with earth. The stream itself was deep, narrow, bone dry and almost completely hidden from view by the chestnut trees which soared up into the air from the ravine the stream had carved for itself. The bed of the stream was horrible, filled with the refuse that people further up the hill had chucked into it: bits of plastic sheeting, half buried in the bottom of it, empty bleach containers, rusty tins and other assorted muck.

Now, for the first time, we saw the house.

It stood at the far end of a grassy dell, overlooking the terraced fields that covered the hillside one above the other, and it was surrounded by vines and old olive trees that cast a dappled shade as their branches moved in a light breeze from the west.

The house itself faced south. It was sheltered from all the winds that blew between north-east and south-east by the groves of chestnuts that also rendered it invisible from further up the hillside in summer, and did so even now in what was autumn although the leaves were beginning to thin out.

It was a small, two-storey farmhouse, built of stone partially rendered with a cement that over the years had turned a creamy colour in some places and in others a lichenous green. The overall effect was of a building on the verge of becoming a ruin.

It was roughly rectangular in shape, roughly because it was possible to see where, over the years, other small wings had been added on, which was why the ones that looked the oldest were roofed with stone slabs. Others, of more recent date, were covered with tiles that had either weathered to a faded pink, or else to a yellowish golden colour. To prevent them being whisked away by some freak wind, stones the size and shape of footballs were disposed along their outer edges in what looked like a rather dangerous fashion for anyone standing below if one of them rolled off.

There were no roses, or any other kind of climbing plant winding their ways up the walls, as there would have been in England. No garden. No shrubs, only an orange tree. There was no muck lying about either, apart from that in the stream. Everything else was spotless. This had been up to now a strictly utilitarian establishment.

As soon as we had taken all this in, without even seeing the interior, we both knew that this was the house we had been looking for and this was the house we would have to have if we were going to have one at all.

The first door we came to had the orange tree growing up a wall to one side of it. As was all the other timber used in the construction of the house – floorboards, roof timbers and joists – the door was chestnut.

The planks from which this had been made had faded over the years to a beautiful silver-grey colour but when Signora Angiolina finally succeeded in turning the key in the lock and we went inside, the door shut on us and we found ourselves in what would have been complete darkness, if the door had not been riddled with holes through which the sun shone in long, slender beams as if someone had fired a shotgun at it.

Yet although it looked as if it was on its last legs, as did the bridge over the stream, and one of the first things that would have to be replaced if we bought the house, this door was still there, in the same condition, when we finally left *I Castagni* twenty-five years later.

What we were now standing in was a room about fifteen feet long, ten feet wide and six feet high, what had been a *stalla*, a cowshed, or a stable for mules, or possibly both.

Until very recently the principal means of moving supplies from one place to another in the mountainous areas of Italy had been by pack mules, hand carts, *slitte*, big wooden sledges with sides made of wattle, wooden stakes interwoven with split branches, which were usually drawn by cows. For the rest it was what people could carry on their backs.

A few years before we arrived on the scene the asphalt road up which we had driven, following the bends, had not existed. Neither had the bends. All there had been in those days was a steep, cobbled mule track which went straight up the hill from Caniparola to Fosdinovo without any bends at all, and stretches of this ancient route still existed and were still used by local people travelling on foot.

The floor of the *stalla* was also cobbled, with thin rectangular stones laid edge to edge. Iron rings for tethering the animals were sunk in the rough stone walls in the back part of the *stalla* and there was still a good deal of dung lying about, but so dry and powdery that it was impossible to know what sort of animal had produced it.

The only illumination, apart from that provided by the self-closing door with the holes in it, which was of rather limited usefulness, came from a small, barred window that looked out towards the bridge over the stream some thirty yards away.

Overhead a trap door with a ladder opened up into a room which had been a *fienile*, a hay loft. The *fienile* was almost twice the height of the *stalla* and much brighter, the light entering it through a large opening in one of the walls through which the hay had been forked up. Other illumination was provided by gaps in the tiled roof where the rain had been coming in. Every bit of timber in these two rooms – beams, ceiling joists and floorboards – was riddled with wormholes and you could break off bits as if they were biscuits.

Further investigation was made impossible because someone had had the truly devilish idea of more or less filling the *fienile* with large coils of heavy wire, of the sort used to set up trellises in vineyards, each of which was inextricably interlaced one with another. The only other way in was round the back of the house where there was another door, literally in mid-air, which needed a ladder to get to it.

Meanwhile, as we were taking all this ruin in, lizards, no doubt deluded by the mild November weather into thinking spring had come, or it was still summer, scuttled about upside down on the tiled roof through which daylight was only too clearly visible. Looking at it I felt that one of us would only have to emit one really hefty sneeze to bring the whole lot, beams, floorboards, joists, roof tiles and all, down about our ears. On one beam there was the skin cast by an adder. Every year, even when the beams were put in order, the adder or its descendants continued to shed its skin in this same place.

'*Ma,*' said Signora Angiolina, as we all three gazed at these irrefutable evidences of decay. What she meant by this enigmatic utterance, devoid of the usual exclamation mark and without the shrugging of the shoulders, was not clear, although I could hazard a guess. It was the first observation she had made since we reached the house, though she had made it abundantly obvious that she was not happy about the condition of the stream when we came to it. '*Sono gente ignorante,*' she said, but who she was referring to was not clear. It could have been a whole band of ignorant people.

'Cor!' I said, the English equivalent of Signora Angiolina's epithet. If the first two rooms were like this what on earth would the others be like?

Only Wanda expressed herself clearly and confidently, although she had said 'My God!' when she first saw the *fienile* and its roof; but then she had recovered.

'Providing Signor Botti doesn't want the earth, we'll be all right,' she said.

Having exhausted the possibilities of the *stalla* and the *fienile* for the time being, we moved on westwards to the main door of the house, passing on the way a bread oven that was built into the wall with a brick chimney rising above it to the height of the upper storey. According to Signora Angiolina it was out of action and was likely to remain so. The only man capable of repairing it had contracted a painful skin disease of a sort that repairers of ovens and users of cement are apparently liable to and was unable to carry out any more work of this sort.

To the right of the door a flight of stone steps led to the upper floor where the chimney of the oven terminated. Originally these steps had been protected from the elements to some extent by a tiled roof but the main support of it, a long beam, had collapsed, taking all the tiles with it and smashing most of them.

High overhead the main chimney stack rose into the air. It had a flat stone on top of it, supported by four rough brick columns, each about a foot high, to stop it smoking. To me it looked more like a tabernacle of the Israelites than a chimney.

Now we waited outside the front door while Signora Angiolina, Mistress of the Ceremonies, a role she enjoyed much more than being in mourning, selected the right key to open it. This was the finest door in the house. In fact, although rough and primitive, it was one of the best of its kind in the entire neighbourhood, apart from those we saw in some houses up the hill in Fosdinovo, but those were doors of town houses rather than rustic ones. It was difficult to imagine one more rustic than ours. Subconsciously, we were already beginning to refer to objects such as the doors at *I Castagni* as 'ours'.

This door consisted of a number of large slabs, probably cut from a single tree and set up horizontally, one above the other, on a stout frame. These slabs were of a beautiful dark colour and looked as if they had been soaked in oil. And this is what we later discovered they had been treated with, linseed oil over a long period, a treatment which we ourselves were to continue.

Such a door would have been irreplaceable if it had been damaged and every time we came back to the house from England our preoccupation was always with the door. Had it fallen to pieces? Had it been damaged by vandals? These were the questions we always used to ask ourselves while descending the bends and crossing the stream. In fact, like most other objects at *I Castagni* which we took over, it outlasted us.

The key for this door, which like all the others, was of hand-forged iron, was the biggest of the lot. It was a key that was easily identifiable, even in the dark, not only because it was the biggest but because someone at one time had attempted to turn it in the lock, or perhaps another lock, and when it had failed to open had inserted a metal rod through the ring at the end of the shaft and twisted that a full half turn without breaking it. Now, in order to turn the key in the lock, it had to be inserted upside down and then jiggled about for what could be ages. Yet we never considered the possibility of changing the key and the lock for a new one. The key was much too beautiful. In fact there was another complete set of keys but I lost them the first day we took over the house and we never found them again.

This lock had the peculiar foible that when the wind was blowing from the south-west it would open itself. The only way to prevent this happening was to secure the door to a ring-bolt in the outer wall of the building using the wire of which there were great coils in the *fienile*.

This door opened into a living room of an unimaginably primitive kind, with a floor made from rough, irregular stone slabs on which it was difficult to set a chair without it wobbling.

To the left, as we went in, there was an old, varnished wood, glass-fronted cupboard with blue-check curtains, what is known as an *armadio a muro*; and against the far wall there was something known as a *madia*, of which this was a very ancient example, a kneading trough for making pasta with a removable top, which could also be used as a table.

To the right of the door there was a charcoal-burning stove, built of brick, and next to it was an open fireplace, with a shelf over it. At one time, what must have been a long time ago, the walls, the stove and the fireplace had all been whitewashed but by now the smoke of innumerable fires had dyed them all a uniform bronze colour.

Inside the fireplace a long chain extended up the chimney into the darkness from which was suspended a large copper pot, and round about the fireplace were disposed a number of cooking utensils, all of them archaic but all of them still in use. The ashes in the fireplace were fresh and there was plenty of kindling and enough logs to make another fire stacked to one side of it.

The other furniture, all of it apparently homemade, consisted of a small table with a plate, a bowl and a knife, fork and spoon set on it, a chair and a minute stool that looked as if it had been made for a child, for sitting in front of the fire. But although they were homemade these items had been constructed and repaired with great skill by whoever had undertaken the work.

The only window was small and barred with metal slats, like the one in the *stalla*. Beneath it there was a small marble sink with a brass tap that was working; above it was an extremely dangerous-looking electric light fitting, which consisted of a bulb connected to the two naked wires which supported it by a couple of blobs of solder, a lighting system that was not at that moment working, although Signora Angiolina said she knew how to get it going.

The only other illumination was provided by several small, homemade brass lamps, fuelled with olive oil, that looked as if they might have been looted from an Etruscan tomb.

'Who has been living here?' Wanda asked Signora Angiolina. This was the first intimation we had had that someone might already be in residence at *I Castagni*.

'This is the room,' Signora Angiolina said, with a certain air of surprise, as if this was something that was common knowledge, 'in which Attilio lives.'

'But who is this Attilio?' Wanda asked. By the way she spoke I knew that she was worried. Neither of us had envisaged the existence of a sitting tenant or, even worse, a squatter. 'Attilio is the brother of the wife of Signor Botti, the *padrone*, the owner. He is only a little man,' she said, referring to him as an *ometto* – as if his smallness was some sort of recommendation. '*Ma lui è molto bravo.*' He knows how to do everything. '*Sa fare tutto,* Attilio.'

What we had already been forced to designate mentally as 'Attilio's Room' – were we really going to have him as a sitting tenant, even though he was '*molto bravo*'? – was separated from the back part of the premises by a partition made from what is known as *canniccio*, wattle and daub. *Canniccio* was made with interwoven canes, the thinnest of the giant reeds that grow everywhere in this part of the world, plastered with a mixture of clay, lime, dung and chopped straw. These reeds, which grow to a great height, fifteen feet or more, were everywhere on the hillside and once established spread like wildfire. Their roots had the consistency of cast iron and in trying to eradicate them I succeeded in bending a pick.

These canes had dozens of uses: as supports for clothes lines, for supporting vines and making pergolas, for fencing in earth closets and rendering the user invisible to the vulgar gaze, for picking fruit from tall trees (by attaching a little net to the end of one of them). And when they finally rotted and broke they made good kindling. Meanwhile, unless ruthlessly controlled, they devastated the countryside.

Now the whole of this partition wall made with *canniccio* was riddled with woodworm and was beginning to fall apart. A ruinous door in the left hand side of this partition wall opened into what had been another *stalla*. It was difficult to imagine domestic animals, however domesticated, walking through one's kitchen/living room on their way in from the fields in the evening to their sleeping quarters and each morning going the other way, back into the open air, but this was presumably what had happened.

This *stalla* was also cobbled. It was also completely window-less. These downstairs rooms were so dark that I began to wonder if the inhabitants had been spiritualists. What was good news was that the floorboards overhead and the beams that supported them were in quite good condition.

The key that opened the door of the room at the top of the outside staircase was the most complex and beautiful of all the keys and the easiest to use. There was no juggling or jiggling necessary. The signora inserted it the right way up and it opened first time.

Inside there were two rooms, back and front, divided from one another by a less ruinous version of the *canniccio* partition on the ground floor but reinforced with wooden uprights that gave it a slightly olde Englishe, half-timbered appearance. To the left of it, another rickety, lockless door similar to the one on the ground floor, separated the two rooms, front and back, both of which had two windows. All four were minute. It was obvious that if we were going to be able to read in either one of them, even in broad daylight, we would have to have bigger windows and these walls would take some excavating as all of them were composed of large stones and were more than two feet thick.

The roof itself appeared to be more or less sound but the main beam which supported it, a really hefty piece of chestnut, would have been more reassuring if it hadn't had a great crack in it.

Looking at it, as I already had at numerous other beams and boards during this tour of inspection, I found it difficult to decide whether *I Castagni* might be good for another hundred years, or might collapse altogether in the course of the next couple of hours.

The view from the outside balcony of this upper floor was terrific. Here we were about eight hundred feet above the sea. It was a beautiful afternoon and the sun shone from a cloudless sky, flooding the front of the house with a brilliant golden light.

To the west, beyond the house, the grassy track that led past the front of it from the stream, gradually descended a hundred yards or so beyond it between lines of vines to a pretty two-storeyed building, a smaller version of *I Castagni*; and some fifteen miles or so beyond it were the mountains of the Cinque Terre beyond La Spezia, behind which the sun was now beginning to sink, like a huge orange.

Far below to the south-west was the Plain of Luni, with its innumerable small holdings and market gardens. And beyond them were the wooded heights that rose steeply above the far, right bank of the Magra, here running down through its final reach before entering the Ligurian Sea.

It was at this moment that I took a black-and-white photograph of the house which, when it was printed had more of the quality of an engraving than a photograph, a magical effect, but one that I was never able to emulate, however hard I tried.

Down on the ground floor, at the foot of the outside staircase, next to the front door and at right angles to it, there was another door that opened into what was a miniature, protruding wing of the house. This part of it was almost completely severed from the main part of the building by a frightful fissure that ran from top to bottom of it.

According to Signora Angiolina, who had been living in the neighbourhood when it occurred, it had been caused by the great earthquake of 1921, which had damaged or destroyed a number of houses in the region. Again I had the feeling that yet another part of the building might be about to collapse.

This was the only room in the house to which Signora Angiolina did not have a key, apart from the one that opened the door to the *fienile* at the back of the house, the one that was going to need a ladder to get to it.

The only way one could see into this little room was through a heavily barred window; fortunately the wooden shutters were open.

It was a very small room, freshly whitewashed and lit by the same sort of oil lamps we had seen in the kitchen. The few bits of furniture, which almost completely filled it, consisted of a large, old single bed of polished wood with a high back inlaid with mother-of-pearl; made up with clean white linen sheets which were turned back, ready to receive whoever was going to sleep between them. Alongside the bed there was a little stool covered with a worn fragment of carpet, and on the wall next to the bed there was a crucifix and an oleograph of La Santissima Vergine del Rosario di Fontanellato, Wanda's village near Parma, where I had been a prisoner-of-war in 1943, and below it there was a small, circular, marble-topped table, which it later transpired contained a *vaso da notte*, a chamber pot.

On the other side of the bed there was a very old wooden chest. Overhead the whitewashed ceiling looked decidedly wonky, with big patches of damp where the rain had penetrated; but in spite of this the room was a lap of luxury compared with the rest of the house, and the only part remotely ready for occupation.

'And who sleeps in this room?' Wanda asked superfluously. Like me she already knew the answer before Signora Angiolina confirmed that this was the bedchamber of Attilio. It was also unnecessary to ask who washed and ironed his sheets. '*Sta arrivando adesso*, Attilio,' she said. ('He is coming now.')

*          *          *

Emerging from the deep shadow cast by the trees on the banks of the stream we could see a small figure travelling towards us across the grass at a tremendous rate, rather like one of those *gompa lamas* who move across the Tibetan plateau at high speed, negotiating what would seem to be impossible obstacles on the way. A method of progression made possible only because they are in a trance state.

Soon we could see him clearly. A tiny, wizened man, bent by a lifetime of toil, toothless so that in profile his mouth looked like a new moon. He was old, how old it was impossible to say, anything between seventy and eighty, quite possibly even more.

As he drew near we could hear him talking to himself in an animated way, and occasionally laughing at some private joke. He was certainly nothing like a *gompa lama*, more like a benevolent gnome.

He was dressed in a pale-coloured jacket, baggy trousers, a white, open-necked shirt and on his head he wore a big, pale-coloured cap that looked a bit like an unbaked sponge cake. Everything about him was very clean looking.

Now he was abreast of us and I prepared to welcome him, or for him to welcome Signora Angiolina, or welcome the three of us. But he did neither of these things. Instead, he looked at us benevolently, cackled a bit while fishing a modest-sized key from a pocket, said something that sounded like '*Bisogna vedere un po*", the equivalent of 'I'll have to think this out a bit', then opened the door to 'Attilio's Bedroom', took the key out of the lock and went in and shut the door, still continuing to chuckle away on the other side of it.

'What we've got to do, before we buy the house, is to talk to him,' Wanda said; but trying to interview Attilio proved to be like trying to interview a will o' the wisp.

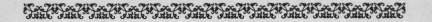

# Index